6.50
19
E

W9-CKD-973

THE UNITY OF PLATO'S THOUGHT

THE
UNITY OF
PLATO'S
THOUGHT

PAUL SHOREY

ARCHON BOOKS, 1968

First published 1903
The University of Chicago Press
Reprinted 1968 in an unaltered and unabridged edition

Library of Congress Catalog Card Number: 68-12527
Printed in the United States of America

THE UNITY OF PLATO'S THOUGHT

Paul Shorey

PART I

INTRODUCTION

During the past twenty years Platonic *Forschung* has come to mean the investigation of the relative dates of the dialogues by the statistical study of vocabulary and idiom. The general trend of modern philology and the reaction against mystical and metaphysical Platonism favored this tendency, and the work would perhaps not have been done at all if the workmen had not cherished illusions as to its value. To combat these illusions or to test in detail the logic of *Sprachstatistik* is not the purpose of this paper. A merely negative attitude toward any harmless form of human endeavor is unfruitful. But granted, since life is short, all that is claimed by the enumerators of καθάπερ and τί μήν, the essential quality of Plato's thought remains for some Platonists[1] a more interesting topic of discussion than the conjectural chronology of his writings. It has become the fashion to assert that the one depends upon the other, that we cannot interpret Plato's philosophy until we have determined the historic sequence of the dialogues, and with it the true order of development of his thought. But we have always known that the *Laws* and *Timæus* are late, that the *Republic* belongs to Plato's full maturity, and that the minor Socratic dialogues are as a whole presumably early. To affirm that more is necessary is to beg the question; it is to assume the very point in controversy that the philosophy set forth in the dialogues did develop in the sense required by the argument. The question is partly verbal. Every man's thought is developed out of nothing somewhere between infancy and maturity. Any author whose literary activity, like that of Plato, extends over half a century undergoes many minor changes of opinion, and reflects many varying moods of himself and his contemporaries. But it is not true of all, or of a majority, of the world's great thinkers that their first tentative gropings toward a philosophy and a criticism of life are depicted as in a votive tablet in their earliest published writings, or that the works of their riper years present a succession of shifting and dissolving views. Yet something like this is the assumption made by the increasing number of investigators who, in emulation of the triumphs of the statistical method, are endeavoring to confirm, refute, or correct its results by a study of alleged inconsistencies, contradictions, or developments in Platonic doctrine. Abstractly the followers of this method would probably repudiate the principle here attributed to them. In their practice the desire for striking arguments and definite results leads them to assume that Plato was capable of producing a masterpiece like the *Protagoras* before his most characteristic philosophical and ethical conceptions had taken shape in his mind, and

---

[1] Notably for Bonitz ; see the judicious observations in *Platonische Studien*, 3d ed., pp. 270 ff. and *passim*.

that throughout the period of his maturest writings his leading ideas were in a state of Heraclitean flux, or were being casually developed from year to year. This method misleads scholars of great acumen and erudition to make false points, to labor fantastic analogies, and to cite irrelevant parallels. It betrays them into misplaced emphasis, disregard of the context, and positive mistranslation. In short, it necessitates the systematic violation of all the canons of the simple, sane, and natural interpretation of literature.[2] Plato avoided rather than sought a rigid technical terminology, and prodigally varied the language and imagery in which he clothed his most familiar thoughts. Every variation of phrase and imagery is pressed to yield significant contradictions or developments. The most far-reaching conclusions are drawn from the different shades of meaning attached to such words as "opinion," "dialectic," "philosophy," "sensation," "reminiscence," "participation," "presence," "communion," freely and untechnically employed by Plato to suit the theme and context.[3] The absence in any work of explicit insistence on a thought is supposed to prove the absence of the thought from Plato's mind at the time, and as a consequence, we are expected to believe in the most incredible combinations of maturity and naïveté within the same writing. Or we are taught that Plato's development, like some Sophoclean sentences, proceeds in the order *aba*, and consisted in the acceptance, the rejection, and the re-acceptance of the same idea. The most reckless assertions are made that certain elementary thoughts appear for the first time in certain dialogues. The emphatic introduction of a term or idea is, according to the exigencies of the theory, now taken as proof that it is a novelty, and now explained away as a mere dramatic artifice. The rapid outline of an argument is alternately regarded, according to the requirements of the "chronology," as an anticipatory germ or a later résumé of the fuller treatment found elsewhere. Fantastic conceits or bare possibilities as to Plato's literary motives and polemical intentions are treated as absolute psychological and historical certainties and made the basis of serious arguments.[4]

May there not be some πρῶτον ψεῦδος involved in a conception that thus betrays its advocates? It is of course *a priori* conceivable that Plato's thought did unfold itself in this tentative and fumbling fashion. Examples of such mutations and nutations can be found among the Fichtes and Schellings of modern philosophy. They are still more frequent, as Professor Gildersleeve has wittily shown, in the history of modern philology, and, as I may add, in the interpretation of Plato. But it is at least equally probable that Plato's philosophy and his conception of life had taken shape at the age of thirty or thirty-five, and that his extant works, though not of course a predetermined systematic exposition, are the naturally varied reflection of a homogeneous body of opinion, and of a consistent attitude in the interpretation and criticism of

---

[2] Examples throughout the paper.

[3] *Infra*, and LUTOSLAWSKI, *Origin and Growth of Plato's Logic, passim.*

[4] To this category belong nearly all conjectures as to the particular philosophers referred to in Plato's generalized statements and criticisms of tendencies in the thought of the time, and especially the hypothesis that he satirized contemporaries under the names of earlier Sophists. Such hypotheses will be wholly disregarded in the following study, as a mere hindrance to the apprehension of Plato's own meanings.

contemporary life. And if this were the fact, it would be a far more important fact for the interpretation of his writings than the determination of the relative dates of the *Phædo* and *Symposium* or even than the demonstration that the *Sophist, Statesman* and *Philebus* follow rather than precede the *Republic.* I am not arguing against such a dating of the dialectical dialogues. I do not deny the value of the more vivid conception that we gain of Plato's later mood and manner by combining and comparing the traits of these dialogues with those of the *Laws* and *Timæus.* This is no ἀργὸς λόγος directed against all sober critical investigation of the difficult problem of Plato's chronology. But the attempt to base such a chronology on the variations and developments of Plato's doctrine has led to an exaggeration of Plato's inconstancy that violates all sound principles of literary interpretation and is fatal to all genuine intelligence of his meaning. The implicit canon of this method is that variation in literary machinery and expression must be assumed to imply divergence or contradiction in thought. To this I wish to oppose an interpretation based on the opposite canon: that we are to assume contradiction or serious alteration in Plato's thought only in default of a rational literary or psychological explanation of the variation in the form of its expression. As Professor Maguire says in his forgotten but very acute essays on the Platonic ethics: " If we are anxious to find out inconsistencies in appearance, we shall find them in abundance. But the student of Plato will perhaps discover that it is more fruitful, because more philosophical to commence with the points of agreement." The ultimate test of the two methods must lie in the appeal to specific texts and contexts, and there will be no lack of this in the following pages. But by way of preparation it is first advisable to enumerate some of the general features of Plato's writings that make the sane and simple literary interpretation of his meaning so difficult and so rare.

1. Plato is not only a thinker, but also a dramatic artist and an impassioned moral and religious teacher. Although, as Schopenhauer says, he is really the most severe and consistent of logicians, and holds the threads of his design in an iron hand, his *dramatis personae* affect to follow whither the argument blows,[5] and he often seems more concerned to edify or entertain than to demonstrate and conclude. Wherever his æsthetic or moral preferences are involved he cavils on terminology and breaks into seemingly irrelevant eloquent digressions in a Ruskinian fashion sorely puzzling to those not in sympathy with his mood. If forced to accept the substance of a repugnant theory, he translates it into language more consonant with his feelings. This peculiar mixture of rhetoric and logic, of edification and science, misleads both the sentimentalist and the scientific puritan. The one often mistakes the ornament for the substance, the other distrusts perfectly sound reasoning because of his distaste for its emotional accompaniment.

Again, Plato stimulates our own speculation in so many ways that we are apt to mistake the drift of his meanings not because it is not clearly defined, but because we abandon

[5] Not only in the earlier dialogues, but in *Rep.*, 394 D ; *Theætet.*, 172 D ; *Laws*, 667 A.

it to pursue our own.   The clever essayist tells us what he himself thought *à propos* of this or that brilliant suggestion.   The investigator too often begins by selecting a few detached notions and formulas as adequately representative of each dialogue, and then proceeds to juggle with ingenious combinations of these and the interpretations put upon them by his predecessors.   Neither interprets Plato's real thoughts as they lie open to any competent reader who will patiently study him to the end and report the things on which he lays most stress.[6]

2. In the second place, Plato's dramatic quality affects not only the artistic setting and the personages, but the ideas which he brings upon the stage.   Plato's serious meaning detaches itself with perfect distinctness for the faithful student.   But the hasty reader is more likely than not to receive as Platonic ideas that have a purely dramatic significance; or that are falsified by isolation from their context.[7]   And the investigator in pursuit of a thesis too often attributes specifically to Protagoras, Antisthenes, Euclid, or Isocrates ideas that Plato has generalized and decked out beyond all recognition, as representatives of the spirit of the age.

Again, arguing for victory, the maintenance of a thesis in jest to test an opponent's metal or display one's own ingenuity was a common practice in the world which Plato depicts, and is frequently illustrated in his writings.   The Platonic Socrates, under cover of an ironical profession of ignorance, employs a similar method to expose showy pretenders to universal knowledge, to produce a salutary conviction of ignorance, or to stimulate youthful thought, and prepare the way for a more serious analysis by an exposition of the antinomies latent in conventional opinions.   It follows that the ostensible failure to conclude an argument, the avowal of bewilderment and perplexity, the admission even of positive fallacies of logic in any given dialogue prove nothing as to the stage of development of Plato's own thought at the time.   The hypothesis that the fallacy was intentional, and that the ἀπορία was affected for a purpose, has at least an equal claim to be tested by all the probabilities in each case.

3. Expositors of Plato seem strangely oblivious of the limits thus far set to all systems of philosophy.   They treat as peculiar defects of Plato the inconsistencies which they detect in his ultimate metaphysics after they have elaborated it into a rigid system which he with sound instinct evaded by poetry and myth.   They habitually write as if they themselves and their intelligent readers were in possession of a final philosophy which reconciles all conflicting claims of metaphysical analysis and common sense, and from the heights of which they may study merely as a historical phenomenon Plato's primitive fumbling with such problems as the nature of

---

[6] Such a reader is Bonitz for the most part in his admirable analyses.

[7] A notable example is Herbert Spencer's inference from *Rep.*, 339 D, that Plato, like Hobbes, makes state enactments the source of right.   So President Eliot has been recently misled by ZELLER's misuse of *Rep.*, 421 A (*Phil. der Griechen*, 4th ed., Vol. II, No. 1, p. 890), to prove that Plato would not educate the masses.   Many scholars still seem to think that the etymologies of the *Cratylus* were intended seriously, and not a few continue to quote *Theœtet.*, 156 ff., as Platonic doctrine.   Under this head fall most of the "fallacies" discovered in Plato: those of the *Parmenides*, which, as we shall see, are intentional; those of the *Gorgias*, dramatically justifiable against the extreme thesis maintained by Callicles; those of *Rep.*, I, 333 E, and 349 B, which Zeller (p. 652) thinks Plato did not perceive.

universals, the antinomy of unity and plurality in thought and things,[8] the relation of mind and body, the possibility of a consciousness of self or a knowledge of knowledge, the proof of immortality, the freedom of the will, the difficulty of conceiving or defining good except in relation to evil, the alternative of excepting thoroughgoing relativism and phenomenalism or of positing a *noumenon* that cannot be described or brought into intelligible relation with phenomena. We are told that he has "keine Ableitung des Sinnlichen," as if there were somewhere extant a satisfactory deduction of the sensible world from some higher metaphysical principle. It is objected that the relation of the ideas to the Deity is undefined, and that the personality of God is not investigated, as if any results could follow from an attempt to define the relation of the metaphysical *noumenon* to the Deity, or from an investigation of the personality of God. The absence of a complete table of categories is taken as a defect in Plato's system or as a proof of the immaturity of the *Phædrus*, as if the Aristotelian and Kantian categories were not mere illusions of the metaphysical instinct, and Plato was not far wiser in proposing only such categories and classifications as the argument in hand required.

A chief merit of Plato is that he clearly recognizes and sharply defines the limits of scientific thought in these matters. When the interests of the moral and religious life, as he conceives them, are at stake he resorts to myth to express his hopes and aspirations. Where the epistemological problem compromises the foundations of practical certainty and sound method, he arbitrarily postulates the solution that will best serve his chief purpose — the extrication of a practicable working logic from the hopeless dialectical muddle of his time. But he is always careful to distinguish his necessary practical postulates from his mythical and metaphysical assumptions.[9] The dogmatism of his later works has been as much exaggerated as the Socratic doubt of the minor dialogues.[10]

4. As a fourth cause of misapprehension we may count a certain quaint and curious subtlety in the use of abstraction and antithesis characteristic of all Greek writers, but carried to its farthest extreme in Plato. His reasoning often proceeds by what seem to us excessively minute verbal links. This is generally thought to mean merely that the modern mind has learned to abridge the formal process by taking some things for granted. But it is often due to Plato's anxiety to anticipate the cavils and quibbles of the age before logic; or his wish to bring out neglected shades of meaning.

Again, Plato, like all serious reasoners, employs unreal abstractions to express ideals and test hypotheses by extreme cases.[11] But in addition to this the Platonic Socrates meets a fallacious and fantastic abstraction from the conditions of reality, not

[8] Astonishment is often expressed at the attention bestowed by Plato upon the problem of the one and the many, as if, transferred to psychology, it were not still the crux of all our metaphysics.

[9] *Meno*, 86 B; *Phædr.*, 252 C, 265 C, 274 C ; *Rep.*, 416 B C, 517 B, 506 C.

[10] *Tim.*, 72 D, *Laws*, 641 D, 799 D, 812 A. The percentage of apodictic replies in the "later" works proves nothing that is not already involved in the fact that they are not dramatic disputations. A consenting respondent naturally gives "apodictic" answers.

[11] *E. g.*, the isolation of pleasure and intelligence in *Phileb.*, 21, to which Grote objects.

by exposing the fallacy, but by translating all the real facts into the language of abstraction. There is no real fallacy in such procedure, but a sense of fallacy results for the modern reader.[12] Allied to this is the use or abuse of antithesis. Opposite views are first stated with ruthless consistency in their most abstract and extreme form. And the truth is approached through a series of compromises and mediations.[13] Dramatically, Plato is right. This is the course of discussion among ordinary men in all ages. But the elaborate refutations which Plato thinks fit to give of the crudest form of hostile theories sometimes produces an impression of unfairness upon modern critics.[14] They forget two things : first, that he always goes on to restate the theory and refute its fair meaning; second, that in the case of many doctrines combated by Plato there is no evidence that they ever were formulated with the proper logical qualifications except by himself.[15]

5. In the fifth place, and finally, we may mention the difficulty of confining the infinite variety and suggestiveness of Plato's thoughts in the framework of any system either of philosophy or of exposition. It is possible to present Plato's ethical and social ideals in a fairly systematic résumé. The theory of ideas may be restated in the Platonic terminology, which does not teach us much, or analyzed in relation to the underlying psychological and ontological problems. Special chapters might be written on Plato's attitude toward inchoate physical science, the temper in which he faced the religious problems of an age of transition, his portrayal and criticism of the literary and artistic life of his time. But a complete system of philosophy with principles subordinate, derivative, and interdependent, and a fixed technical terminology, cannot be extracted from the Platonic writings. This will not greatly grieve those who are aware of the perfect futility of all such system-building, even when the architect possesses the genius of a Spinoza, a Kant, or a Schopenhauer. But the expositor of Plato can hardly avoid attempting to cast his exposition into some systematic form, and the recalcitrance of his material is to him a serious problem. No method is quite satisfactory. The atomism of Grote, Jowett, Bonitz, and Horn, that treats each dialogue as an isolated unit, is the renunciation of all method. The clever attempts of a succession of French expositors to deduce all Platonism symmetrically from a few principles are more ingenious than convincing.[16] The exhaustive schematism of Zeller, applied alike to all philosophers from Thales to Plotinus, is philologically a masterly achievement of German erudition. But, though

---

[12] E. g., in Rep., I, 346, the separation of μισθωτική, the wage-earning power, from the other functions of each art and craft.

[13] Philebus, Theœtetus, Rep., I and II, Gorgias.

[14] E. g., in the Cratylus, 385 A, the theory that language is a mere convention is first stated in the most extreme form. In the Gorgias a long argument is spent to drive Callicles from a position which he affirms was assumed in jest (499 B). In Rep., 338 C., Thrasymachus's definition of justice is taken in a grotesquely unfair sense in order to force him to state it more clearly. Cf. Laws, 714 C; Gorg.,

451 E, 453 B, 489 D. Similar is the treatment of Homo Mensura in the Protagoras, and the claim of pleasure to be the chief good in the Philebus.

[15] Plato may have found hints and suggestions of the views he brings on the stage in Euripides and the Sophists (DÜMMLER, Prolegomena zu Platons Staat). But so far as we know, he is the first thinker who could present a complete logical statement of any philosophical theory in all its bearings.

[16] See my review of HALÉVY, Théorie platonicienne des sciences, Philosophical Review, Vol. V, p. 522.

rarely admitting gross and palpable errors, Zeller's exposition frequently misses the true proportions, perspective, and emphasis that would be brought out by a more flexible literary and philosophic interpretation.

The present study, though it touches on most topics of the Platonic philosophy, does not attempt a complete historical survey. Some subjects I have discussed elsewhere. There are many details (in the *Laws* and *Timœus, e. g.*) which would be irrelevant to the main purpose of emphasizing the unity of Plato's thought. The order of presentation adopted after many attempts is a compromise between the systematic and the atomistic. The Platonic ethics, the theory of ideas, and an outline of the psychology will first be set forth as a whole. A group of logical and metaphysical problems will be discussed in connection with the *Sophist* and *Parmenides*. Other topics and some repetitions from a different point of view will follow in a survey of the principal dialogues taken one by one.

I. ETHICS

The chief topics of the Platonic ethics are these: (1) the Socratic paradoxes; (2) the definition of the virtues, and, more particularly, the determination of their relation to a postulated supreme science or art, to happiness, to the political or royal art, to the idea of good; (3) the problem of hedonism; and (4), associated with it, the attempt to demonstrate the inseparability of virtue and happiness.[17]

1. Plato always formally maintained that all wrongdoing is involuntary;[18] that virtue is insight or knowledge, is in its essence one, and can in some sense be taught.[19] Sometimes he merely dramatically illustrates the conflicts that arise between these paradoxes and common-sense. Elsewhere, most explicitly in the *Laws*,[20] but by implication even in the minor dialogues, he reveals his perception that these propositions can be reconciled with experience only by the conscious employment of words in a special sense.[21] Wrongdoing is involuntary (1) because all men will the good or what they deem the good;[22] (2) because no man who knows the right will do the wrong, if we take knowledge in the highest sense, or refuse the term to any cognition that does not control the will;[23] (3) because the conditions that shape conduct lie far more in heredity, education, and environment than in our conscious wills.[24] The contradiction noted by Aristotle between this charitable principle and the edifying proclamation "virtue is free,"[25] is emotional rather than scientific.[26] The modern free-will controversy arises out of two conceptions not connected with this problem by Plato: the

[17] These are, as a matter of fact, the chief topics of the ethical dialogues. If we base Plato's ethics on the idea of good, or on any other metaphysical principle or schematism, we shall distort his meanings.

[18] XEN., *Mem.*, 3, 9, 4; 4, 6, 6; *Apol.*, 26 A; *Protag.*, 345 D, 358 C D; *Meno*, 77, 78; *Gorg.*, 466 E, 467 B=*Rep.*, 577 E=*Laws*, 688 B; *Rep.*, 382 A (?), 413 A (?), 492 E (?), 589 C; *Phileb.*, 22 B; *Soph.*, 228 C, 230 A; *Tim.*, 86 D; *Laws*, 731 C, 734 B, 860 D.

[19] *Euthydem.*, 282 C; *Laws*, 644 A, ὡς οἵ γε ὀρθῶς πεπαιδευμένοι σχεδὸν ἀγαθοὶ γίγνονται.

[20] 689 D, 696 C, 710 A, ἤν τις σεμνύνων ἂν λέγοι, φρόνησιν προσαναγκάζων εἶναι τὸ σωφρονεῖν.

[21] *Laches*, 196 E; *Laches*, 191 E, ἀνδρεῖοι . . . . ἐν ἡδοναῖς, cf. *Laws*, 633 D E, and *Rep.*, 429 D; *Rep.*, 443 E, 444 A; *Theœtet.*, 176 C; *Polit.*, 306 A.

[22] *Meno*, 77; *Euthydem.*, 279; *Symp.*, 205 A; *Gorg.*, 468.

[23] *Protag.*, 352 B; *Laws*, 689; *Theœtet.*, 176 C.

[24] *Tim.*, 86 D.   [25] *Rep.*, 617 E, ἀρετὴ δὲ ἀδέσποτον.

[26] Cf. my note in *A. J. P.*, Vol. X, p. 77.

infinite foreknowledge of God, and the absolute continuity of physical causation. It is, then, unprofitable to inquire whether Plato taught free-will or determinism.[27] But it should be distinctly noted that in the *Laws* he employs precisely the logic of modern determinism to prove that the involuntary character of wrongdoing is compatible with the distinction for legal purposes of voluntary and involuntary acts.[28]

Virtue is knowledge because it must be assumed to be a good, and the only certain good, the only sure guide to the good use of what the world calls good, is knowledge.[29] Opinion and habit may often suffice to regulate action, but persistent right opinion presupposes knowledge in its teachers, and the highest rule of conduct must be deduced from and referred to a rational apprehension of ultimate good.[30] Virtue is one because each of the virtues is a form of knowledge,[31] or because each, when taken in the highest sense, involves all the others.[32] Virtue is teachable in the senses in which knowledge and right opinion may be taught. The capacity for knowledge, the divine faculty, is innate, but teaching and guidance may direct it toward the good.[33] The ordinary virtues of habit and opinion may fairly be said to be taught when they are systematically inculcated by superior wisdom enlisting all the forces of society in its service.[34] This is not the case at Athens,[35] and therefore the Platonic Socrates alternately affirms and denies the possibility of teaching "virtue,"[36] and at the close of the *Meno* declares that under present conditions it comes by a grace divine which is equivalent to chance.[37]

Plato uses, but is not himself confused by, the Socratic analogy between the virtues and the arts and sciences.[38] That comparison, though it ignores the distinctively ethical element, contains a certain measure of truth. In a sense, each of us is good in that which he knows.[39] Knowledge as ordinarily understood is not virtue, but it

---

[27] ZELLER, p. 853; JOWETT, Vol. III, pp. 408, 425.

[28] 861–864 C. The meaning of the passage, though often misunderstood, is perfectly clear, and Plato warns us, 864 B, not to cavil about the terminology.

[29] *Euthydem.*, 281, 289; *Meno*, 88 C. *Cf.* from another point of view *Phædo*, 69 A B; *Protag.*, 356, 357, with *Phileb.*, 41 E.

[30] *Meno*, 97 B; *Meno*, 100 A, οἷος καὶ ἄλλον ποιῆσαι, etc. *Cf. Euthyd.*, 292 D; *infra*, p. 16; *Laws*, 951 B.

[31] *Laches*; *Protag.*; *Phædo*, 69 A B. *Meno*, 71 D ff., is logical rather than ethical. The unity of ἀρετή is postulated, like that of any other abstract idea, as a precondition of a definition.

[32] *Gorg.*, 507 A; *Laws*, 696 C. There is a suggestion of this also in the (of course intentional, BONITZ, *Platonic Studies*, p. 265) fallacies of *Protag.*, 330, 331.

[33] *Rep.*, 518 B, 519 A. This apparently contradicts the statement of the *Meno*, 99 A, and *Protag.*, 361 B, that ἐπιστήμη alone can be taught. But the objection is captious. The *Republic* is satirizing the exaggerated claims of the Sophists and is speaking of the faculty, not the content, of knowledge. The whole higher education is a teaching of knowledge in a sense. And, on the other hand, though both Plato and Aristotle limit teaching in the strict sense

to knowledge, opinion is imparted ἐν τῇ παιδείᾳ, 429 C, *i. e.*, is virtually taught.

[34] *Rep.*, 500 D, 429 C D; *Polit.*, 309 D; *Laws*, *passim*.

[35] *Rep.*, 492 E; *Tim.*, 87 B; *Meno*, 93 B ff.; *Protag.*, 320; *Rep.*, 520 B; *Euthyphro*, 2 C D; *Gorg.*, 521 D; *Apol.*, 24, 25; *Laches*, 179 C D.

[36] *Protag.*; *Meno*; *Euthyd.*, 282 C (274 E).

[37] For this interpretation of θείᾳ μοίρᾳ see MAGUIRE, p. 63, and ZELLER's full refutation of other views, p. 594, n. 4, *Rep.*, 492, 493. At present good men spring up αὐτόματοι (*Rep.*, 520 B; *cf. Protag.*, 320 A; *Euthyd.*, 282 C); even in vicious states, *Laws*, 951 B, ἀεὶ θεῖοί τινες οὐ πολλοί . . . . φυόμενοι οὐδὲν μᾶλλον ἐν εὐνομουμέναις πόλεσιν ἢ καὶ μή.

[38] The lesser *Hippias* (certainly by Plato) presents the fallacy in its most paradoxical form (the voluntary lie better than the involuntary) and by its obvious irony (372 D E, 376 C) shows that Plato "already" in the Socratic period does not take it seriously, but merely uses it for dramatic or propædeutic purposes. ZELLER, p. 597, takes this as Plato's real opinion, citing *Rep.*, 535 D and 382, which merely use the paradoxical terminology to emphasize the thought, acceptable to Mill or Huxley, that the mere intellectual love of truth (knowledge) ought to be counted a virtue as well as the ordinary virtue of truthfulness.

[39] *Laches*, 194 D; *Lysis*, 210 D; *Rep.*, 349 E.

does away with many forms of wrongdoing. It is not courage, but the man who knows how is less likely to be afraid.[40] It is not σωφροσύνη, but it is incompatible with many forms of ἀφροσύνη. The wise man knows his own limits, and will undertake only what he can perform.[41] Partly for these reasons, and partly because he did not or, in ironical assumption that others were even as himself, would not recognize that men know the right and yet the wrong pursue, the Platonic Socrates seems to ignore the chief ethical factor, a virtuous will, and argues that he who knows justice is just.[42] But such "fallacies" are for Plato merely the starting-point of a fuller analysis. All knowledge is good and commendable,[43] but the supreme knowledge that may be identified with "virtue" is plainly something different from the specialties of the arts and sciences.[44] Courage, for example, apart from mere animal and temperamental fearlessness, may be defined as knowledge of what is and is not to be feared. But this involves real knowledge of good and evil, a complete ideal of life, either that of the Sophists and average Athenian opinion, or that unfolded by Plato himself in the *Republic*. The attempt to define courage in the absence of these distinctions merely illustrates the inadequacy of conventional ethical thought.[45]

The effective application to these problems of the obvious distinction between science and right opinion requires the larger canvas of the *Republic*. And even then it remains true that the courage most worthy of the name implies a complete philosophic mastery of the conception of life that educates the masses in such right opinion.[46] Plato tacitly assumes that this supreme knowledge will be inseparable from the virtuous will in his philosophic statesmen as it is in Socrates.[47] And thus on this higher plane the Socratic paradox becomes true again.

It matters little to the consistency and unity of Plato's thought whether we regard this harmony of the intellect and the will as a mere ideal or as a practicable postulate realized in Socrates and to be fulfilled by others in a reformed society. The distinction once drawn, the ideal once affirmed, Plato can afford to make concessions to common-sense. He can admit that in present experience a kind of bravery is

[40] *Laches*, 193; *Protag.*, 350.

[41] XEN., *Mem.*, 2, 2, 24; *Charm.*, 171 D E; *Alc.*, I, 117 D E; *Sophist*, 229 C; *Laws*, 732 A.

[42] *Gorg.*, 460 B. The fallacy, so far as it is one, is intentional. Observe κατὰ τοῦτον τὸν λόγον, and the explanation in *Rep.*, 438 D E, that the knowledge of health, though differentiated from knowledge in general, is not necessarily healthful. *Cf.* also the recognition of common-sense in 444 D, τὸ μὲν δίκαια πράττειν δικαιοσύνην ἐμποιεῖ. But for the broad purposes of the argument of the *Gorgias* it is true (460 E) that rhetoric, if really the science of the just, could not be the instrument of injustice which Gorgias with unconscious immorality complacently represented it to be. Socrates is οἷος τῶν ἐμῶν μηδενὶ ἄλλῳ πείθεσθαι ἢ τῷ λόγῳ, *Crito*, 46 B; *cf. Laches*, 188 D E; *Gorg.*, 488 A. Hence, as Aristotle (*Eth. nic.*, 7, 2, 1), quoting *Protag.*, 352 B, says, he thought it monstrous that any other impulse in man should prevail over his better knowledge. And Plato in his latest work refuses the term "knowledge" to any belief that does not control the will, and pronounces discord between the desires and the ethical convictions the grossest form of "ignorance."

[43] *Protag.*, 318 B; *Laches*, 182 D.

[44] *Charm.*, 165 C; *Euthydem.*, 282 E, 290; *Protag.*, 311, 312, 319 A; *Laws*, 961 E ff.

[45] *Laches*; *Protag.*, 349, 350, 360 D; *Rep.*, 429, 430.

[46] The courage defined in 429 C is only πολιτικήν γε. *Cf.* δημώδη γε, *Laws*, 710 A; *Polit.*, 309 E; *Phædo*, 82 A. There are, strictly speaking, three or four grades; brute animal courage, the courage of soldiers and citizens in ordinary states, the citizen courage of the Platonic state, the philosophic courage.

[47] This harmony is the chief point in the selections and tests applied to them; *Rep.*, 485, 486, 539 D ff. *Cf. Polit.*, 309 A B. The *Laws* emphasize character, as compared with intellect, still more, and preserve the identity of the moral and the intellectual "which are ever dividing, but must ever be reunited" (Jowett), by reserving the word "wise" for the virtuous, 689 D.

found dissociated from the other virtues.[48]   He can allow the word σωφροσύνη to be used merely for the instinctive temperamental moderation in appetite that is the fortunate endowment of some children and animals.[49]   He can recognize that knowledge, or at least quickness and acumen of thought, is not infrequently associated with intemperance and injustice.[50]   But he prefers to translate the facts into a more edifying terminology.   Conventional virtue is a worthless currency unless redeemable and redeemed by and in the coin of wisdom.[51]   And, on the other hand, we will refuse the name of wise to him whose will does not follow his judgment of right; and we will grant it to the man who knows enough to obey his acquired belief in the good rather than the innate promptings of appetite, though he know not how to swim or recite the alphabet.[52]

2. Plato found the suggestion of the cardinal virtues and of the predominance of justice in the poets.   He also mentions ὁσιότης[53] and μεγαλοπρέπεια, the latter sometimes with irony.[54]   But the number four was consecrated by its incorporation in the scheme of the *Republic*.   This implies no change of doctrine.   Even in the *Republic* other virtues are mentioned.[55]   And in the *Euthyphro* it is hinted that piety is a form of justice.[56]

Plato would always recognize piety as one of the chief virtues, or perhaps as a synonym of all virtue,[57] and he would always shrink from giving so problematical a concept a place in a scientific scheme.[58]

Several of the minor dialogues turn on the attempt to define the virtues and allied notions.   The *Laches* and *Charmides* are both Socratic quests for definition — of courage in the one case, of temperance in the other.   Both involve the antithesis of the quiet and the energetic temperament.[59]   Both terminate in perplexity — in the puzzle that, if any one virtue is identified with the supreme knowledge that will make

[48] Protagoras maintains this view, *Protag.*, 350, and is not answered by Socrates, who refutes him only indirectly by the proof that all virtue is one — the science of measuring pleasure and pain.   But the obvious fact of experience is presumably as clear to Plato when he allows Protagoras to state it as when it is enunciated more explicitly in the *Politicus*, 306 B, or the *Laws*, 631 C.   ZELLER (p. 599) incomprehensibly affirms that the plurality in unity of virtue is found only in the *Republic*!

[49] *Laws*, 710 A B.

[50] *Rep.*, 519 A; *Laws*, 689 D, ὅσα πρὸς τάχος τῆς ψυχῆς; *Theætet.*, 176 C.

[51] *Phædo.*, 69 B.

[52] *Laws*, 689 D, μήτε γράμματα μήτε νεῖν.   Cf. *Theætet.*, 176 C, τῷ οὖν ἀδικοῦντι . . . . μακρῷ ἄριστ' ἔχει τὸ μὴ συγχωρεῖν δεινῷ ὑπὸ πανουργίας εἶναι.   The whole passage is in the mood and temper of the *Laws*.

[53] *Protag.*, 329 C; *Meno*, 78 D; *Laches*, 199 D.

[54] *Meno*, 74 A; *Rep.*, 560 E.   In *Meno*, 88 A, εὐμάθεια and μνήμη are included.

[55] 402 C, ἐλευθεριότης, μεγαλοπρέπεια 536 A.

[56] Cf. also *Protag.*, 331 A.

[57] If it were desirable to produce a Platonic definition

of piety, I should accept that of Bonitz as formulated by PROFESSOR HEIDEL (introduction to his edition of *Euthyphro*, p. 24).   It is the endeavor to realize the good felt as the service of God, and as a willed co-operation with Him.   But this is a mood in relation to, or an emotional synonym of, all virtue.   It is not one aspect of virtue which it is necessary to distinguish in relation to a special field of conduct or a particular classification of the faculties of the soul.

[58] The suggestion that the *Euthyphro* " eliminates " piety, and that the *Meno* may be dated by its recognition of ὁσιότης (78 D) is utterly fantastic.

[59] Cf. *Charm.*, 159 B ff., with *Polit.*, 307 A B.   Temperament is not virtue, but is the basis of the seeming opposition between bravery and temperance (*Polit.*, 306, 307; *Rep.*, 410 D E, 503 C D; *Laws*, 735 A, 681 B, 773 B, 831 E; *Protag.*, 349 E).   Nicias and Laches, for want of this distinction, maintain opposite paradoxes.   Socrates calls our attention to this by attributing to Nicias the doctrine ὁμοίως λέοντα καὶ ἔλαφον . . . . πρὸς ἀνδρείαν — πεφυκέναι (196 E).   In the *Republic* (430 B), Plato chooses to deny the term " bravery " to mere animal courage.   In the *Laws*, 963 E, he attributes a kind of courage to children and animals.   But ὁμοίως πεφυκέναι pointedly ignores the distinction of temperament.

us happy, the distinction between the virtues vanishes;[60] or in the tautology that the knowledge that is good is knowledge of the good.[61]

It is often assumed (1) that Plato was serious in these attempts to express by a phrase or a substituted synonym the essence of a virtue and the various and contradictory meanings of its conventional name; (2) that the failure and pretended perplexity of Socrates at the close mark the point reached by Plato's own thought at the time. This is *a priori* conceivable. But the following considerations make it highly improbable:

a) Plato, in this unlike Xenophon,[62] always proceeds as if he were aware of the true theory and use of the definition and of the multiple meanings of ethical terms. All attempts in his writings to work out absolute and isolated definitions fail.[63] His own definitions, when not mere illustrations,[64] are always working hypotheses[65] or epigrammatic formulas, subordinate to and interpreted by the argument of which they form a part, and recognized as imperfect, but sufficient for the purpose in hand.[66] The definitions of the virtues in *Rep.*, 429 ff. cannot be understood apart from their context, and are never used again. They are declared to be a mere sketch— ὑπογραφήν, 504 D.[67] How shall we explain this on the supposition that he was under any illusion as to the value of absolute and isolated definitions?

b) Plato repeatedly refers in a superior way to eristic, voluntary and involuntary,[68] and more particularly to the confusion, tautology, and logomachy into which the vulgar fall when they attempt to discuss abstract and ethical problems.[69] Some of these allusions touch on the very perplexities and fallacies exemplified in the minor dialogues.[70] They do not imply that Plato himself had ever been so confused.[71] Why should we assume that he deceives us in order to disguise his changes of opinion, or

---

[60] *Laches*, 199 E.

[61] *Charm.*, 174 B; *cf. Rep.*, 505 B C — a connection generally missed.

[62] The Xenophontic Socrates perceives no difficulties, is never in doubt, and propounds dogmatically such definitions as νόμιμον = δίκαιον, *Mem.*, IV, 4, 12.

[63] Except the not quite serious definitions reached by dichotomy in the *Sophist* and *Politicus*. *Cf. Charmides, Laches, Lysis, Meno, Theœtetus, Euthyphro, Hippias Major.*

[64] τάχος, *Laches*, 192 B; σχῆμα, *Meno*, 75, 76; πηλός, *Theœtet.*, 147 C; ἥλιος, *ibid.*, 208 D.

[65] *Phœdr.*, 237 D, ὁμολογίᾳ θέμενοι ὅρον. *Cf.* 263 D E.

[66] *E. g.*, ῥητορικὴ=πολιτικῆς μορίου εἴδωλον, *Gorg.*, 463 D, but in *Phœdr.*, 261 A, ψυχαγωγία τις διὰ λόγων. *Cf.* the definitions of σωφροσύνη, *Phœdr.*, 237 E.

[67] The *Laws* repeats the substance of the definition of justice, 863 E: τὴν γὰρ τοῦ θυμοῦ . . . . καὶ ἐπιθυμιῶν ἐν ψυχῇ τυραννίδα . . . . πάντως ἀδικίαν προσαγορεύω. *Cf.* 689 A B, τὸ γὰρ λυπούμενον καὶ ἡδόμενον αὐτῆς (*sc.* τῆς ψυχῆς) ὅπερ δῆμός τε καὶ πλῆθος πόλεώς ἐστιν. *Cf. Rep.*, 442 A, ὃ δὴ πλεῖστον τῆς ψυχῆς, etc.

[68] *Rep.*, 454 A; *Phileb.*, 14 C, ἑκοῦσί τε καὶ ἄκουσιν; *Theœtet.*, 206 B, ἑκόντα ἢ ἄκοντα παίζειν; *Theœtet.*, 167 E; *Sophist*, 259 D; already in *Lysis*, 216 A B. *Cf. infra*, p. 19.

[69] *Phœdr.*, 237 C, 263, and, from a slightly different point of view, *Rep.*, 538 D; *Phœdo*, 90 C. This is largely due to a false conceit of knowledge, *Phœdr.*, 237 C, which the Elenchus as described in *Soph.*, 230 B, and practised in the minor

dialogues cures. *Cf. Meno*, 84 A B. So *Soph.*, 232 A B, gives the *raison d'être* of passages (*Gorgias, Protag., Ion*) in which a pretender to universal knowledge is pressed for a specific definition of his function which he naturally is unable to give.

[70] *Polit.*, 306 ff., especially 306 A, τὸ γὰρ ἀρετῆς μέρος ἀρετῆς εἴδει διάφορον εἶναί τινα τρόπον τοῖς περὶ λόγους ἀμφισβητικοῖς καὶ μάλ' εὐεπίθετον πρὸς τὰς τῶν πολλῶν δόξας. *Cf. Laws*, 627 D, εὐσχημοσύνης . . . . ῥημάτων πρὸς τὸν τῶν πολλῶν λόγον. *Repub.*, 348 E, εἴχομεν ἄν τι λέγειν κατὰ τὰ νομιζόμενα λέγοντες, with reference to the arguments of *Gorg.*, 474 C ff. *Cf. Laws*, 837 A, with reference to the problem of the *Lysis; Laws*, 661 B, 687, 688, 688 B, where the paradox of *Gorg.*, 467, is reaffirmed, εἰ μὲν βούλεσθε ὡς παίζων, εἰ δ' ὡς σπουδάζων; *Republic*, 505 B, with *Charm.*, 173 E–174 B; *Rep.*, 505 C, with *Gorg.*, 499 B, where Callicles is forced to admit that some pleasures are bad. ZELLER (p. 604) thinks that *Rep.*, 505 C, refers to the *Philebus*. But the advocates of a late date for the *Philebus* rightly deny any specific parallel.

[71] Even after the *Republic* and *Politicus*, Plato in *Laws*, 963 ff., approaches the problem of the "political art" and the unity of virtue precisely in the manner of the tentative dialogues. There is no reason for taking seriously Socrates's dramatic bewilderment as to the "political art" in *Euthydem.*, 292 D E, that would not apply equally to the avowal of ignorance in *Laws*, 963 B, or in the *Politicus* itself, 292 C. The political art, *i.e.*, ultimate ethical and social "good," was always a problem to Plato, as it must be to any thoughtful, conscientious man (*Rep.*, 451 A). In the *Laws*,

obliterate the traces of his mental growth?   Have we not a right to expect dramatic illustration of so prominent a feature in the intellectual life of the time, and do we not find it in the *Laches, Charmides, Lysis,* and the corresponding parts of the *Protagoras?*   In brief, the *Euthydemus,* 277, 278; *Phœdrus,* 261, 262; the *Theœtetus,* 167 E; the *Republic,* 454, 487 B C; the *Sophist,* 230 B, 251 B, 259 C, and *Philebus,* 20 A, 15 E, show a clear consciousness of dialectic, not merely as a method of truth, but as a game practiced for amusement or eristic, to purge the conceit of ignorance or awaken intellectual curiosity.   When we find this game dramatically illustrated why should we assume naïve unconsciousness on Plato's part?

c) The *Republic,* in which Plato explicitly states his solution of these problems, is a marvelous achievement of mature constructive thought.   But the ideas and distinctions required for the solution itself are obvious enough, and it is absurd to affirm that they were beyond the reach of a thinker who was capable of composing the *Protagoras,*[72] the subtle *Lysis* and *Charmides,* or the eloquent and ingenious *Gorgias.* That the highest rule of conduct must be based upon complete insight and is the possession of a few; that the action of the multitude is determined by habit and belief[73] shaped under the manifold pressure of tradition and public opinion; that the virtues may be differently defined according as we refer them to knowledge or to opinion and habit; that opinion in the Athens of the Sophists and of the Peloponnesian war was not guided by true philosophy, and therefore was not the "right opinion" which should become the fixed habit of the populace in a reformed society; that the Sophists who professed to teach virtue taught at the best conformity to the desires and opinions of the many-headed beast, and that therefore in the proper sense virtue was not taught at all at Athens;[74] that virtue is one regarded as knowledge, or as the spiritual harmony resulting from perfect self-control (443 E), but many as expressing the opposition of contrasted temperaments and different degrees of education; and that endless logomachies result from the inability of the average disputant to grasp these and similar distinctions[75]— these are reflections that might present themselves to any intelligent young man who had listened to Socrates, and surveyed the intellectual life of the time, though only the genius of Plato could construct a *Republic* from them.   They could occur to Plato at the age of thirty or thirty-five as well as at forty or forty-five; and it is extremely naïve to assume that so obvious a distinction as that between science and opinion, familiar to every reader of *Parmenides,* and employed to bring the *Meno* to a plausible dramatic conclusion, was a great scientific discovery, marking an epoch in Plato's thought.[76]

964 ff., as in the *Republic,* he finally limits himself to indicating the kind of training that will prepare the mind to apprehend it best.   But as against the ideals of Athenian sophists and politicians, his beliefs were defined "already" in the *Euthyphro,* 2 C, and the *Gorgias,* 463 D ff., 521 D.

[72] "One of the finest specimens of analysis in all his writings."—JOHN STUART MILL, *Dissertations and Discussions,* Vol. IV, p. 250.

[73] *Phœdo,* 82 A; *Rep.,* 522 A, 619 C; *Laws,* 966 C.

[74] *Rep.,* 492, 493.

[75] *Laws,* 964 A, διανοοῦ δὲ ὡς ἐρῶν καὶ ὅπη τέτταρα ὄντα ἔν ἐστι, καὶ ἐμὲ δὲ ἀξίου, σοῦ δείξαντος ὡς ἔν, πάλιν ὅπη τέτταρα.

[76] Not to dwell on the resemblance of *Meno,* 99 C, and *Apology,* 22 C (*cf.* also the *Ion*), why, if Plato has no dramatic reserves, is ὀρθή δόξα ignored in the *Euthydemus?* Or is the *Euthydemus,* with its mature logic and its assumption that virtue can be taught, earlier than the *Meno?*

d) Lastly the structure and logic of the minor dialogues are indicative of dramatic design rather than of tentative inquiry. The systematic evolution of the argument and of the antitheses which it involves;[77] the emphasis laid on the very difficulties elucidated by the latter theory;[78] the reserves and qualifications of the argument and the hints of dramatic purpose[79]—all point to Plato's possession of the clue. The argument based on the absence from the "Socratic" dialogues of certain features of the longer works begs the point at issue.

Assuming that Plato undertook to illustrate in brief dramatic discussions the ethical logomachies of the day, he would by hypothesis as a rule abstain from Pythagorean myths, criticism of pre-Socratic thinkers, demonstrations of immortality, psychological or physiological digressions, and dogmatic developments of his own philosophy. It may be argued that such dramatic dialogues form as a whole an earlier group. It cannot be maintained that they mark the stages of Plato's own progress.[80] The definitions of the virtues proposed in the fourth book of the *Republic*, interpreted by their context, meet the dramatic difficulties of the *Laches, Charmides, Protagoras*, and *Meno*. Courage is not animal fearlessness, neither is it precisely knowledge of things terrible and the reverse. But the courage to be expected of the masses in a reformed state is the conservation by disciplined feeling of the opinion about things terrible or not terrible inculcated by the possessors of such knowledge.[81] Σωφροσύνη is not precisely quietness, nor doing one's own business, nor self-knowledge, though each of these definitions emphasizes one of the shades of meaning which Greek usage assigned to this "mixed mode." It is in man and state the willing acceptance by all the psychic faculties and the corresponding classes in the population of a harmonious scale of

---

[77] In the *Charmides* σωφροσύνη is first defined by the quiet temperament, 159 B, then by the associated modesty, αἰδώς, 159 E, which is elsewhere its virtual synonym, *Protag.*, 322 C D E; then by τὰ ἑαυτοῦ πράττειν, 161 B, another rhetorical equivalent, *Tim.*, 72 A, which, however, requires an interpretation that Critias is unable to give, even though assisted by a hint from Socrates (161 E). He cannot generalize minding one's own business, and distinguish (1) the economic, (2) the social and political, (3) the psychic division of labor; *Rep.*, 443 C. The formula is allowed to drop, and the equally ambiguous expression "self-knowledge" is substituted (164), which is found to involve puzzles that Critias can neither untie nor cut (*cf.* 167 A with *Meno*, 80 E; *Theætet.*, 188 A).

In the *Laches*, Laches insists exclusively on the temperamental aspect of bravery which opposes it to other virtues, Nicias on the cognitive element which identifies it with them. Laches's theory tends to show how the virtues are many, that of Nicias how they are one (*Laws*, 963 E ff.). But neither can expound his own view completely, still less reconcile it with the truth of his adversary. They exemplify the logomachy described in *Polit.*, 306, 307. This is the chief object of the dialogue, and not the reduction of all virtue to knowledge (Zeller), nor the unity of virtue (Horn), nor even the establishment of the definition φρόνιμος καρτερία which Bonitz says is the only suggestion not disproved.

In the *Lysis* we begin with purely verbal quibbles, pass to the suggestive antithesis of the attraction of like and unlike in nature and man (214, 215), and conclude with the problem of good and evil, and the ultimate nature of desire and the good.

[78] Note the repeated demand that it be shown how σωφροσύνη is a good, *Charm.*, 159 C, 161 A, 165 D, 172 D, 174 B, with *Rep.*, 50. *Cf. infra*, p. 17. Also *Laws*, 710, when, even after the *Republic*, it is recognized that σωφροσύνη as the mere passive *conditio sine qua non* of the usefulness of the active virtues ἀλόγου σιγῆς ἄξιον ἂν εἴη. Again, *cf.* the association of τὰ ἑαυτοῦ πράττειν in 161 with the division of labor, and *Rep.*, 370 A, 432 A, 434 C, 443 D. So in the *Laches*, Nicias is driven to admit that the knowledge of things really terrible and the reverse is not the property of any craftsman even in his own field, but is some higher knowledge of final ends which he cannot define — *i. e.*, obviously the "political art" or the idea of good.

[79] *Charm.*, 160 B, ἔκ γε τούτου τοῦ λόγου; the obvious design of humbling Critias, 162 C D; Charmides's disbelief in Socrates's ignorance, 176 B. *Cf. Phædr.*, 262 D, ὡς ἂν ὁ εἰδὼς τὸ ἀληθὲς προσπαίζων ἐν λόγοις παράγοι τοὺς ἀκούοντας, Laches's unfamiliarity with dialectic and the awakening effect of the Elenchus upon him; 194 A B.

[80] As UEBERWEG says (*Untersuchungen*, p. 280): "Für das Verständniss des Platonismus ist kaum ein anderer Irrthum gefährlicher, als der, eine Zurückhaltung, die Plato aus methodischen Gründen übte, mit einem Nochnichtsein zu verwechseln."

[81] *Rep.*, 429 C D, 442 C.

subordination from higher to lower.[82]   It is thus the precondition and obverse aspect of justice which is the fulfilment of its own function by each faculty and class—a higher than the economic division of labor in the soul and in society.[83]   These definitions are stated in terms of being rather than of doing, and Plato preferred this form of statement to the end.[84]   But he is careful to add that the one includes the other and that the justice within the soul will express itself in just action.[85]

3. These definitions, then, meet the chief difficulties of the minor dialogues and fill their place in the literary economy of the *Republic*.   But Plato warns us that they are not the final definitions of a complete philosophy.[86]   It is not enough to define the virtues psychologically on the assumption that their sum is good.[87]   A final definition must relate virtue to, and deduce its utility from, an ultimate standard or ideal of good.[88]   Such a definition is rather a regulative conception than a practical possibility. The Platonic Socrates is always prepared to silence by dialectic or overwhelm by his eloquence those who deny that "virtue" is a real good.[89]   But a formal, positive enumeration of the reasons why courage and justice are good and desirable can never be complete, and will always prove unedifying: "Does law so analyzed coerce you much?"   Plato wisely attempts nothing of the kind.   He merely describes the discipline and education[90] that will enable his philosophic rulers to prove, if required, the coincidence of virtue and happiness, and systematically inculcate efficacious right opinion, thus teaching virtue and molding character and institutions in the light of a reasoned and unified conception of the true scope and good of individual· and public

---

[82] 432 A, 442 D. This definition is adapted to the literary machinery of the *Republic*. It does not estop Plato from employing the word in its normal Greek sense (*Rep.*, 389 D E, ὡς πλήθει, etc.), or from recognizing that it is a condition of virtue rather than an active virtue; *supra*, p. 12.

[83] Allowance once made for the literary schematism of the four virtues, the three faculties, and the analogy between the man and the state, and account once taken of *Laws*, 696 C, 710, and *Politicus*, 306 ff., it becomes a little naïve to complain that the distinction intended between σωφροσύνη and δικαιοσύνη is not clear, and a little pedantic to institute a learned philological inquiry to ascertain it.

[84] *Laws*, 864 A, τὴν δὲ τοῦ ἀρίστου δόξαν . . . . ἐὰν αὕτη κρατοῦσα ἐν ψυχαῖς διακοσμῇ πάντα ἄνδρα, κἂν σφάλληταί τι δίκαιον μὲν πᾶν εἶναι φατέον τὸ ταύτῃ πραχθέν.

[85] 442 E, 443 A.

[86] Grote, followed by many others, denies this. But that is because he persists in attributing to Plato the doctrine that ethical abstractions ("mixed modes") have one meaning only which can be expressed in an absolute definition; *cf. supra.* But, on the contrary, the very cause of the confusion, according to Plato, is that men fail to take notice of the different meanings and sub-species covered by one generic term (*Phœdr.*, 161, 162; *Euthydem.*, 277, 278; *Laws*, 837 A; *Phileb.*, 12 E ff.; *Euthyphro*, 7 D. with *Phœdr.*, 263 B, and *Polit.*, 285 E; *Polit.*, 306 A). Laches, Nicias, Charmides, Critias, discuss the virtues without distinguishing temperament, convention, habit, systematic discipline, opinion, and complete insight. They are unable to attach any precise meaning to the conventional phrases

"know thyself" and "minding one's own business." There is not one temperance or bravery, but three or four. There is no incompatibility between this view and Plato's insistence on the necessity of the definition and the final unity of virtue. If the word has many meanings, the first step in rational argument is to define the one intended. And the unity of virtue is to be sought, not in a verbal definition, but in the unity of the moral life, the idea of good, the political art, the σκοπός (*cf. infra*, n. 102). The definition is a hypothesis at the beginning, or a stage in the progress of the argument (*Charm.*, 163 A; *Euthyphro*, 9 D, 11 C; *Phœdr.*, 237 D, ὁμολογίᾳ θέμενοι ὅρον, 263 D E). It cannot be an end, and for this reason dialogues that seek a definition fail. This dialectical relativity of the definition, of course, does not preclude Plato from arguing that his ideal of the moral and social life is better than that of average Athenian opinion, and that the definitions which embody it are right as against formulas that express some aspect of the traditional belief.

[87] *Rep.*, 427 E, οἶμαι ἡμῖν τὴν πόλιν . . . . τελέως ἀγαθὴν εἶναι. δῆλον δὴ ὅτι σοφή τ' ἐστὶ καὶ ἀνδρεία καὶ σώφρων καὶ δικαία.

[88] *Ibid.*, 504 B C D, 505 A, ἡ τοῦ ἀγαθοῦ ἰδέα . . . . ᾗ δίκαια καὶ τ'ἄλλα προσχρησάμενα χρήσιμα καὶ ὠφέλιμα γίγνεται.

[89] *Gorgias; Rep.*, I.

[90] The "longer way," *Rep.*, 504 C, is for the guardians, not for us who are reading the *Republic*. See *Laws*, 964. 966 C. Neglect of this point has caused much misinterpretation. See *Idea of Good*, in "University of Chicago Classical Studies," Vol. I, p. 190.

life. The attainment of this mastery he poetically describes as the vision of the Idea of Good. But it must never be forgotten that all this mysticism culminates in the precise and purely logical statement of 534 B C, which affirms little more than *Phœdrus*, 278 C, or than Mill when he says: "There is no knowledge, and no assurance of right belief, but with him who can both confute the opposite opinion and successfully defend his own against confutation.[91] Many secondary suggestions attach themselves to the phrase by association with the goodness of God, the universal cause, in the *Timœus*,[92] the vision of the absolute ideas in the *Phœdrus* and *Symposium*, the fantastic enumeration in the *Philebus* (66) of the elements of "good" conceived at once as an ethical and a cosmical principle.[93] Its chief logical and ethical significance for the *Republic* has been hopelessly misunderstood, owing to the failure to connect it rightly with the problem of the "good" as presented in the minor dialogues.[94] In these dialogues Socrates repeatedly tests definitions of the virtues by demanding that they be related to happiness, the political or royal art, or the good. A virtue by hypothesis must be a καλόν and ἀγαθόν.[95] The definitions proposed repeatedly break down because Socrates is able to instance cases in which the rule prescribed does not conduce to happiness—is not good.[96] Similarly the rhetorician, the sophist, and other pretenders to some supreme knowledge are confounded by Socrates's demand that they shall sharply discriminate their art and science from all merely instrumental and technical specialties which effect good or evil according as they are rightly or wrongly used, and show its identity with the art of arts, the art of final ends, the political art, the good.[97]

In some of the minor dialogues the negative dialectic seems to go too far, and Socrates makes demands that neither Platonism nor any other doctrine can meet. Thus in the *Charmides* the familiar expression "knowing one's self," "knowing one's limits," "knowing what one can or cannot do," is made a puzzle by confounding it with the psychological question of self-knowledge or self-consciousness, and the fallacy or problem about knowing and not knowing the same thing;[98] and, waiving this point, Socrates demands proof that knowing the things one cannot do and intrusting them to experts is a good—a fundamental axiom of Platonism.[99] The explanation is that the phrase, like τὰ ἑαυτοῦ πράττειν above, is taken externally of adminicular and

[91] *Dissertations and Discussions*, Vol. IV, p. 283.

[92] 23 E, ἀγαθὸς ἦν. On the identification of the good with God see *Idea of Good*, pp. 188, 189.

[93] Fantastic because due (1) to the wish to depress ἡδονή to the fifth place; (2) to the neo-Platonic device of extending the intelligible hierarchy by the interpolation of new members between the highest and the lowest. It belongs to rhetoric or religious emotion, then, not to Plato's scientific ethics.

[94] *E. g.*, one hundred and fifty pages separate ZELLER's treatment of the idea of good (p. 707) from his discussion of the ethical good (p. 867). In elucidation of the former he quotes little or nothing from the ethical dialogues and cites neither *Phœdo*, 99 A, nor any other passage in which

the "opinion of the best" is treated as a potent cause. Finally he identifies the idea of good with God by a sophistical interpretation of παραπλήσια ἑαυτῷ (*Tim.*, 29 E) and a false construction of (92 B) εἰκὼν τοῦ νοητοῦ (sc. ζῴου not θεοῦ, cf. 38 C D).

[95] *Meno*, 87 D; *Laches*, 192 C, 193 D; *Protag.*, 349 E; *Hipp. Maj.*, 284 D; *Rep.*, 332, 333.

[96] See *Idea of Good*, pp. 200-204.

[97] *Euthyd.*, 282 E, 290, 291 C; *Charm.*, 170 B; *Protag.*. 319 A; *Gorg.*, 501 A B, 503 D; *Polit.*, 289 C, 293 D, 309 C; *Rep.*, 428 D.

[98] *Cf. Meno*, 80 E; *Euthydem.*, 286 D., *Theœtet.*, 191 B, 196 C.

[99] *Cf.* XEN., *Men.*, 4, 2, 24; *Alc.*, I, 117 D E; *Laws*, 732 A.

mechanical arts and sciences, not as in the *Republic*, with reference to the division of labor or function in the soul and the supreme arts of life and government.   To ask why Critias is allowed to be baffled for lack of this distinction is to ask why Plato wrote short dramatic dialogues at all—why he did not incorporate the fourth book of the *Republic* in the *Charmides*.   So in *Euthydemus*, 292 E, the suggestion that the good achieved by the possessors of the political art will be the training up of successors to know it is treated as a vicious circle or an infinite regress, although, when accompanied by the fuller explanations of the *Republic*, it is evidently in part the true Platonic doctrine.[100]   And similarly in the *Lysis* the theory, virtually repeated in the *Symposium*, that that which is intermediate between good and evil desires the good as a remedy against evil, is rejected because it makes the good a mere means to an end.[101]   But the general meaning that emerges from the ἀπορίαι of the minor dialogues, and the answer to them given in the *Republic*, is as simple as it is sound.   A philosophic ethics must systematically relate its definitions and prescriptions to some consistent conception of final ends and good—be it the realization of spiritual health and order in a reformed society, the development of personality, the greatest happiness of the greatest number, the fulfilment of the will of God, the renunciation of the will to live, or the survival of the fittest.   The statesman rises above the politician, the thinker and artist above the rhetorician, the true teacher above the charlatan, by his possession of an aim and a standard, his apprehension of a type of perfection toward which all his thoughts, and words, and acts converge.[102]

Plato's own ethical and social conceptions were thus co-ordinated and unified. Those of the brilliant sophists and rhetoricians who figure in his pages were not. They may have been very estimable and ingenious men.   They could not in Plato's judgment be true philosophers, statesmen, or teachers of statesmen, because they lacked both the "idea of good" and the synoptic and unifying dialectic required for its systematic application in ethics and politics, and in the education of the masses to "virtue."   This recognition of the logical significance of the idea of good for the *Republic* and the Socratic dialogues does not commit us to an acceptance of all Plato's social ideals.   It does not even require us to admit that the doctrine of the *Republic* really solves all the difficulties suggested by Plato's "negative dialectic."   But it creates the strongest presumption that it was present to his mind when he wrote the *Laches*, *Charmides*, and *Euthydemus*.

Parallel to the quest for the definition of the cardinal virtues leading to the idea of good is the study of friendship, love, passion, culminating in the apprehension of the idea of beauty at the point where it is hardly to be distinguished from the good.[103] No complete philosophy can ignore these things.   Plato's reflections upon them have

---

[100] Cf. *Meno*, 100 A, οἷος καὶ ἄλλον ποιῆσαι πολιτικόν, etc. Cf. *Rep.*, 412 A B, 497 C D; *Laws*, 950 B ff.; *Polit.*, 309 D, τὸν δὴ πολιτικὸν .... προσήκει .... τῇ τῆς βασιλικῆς μούσῃ τοῦτο αὐτὸ ἐμποιεῖν τοῖς ὀρθῶς μεταλαβοῦσι παιδείας, which, however, refers partly to the lower education as well.

[101] Cf. *Lysis*, 218 A, with *Symp.*, 203 E.

[102] *Gorg.*, 503 E, 501 C, 517, 518; *Rep.*, 484 C, 500 D E, 520 C; *Laws*, 625 E, 630 C, 688 B, 693 B, 706 A, 717 A, 733 C D, 962 A.

[103] *Lysis*, 219, 220; *Symp.*, 205 D, 210, 211; *Phœdr.*, 250 D ff.; *Phileb.*, 64 E.   νῦν δὴ καταπέφευγεν ἡμῖν ἡ τοῦ ἀγαθοῦ δύναμις εἰς τὴν τοῦ καλοῦ φύσιν.

become the commonplaces of the philosophy and poetry of modern Europe: the strange antinomy between the love of like for like and the attraction of dissimilars in man and nature; the exaltation of character and mood in passionate love and friendship; the transfiguration of the passion in the love of æsthetic, moral, and intellectual beauty;[104] the overloading of the instinct to achieve the ends of nature — the immortality of the species.[105]   The student of the *Lysis, Phœdrus, Symposium, Republic,* and *Laws* will find it impossible to fix a date at which these ideas first presented themselves to Plato's mind.[106]   The mood, the treatment, the emphasis varies.   Some of the thoughts are omitted in each dialogue, none are treated in all, and contradictions and developments may be "proved" by uncritically pressing the language and the imagery.   But the differences between the *Symposium* and *Phœdrus*, both presumably works of the middle period, are as noticeable as those found in any other works that touch on the theme.   The *Symposium* mentions one idea, the *Phœdrus* several; the former ignores immortality and ἀνάμνησις, the latter is one of the chief sources for both.[107]   The *Phœdrus* ignores the thought that love is the yearning of the mortal for immortality, the *Symposium* virtually omits the doctrine of μανία and enthusiasm.   In the *Symposium* love is not a god, but a demon; in the *Phœdrus* he is θεός or (to escape explicit contradiction) τι θεῖον.   These and other differences present no difficulties to a rational literary interpretation.   On no reasonable theory of Plato's development can they signify real changes in Plato's beliefs in the interval between the composition of the two dialogues.

The *Lysis*, though a slight Socratic dialogue, displays extreme subtlety of dialectic,[108] and implies some of the most characteristic thoughts of the *Symposium.*[109]   The failure to establish a formal definition, and the Socratic avowal of ignorance at the end prove nothing.   There is a plain hint that Menexenus is an "eristic," and Socrates's treatment of him, so different in tone from the edifying little conversation with Lysis, is a mere dramatic illustration of the πλάνη or ἀπορία that results from failure to discriminate the different meanings of an ambiguous term.   Love, as the *Phœdrus* tells us, is such a term — including subordinate and contradictory species.[110] For, as the *Laws* say, 837 A, δύο γὰρ ὄντα αὐτὰ καὶ ἐξ ἀμφοῖν τρίτον ἄλλο εἶδος ἐν ὄνομα

---

[104] Zeller's theory that Eros is *der philosophische Trieb* is a somewhat rigid and matter-of-fact interpretation of this poetry.

[105] *Symp.,* 207 D; *Laws,* 721, 773 E.

[106] *Cf. Rep.,* 402, 403, with *Symp.,* 210 C; *Rep.,* 490 A B; *Laws,* 688 B, φρόνησις . . . . καί νοῦς καί δόξα μετ' ἔρωτός τε καί ἐπιθυμίας; *Rep.,* 499 C, with *Laws,* 711 D, ὅταν ἔρως θεῖος τῶν σωφρόνων τε καὶ δικαίων ἐπιτηδευμάτων ἐγγένηται. *Laws,* 841 D, 636 C, παρὰ φύσιν, with *Phœdr.,* 251 A; *Laws,* 837; *Gorg.,* 474 D E, generalization of καλόν as in *Symp.*

[107] LUTOSLAWSKI (p. 242) fails to tell us where ἀνάμνησις is "alluded to in the speech of Aristophanes."

[108] The conception of eristic, 216 A B, arguing to the word, not the meaning, is as clear as it is in *Rep.,* 454 A, or *Euthydem.,* 295 B C, and the fallacy by which it is illus-

trated, the identity of opposites as such, recurs in substance in *Parmen.,* 148 A B, and belongs to the same class as the quibble on ἔτερον, *Euthydem.,* 301 B; *Theætet.,* 190 C; *Parmen.,* 147 E.   *Cf.* also ἀνομοιότατον, *Phileb.,* 13 D; *Parmen.,* 127 E, 148 B C.

[109] *E. g.,* θεῶν οὐδείς φιλοσοφεῖ, etc , *Symp.,* 203 E, which LUTOSLAWSKI (p. 239) thinks an important new point, in advance even of the *Cratylus,* is "already" in *Lysis,* 218 A. Zeller, who is "unable to suppose" that Plato had "already" attained the guiding thoughts of his later system (p. 614), argues that in the *Lysis* the psychological analysis is carried as far as is possible on a Socratic basis, but that the metaphysical explanation was revealed later.   If Plato must tell all he knows in every dialogue, why is ἀνάμνησις not associated with ἔρως in the *Symposium* and *Republic?*

[110] 263 C, 265 E.

περιλαβὸν πᾶσαν ἀπορίαν καὶ σκότον ἀπεργάζεται. How familiar the two εἴδη were to Plato appears from the almost technical use of the phrase δι' ὁμοιότητα φιλίαν in *Phædr.*, 240 C. Menexenus's bewilderment is precisely on a par with that of Kleinias over the two meanings of μανθάνω in the *Euthydemus*.[111] Plato is no more confused in the one case than in the other. The mood of the *Symposium* and *Phædrus* is compatible with youth or maturity, hardly with old age. The thoughts are naturally not repeated in their entirety, but many of them appear in the *Republic*, or are suggested elsewhere. They are nowhere contradicted,[112] and there is no reason to doubt that they were essential permanent elements of Plato's criticism of life. But he was not always in the mood to dwell upon them.

4. In another aspect the Platonic ethics is a polemic against hedonism. This must not be confounded with the modern utilitarian controversy. The modern opponent of utilitarianism is chiefly concerned to prove that the moral law cannot be deduced from experiences of utility, but has an *a priori* origin and requires a supernatural sanction. Plato does not directly discuss the origin of morality, but he explicitly disclaims the necessity of the sanction derived from the hope of immortality,[113] affirms with great emphasis that the useful is the right,[114] and bases all virtue on the supremacy of the λογιστικόν or calculating reason.[115] In the *Protagoras* Socrates is represented as maintaining against Protagoras by purely Benthamite arguments the identity of pleasure and the good.[116]

The seeming contradiction between this and the anti-hedonism of the *Gorgias* and *Philebus* demands explanation. It has sometimes been argued that Plato's own opinions on this point were reversed between the composition of the *Protagoras* and that of the *Gorgias*. Another explanation is that Socrates merely develops a paradox for the bewilderment of the Sophist. And it is true that in some parts of the dialogue Socrates is obviously jesting,[117] and that we are warned against accepting the result too seriously by the reminder that both Socrates and Protagoras have maintained

---

[111] 277 E.

[112] Grote says that in the *Theœtetus* the spectacle of a beautiful youth is not required as the indispensable initiatory stimulus to philosophy. But the *Symp.*, 210 C, κἂν σμικρὸν ἄνθος ἔχῃ, and the *Rep.*, 402 D, emphasize the unimportance of the beauty of the body as compared with that of the mind. And in the same vein Socrates says, καλὸς γὰρ εἶ ὦ Θεαίτητε . . . . ὁ γὰρ καλῶς λέγων καλός, etc., 186 E. The Platonic Socrates is still the ἐρωτικός as he was in the *Lysis*, nor can we suppose that he would ever have found the beautiful *Meno* as helpful an "initiatory stimulus to philosophy" as the snub-nosed Theætetus.

[113] *Rep.*, 363 B C D, 367 E, 612 B C. The *Gorgias* does not differ herein from the *Republic*, as Ritchie (p. 156) seems to think. The argument is complete without the myth, and the phrases at the end about living justly in order to prepare for the judgment of Minos prove no more than the ἵνα of *Rep.*, 621 C.

[114] καλόν, *Rep.*, 457 B.

[115] *Rep.*, 440 E, 571 C, 605 B.

[116] *Protag.*, 353–8.

[117] 340 ff. In 341 D, Protagoras, anticipating *Philebus*, 12 E, and in language suggesting the protest against eristic in *Sophist*, 259 D, points out that (generic) resemblance is compatible with difference and even contrariety (*cf.* also *Meno*, 74 D). He does not explain himself fully, however, and Socrates, ignoring the point, proceeds to trip him up by a fallacious use of the principle that one thing can have only one opposite. Whatever the date of the *Euthydemus*, its author was aware that a word used in two senses may have two opposites, quite as early as he was capable of writing the *Protagoras*. The passage is merely a dramatic illustration of Socrates's superiority in the game of question and answer. Again in 350 B–351 A, when it is argued that bravery is knowledge because knowledge imparts confidence, Protagoras points out that we cannot convert the universal affirmative proposition, "all bravery is confidence," and distinguishes as bravery the confidence that arises from nature and training. Though not a match for Socrates, Protagoras is a far better reasoner than Laches or Nicias, and again Socrates refutes him only by taking

theses incompatible with the positions from which they started.[118] But the full explanation lies deeper. In the *Republic* Plato undertakes to demonstrate the intrinsic desirability of virtue against two forms of disbelief—the explicit skepticism of the cynic, who affirms that natural justice is the advantage of the stronger and human justice an artificial convention, and the unfaith of the ordinary man, who virtually admits this theory by commending justice solely on external and prudential grounds.[119] The Callicles of the *Gorgias* represents the former view, Gorgias himself and (less obviously) Protagoras the latter. Like other Sophists, he is the embodiment of average public opinion which his teaching reproduces.[120] He himself says that all men teach virtue. He modestly claims at the most only to teach it a little more effectively and persuasively than the layman.[121] Plato would admit both assertions, with the reservation that the virtue so-taught hardly deserves the name, and that the teaching is neither systematic nor philosophical.

The molding power of public opinion, operating through countless social and educative agencies, is admirably depicted in the myth attributed to Protagoras, the main thought of which is repeated in the *Republic*.[122] There, however, the philosophic rulers are to employ this irresistible force for the inculcation, not of average Greek opinion, but of Platonic virtue. The *Protagoras* dramatically illustrates the dialectic incapacity and philosophic superficiality of the great popular teacher. His ethical teaching is spiritually and logically on a level with the precepts of the worthy sires and guardians satirized by Adeimantus.[123] However unlike in temper and practical effect, it is philosophically akin to the individual hedonism of Callicles and Thrasymachus who reject all morality as an unreal convention. Protagoras is naturally unaware of this. Like the populace, he recoils from the naked exposition of the principles implied in his preaching and practice. He accepts the terminology of individual hedonism only under compulsion of Socrates's superior dialectic. But Socrates's explicit challenge to him and the assembled Sophists to name any other final good than ἡδονή is a proof that one of Plato's objects was to identify the Sophistic ethics with hedonism.[124] But neither this nor the demonstration of Protagoras's inability to cope with Socrates in dialectic exhausts the significance of the dialogue.

Plato, however reluctantly, always recognized a certain measure of truth in the Benthamite analysis here attributed to Socrates. He knew that "act we must in pursuance of that which (we think) will give us most pleasure" Even the *Gorgias* contains phrases of utilitarian, if not hedonistic, implication.[125] The Eudæmonism of

up a new line of argument—the identity of pleasure and good, and the consequent unity of the virtues in the "measuring art." Plato of course was aware here, and in the *Euthyphro* (12), and everywhere, that a universal affirmative cannot be directly converted. But it is a part of the scheme of the dialogue that Protagoras should make some good points, though defeated in the end. And Socrates is baffled in or fails to complete other proofs of the unity of virtue, and so is driven to rely on the proof from hedonism, which is the chief feature of the dialogue.

[118] *Protag.*, 361.

[119] *Rep.*, 362 E ff. *Cf.* ZELLER, p. 603, n. 1.

[120] *Rep.*, 492 ff.   [121] *Protag.*, 328 B.

[122] RITCHIE (p. 156) says: "The argument of the Sophist Protagoras . . . . is now fully accepted by Plato," etc., as if Plato was not the author of the *Protagoras*.

[123] *Rep.*, 362 E.   [124] 354 D, 358 A.

[125] 499 D. RITCHIE (p. 155) strangely says that in the *Republic* Plato recognizes, in marked advance upon the position of the *Gorgias*, that there are good pleasures as well as bad!

the *Republic* has often been pointed out,[126] and in the *Laws* Plato explicitly declares, in language recalling that of the *Protagoras*, that it is not in human nature to pursue any course of action that does not promise a favorable balance of pleasure.[127] But the inference which he draws is not that it is safe or desirable to proclaim that pleasure is the good, but that it is necessary to demonstrate that the good — the virtuous life — is the most pleasurable.

To a Benthamite this will seem a purely verbal or rhetorical distinction. And Aristotle himself hints that Plato's aversion to the name of pleasure cast a suspicion of unreality over his ethical teaching.[128] But Plato is not alone in his aversion to the word. Matthew Arnold acknowledges a similar feeling. And Jowett, in his admirable introduction to the *Philebus*, has once for all set forth the considerations by which many clear-headed modern thinkers, who perfectly understand the utilitarian logic and accept whatever is true in its psychology, are nevertheless moved to reject its language. The Greek word ἡδονή is much more closely associated with a low view of happiness than the English word "pleasure;" and Plato had, or thought that he had, much stronger reasons than the moderns have, for identifying hedonism with the negation of all moral principle.

The *Gorgias* and *Philebus* nowhere explicitly contradict the thesis of the *Protagoras* that a preponderance of pleasure, rightly estimated and abstracted from all evil consequences, is good.[129] The doctrine which they combat is the unqualified identification of pleasure and good, coupled with the affirmation that true happiness is to be sought by developing and gratifying the appetite for the pleasures of sense and ambition.[130] Plato represents Callicles and Philebus as unable or unwilling to limit these propositions even by the qualifications of the *Protagoras*.[131] It is he, not they, who introduces the distinction of pure and impure,[132] true and illusive,[133] wholesome and unwholesome,[134] necessary and unnecessary pleasures.[135] The modern critic may object that Plato was not justified in attributing to any contemporaries either this dialectical incapacity or this cynical effrontery. Plato thought otherwise. It is a question of historical evidence. But it is not legitimate to attribute to the Callicles and the Philebus of the dialogues the utilitarianism of Grote or John Stuart Mill, or even that of the *Protagoras*, and so convict Plato of self-contradiction.[136]

With these remarks we may dismiss so much of the *Gorgias* and *Philebus* as is merely dialectical, dramatic, or rhetorical, directed against the crudest form of hedonism which Plato chooses to bring upon the stage before grappling with the problem in

[126] 357 B, ἡδοναὶ ὅσαι ἀβλαβεῖς goods *per se; ;* 457 B, 458 E, 581 E (with *Laws*, 732 E), μὴ ὅτι πρὸς τὸ κάλλιον καὶ αἴσχιον ζῆν μηδὲ τὸ χεῖρον καὶ ἄμεινον, ἀλλὰ πρὸς αὐτὸ τὸ ἥδιον καὶ ἀλυπότερον.

[127] *Laws*, 733, 734; *cf.* 663 A.   [128] *Eth. nic.*, X, 1.

[129] *Phileb.*, 60 A B, is verbally a direct contradiction of *Protag.*, 355 B.

[130] *Gorg.*, 495 A, 492 D E; *Phileb.*, 12 A, 12 D, 27 E.

[131] The verbal identification of ἡδονὴ and ἀγαθὸν in 355 has been preceded by such phrases as καθ' ὃ ἡδέα ἐστίν, 351 C,

and the explanation that some painful goods are medicinal (354 A = *Rep.*, 357 C), and is checked by the calculus of all consequences, all of which is ignored by Callicles and Philebus.

[132] *Phileb.*, 51, 52.   [133] *Ibid.*, 36 C ff.

[134] *Ibid.*, 41 A; *Gorg.*, 499 D E.   [135] *Rep.*, 558 D.

[136] Plato, as Jowett says, is "playing both sides of the game . . . . but it is not necessary in order to understand him that we should discuss the fairness of his modes of proceeding."

earnest.[137]   The real arguments which he employs, not so much to refute the thesis of the *Protagoras* as to limit its practicable application and justify his repudiation of its terminology, may be summed up as follows: The distinction between good and bad pleasures once admitted, the statement that pleasure as such is the good, becomes an unreal abstraction.[138]   The reality is specific kinds of pleasure and the principle of distinction, whether intelligence, measure, or the will to obey the "opinion of the best,"[139] becomes more important than the bare name of pleasure, and more nearly allied to the good.[140]   The "measuring art" postulated in the *Protagoras* is impracticable.   Pleasure and pain are, like confidence and fear, foolish counselors;[141] either deprives the mind of the sanity required for a just estimate.[142]   No scale of human judgment can be trusted to weigh the present against the future, and make allowance for all the illusions of memory, hope, and contrast.[143]   The most intense pleasures and pains are associated with a diseased condition of mind and body.[144]   And the habit of pursuing pleasure, of thinking and speaking of it as the good, tends to make the world of sense seem more real than that of thought and spirit.[145]   The contrary is the truth. The world of sense is a pale reflex of the world of ideas,[146] and the pleasures of sense are inherently unreal, illusory, and deceptive, and may in sound logic be termed false, as fairly as the erroneous opinions that accompany them.[147]   They are false because composed of hopes and imaginations not destined to be fulfilled;[148] false, because exaggerated by the illusions of distance in time or contrast;[149] false, because

[137] *Phileb.*, 55 A B, and *Gorg.*, 495 C, 499 B, show that the arguments of *Gorg.*, 495 C–499 B, are, in the main, a conscious dialectical sport. I recur to this point so often because the *Gorgias* and the first book of the *Republic* are the chief source of the opinion, widely spread by Grote, Mill, and Sidgwick, that Plato is a magnificent preacher, but often a weak reasoner. *Cf.* MILL, *Diss. and Discuss.*, IV, 291: "This great dialogue, full of just thoughts and fine observations on human nature, is, in mere argument, one of the weakest of Plato's works." *Cf. Idea of Good*, pp. 213–15.

[138] *Phileb.*, 12 D E. In answer to the question, πῶς γὰρ ἡδονή γε ἡδονῇ μὴ οὐχ ὁμοιότατον ἂν εἴη; Socrates shows that generic (verbal) identity is compatible with specific difference or even opposition, a logical principle "already" glanced at in the *Protag.*, 331 D, with the same illustration of μέλαν and λευκόν. LUTOSLAWSKI, p. 467, misunderstands 13 A, τούτῳ τῷ λόγῳ μὴ πίστευε, τῷ πάντα τὰ ἐναντιώτατα ἐν ποιοῦντι—"we need not attempt a reconciliation of all contradictions!"

[139] *Phædr.*, 237 D, ἔμφυτος . . . . ἐπιθυμία ἡδονῶν . . . . ἐπίκτητος δόξα, ἐφιεμένη τοῦ ἀρίστου. *Cf. Laws*, 644 D, 645 A. *Phædo*, 99 A, ὑπὸ δόξης φερόμενα τοῦ βελτίστου.

[140] *Phileb.*, 64 C, τί . . . . μάλιστ' αἴτιον εἶναι δόξειεν ἂν ἡμῖν τοῦ πᾶσι γεγονέναι προσφιλῆ τὴν τοιαύτην διάθεσιν; with the context.

[141] *Cf. Tim.*, 69 D, with *Laws*, 644 C.

[142] *Rep.*, 402 E; *Phileb.*, 63 D; *Phædo*, 66 B.

[143] *Cf. Phileb.*, 41 E ff., with *Protag.*, 356, 357; *Gorgias*, 500 A, ἆρ' οὖν παντὸς ἀνδρός ἐστιν ἐκλέξασθαι, etc. *Laws*, 663 B,

σκοτοδινιᾶν δὲ τὸ πόρρωθεν ὁρώμενον πᾶσί τε ὡς ἔπος εἰπεῖν . . . . παρέχει, and the rhetorical repudiation of the whole hedonistic calculus, *Phædo*, 69 A B.

[144] *Phileb.*, 45 B–E, ἔν τινι πονηρίᾳ ψυχῆς καὶ τοῦ σώματος . . . . μέγισται μὲν ἡδοναί, etc.

[145] *Cf. Phædo*, 83 D, with JAMES's *Psychology*, Vol. II, p. 306: "Among all sensations, the *most* belief-compelling are those productive of pleasure or pain."

[146] *Rep.*, 509, 510, 514 ff., the allegory of the cave.

[147] *Phileb.*, 36 C ff. As Berkeley and Huxley argue from the subjectivity of pain to that of sensations and ideas; as Epicurus proceeds from the reality of pain to that of the other secondary qualities; so, reversing the order, Plato infers the falsity of pleasures and pains from that of the associated perceptions and beliefs. Grote, Jowett, Horn, and others pronounce the whole train of reasoning fallacious. But it is to be observed: (1) that their objections as usual are anticipated by Plato (*Phileb.*, 38 A), who has a right to use his own terminology provided his meaning is unambiguous (*Charmides*, 163 D); (2) that the epithet "false" is used either with reference to a postulated objective judgment of life as a whole, or as a mere rhetorical expression of the disdain or pity felt by an onlooker. In the first sense it is justified by the argument, in the second by the usage of the poets—*falsa licet cupidus deponat gaudia livor* (*Propert.*, 1, 8, 29); (3) having demonstrated against Sophistic negations that ψευδής applies to δόξα, Plato was naturally tempted to extend it to ἡδονή.

[148] *Phileb.*, 39 E, 40 C. *Cf.* "we are all imaginative, for images are the brood of desire" (George Eliot).

[149] *Ibid.*, 41, 42 B; *Laws*, 663 B.

what we mistake for positive pleasure is usually the neutral state, the absence of uneasiness, the cessation of pain.[150]

This doctrine of the negativity of what men call pleasure is the fundamental basis of Plato's ethics, as it is of Schopenhauer's. On this, in the last instance, rests his refutation of hedonism, and, as we shall see, his demonstration that virtue and happiness are one.[151] Sensuous pleasures are in their nature impure and illusory. They are preconditioned by, and mixed with, desire, want, pain. "Surgit amari aliquid" is ever true of them. They are the relief of an uneasiness, the scratching of an itch, the filling of a vacuum.[152] To treat them as real, or to make them one's aim (except so far as our human estate requires), is to seek happiness in a process rather than a state,[153] in becoming rather than in being. It is to bind one's self to the wheel of Ixion and pour water into the bottomless jar of the Danaids.[154] Far happier, far more pleasurable, is the life that consistently aims at few and calm pleasures, to which the sensualist would hardly give the name, a life which he would regard as torpor or death.[155]

Both the physiology and the psychology of this doctrine have been impugned. It has been argued that, up to the point of fatigue, the action of healthy nerves involves no pain, and must yield a surplus of positive sensuous pleasure. It is urged that the present uneasiness of appetite is normally more than counterbalanced by the anticipation of immediate satisfaction. Such arguments will carry no weight with those who accept Plato's main contention, that the satisfactions of sense and ambition, however inevitable, have no real worth, and that to seek our true life in them is to weave and unweave the futile web of Penelope. Whatever qualifications modern psychology may attach to the doctrine, it is the logical basis of Plato's ethics. The unfeigned recognition of the inherent worthlessness of the lower pleasures removes at once the motive and lures to evil.[156] It is the chief link in the proof that virtue is happiness. It insures the domination of reason over feeling and appetite. It molds man into that likeness to the divine pattern which is Plato's favorite expression for the ethical ideal,[157] for the divine life knows neither pleasure nor pain.[158] It is the serious argument that

[150] *Phileb.*, 42 C ff.; *Rep.*, 583 D.

[151] The argument that pleasure is γένεσις, not οὐσία, is' not, as ZELLER says (p. 604), the nerve of the proof. It is obviously, as the language of 53 C implies, one of those half-serious metaphysical and rhetorical confirmations used to make a strong case where Plato's feelings are enlisted. It does not occur explicitly in the *Republic* which speaks, however, of pleasure as κίνησις, 583 E.

[152] "Already" in the *Gorgias*, 493 E, 494 C, and the *Phædrus*, 258 E, ὧν προλυπηθῆναι δεῖ ἢ μηδὲ ἡσθῆναι, etc.; *Rep.*, 584 A B. It has even been argued that the *Phædrus* passage takes for granted the fuller discussion of the *Philebus* (W. H. THOMPSON, *Phædrus, ad loc.*). And why not? Anything may be argued if the dialogues are supposed to grow out of one another and not out of Plato's mind.

[153] *Phileb.*, 53 C ff.; 54 E virtually = *Gorg.*, 493 E. The literal-minded objection of ARISTOTLE, *Eth. Nic.*, X, 4, and

some moderns, that pleasure is not strictly = κίνησις is beside the point.

[154] *Gorg.*, 493 B, τετρημένος πίθος, etc.; *Phædo*, 84 A, ἀνήνυτον ἔργον . . . . Πηνελόπης — ἱστόν, *Gorg.*, 507 E; *Phileb.*, 54 E.

[155] *Phædo*, 64 B; *Gorg.*, 492 E; *Phileb.*, 54 E, καί φασι ζῆν οὐκ ἂν δέξασθαι, etc. In *Laws*, 733, 734 B, the hedonistic calculus of the *Protagoras* is retained, but is applied not directly to the individual acts, but to types of life. The life of moderate pleasures is *a priori* the more pleasurable because it necessarily yields a more favorable balance than the life of intense pleasures.

[156] *Phædo*, 66 C; *Rep.*, 586 A B, 588.

[157] *Theætet.*, 176 B ff.; *Laws*, 716 D, 728 A B; *Rep.*, 352 B, 612 E; *Phileb.*, 391 E.

[158] *Phileb.*, 33 B.

explains Plato's repudiation of the hedonistic formulas of the *Protagoras*, and justifies the noble anti-hedonistic rhetoric of the *Gorgias*, the *Phœdo*, and the *Philebus*.[159]

4. Plato's insistence on the necessity of proving the coincidence of virtue and happiness marks another difference between him and modern writers. The question is rarely put in the forefront of modern ethical discussion, except for the polemical purpose of proving that an opponent's philosophy supplies no basis or sanction for morality. The majority of modern ethical writers relegate the problem to a digression or a footnote. They are content to establish a "general tendency" or "strong probability." Or they frankly admit that while everybody would be glad if the proposition could be proved, it is not susceptible of mathematical demonstration. But this was not enough for Plato. His own faith was adamantine.[160] He was as certain that happiness is inseparable from virtue as of the existence[161] of the Island of Crete. Even if it were only a probability, he would not permit it to be impugned in a well-ordered state.[162] Just how much positively immoral and cynical philosophy was current in Plato's day is, as we have seen, a disputed historical question. But Plato himself was haunted by the thought of the unscrupulous skeptic who sought to justify his own practice by appeals to the law of nature or theories of the origin of justice in a conspiracy of the weak against the strong.[163] His imagination was beset by the picture of some brilliant young Alcibiades standing at the crossways of life and debating in his mind whether his best chance of happiness lay in accepting the conventional moral law that serves to police the vulgar or in giving rein to the instincts and appetites of his own stronger nature.[164] To confute the one, to convince the other, became to him the main problem of moral philosophy. It is a chief duty of the rulers in the *Republic* and the *Laws*, and the Socrates of the dialogues is at all times ready and equipped to undertake it.

Plato is not always overnice in the arguments by which the skeptic is refuted. It is enough that the "wicked" should not have the best of the argument.[165] Socrates in the first instance puts forth just enough dialectical strength to baffle a Callicles or a Thrasymachus.[166] This, as we have seen, is the quality of much of the argument of the *Gorgias*,[167] though it is intermingled with hints of deeper things, and supplemented

---

[159] *Gorg.*, 507, 512, 513; *Phœdo*, 69; *Phileb.*, 66 A; *Rep.*, 580 B.

[160] *Gorgias*, 509 A; *Rep.*, 360 B, 618 A.

[161] *Laws*, 662 B.

[162] *Rep.*, 392 A B; *Laws*, 663 B, πιθανός γ', εἰ μηδὲν ἕτερον, πρὸς τό τινα ἐθέλειν ζῆν τὸν ὅσιον καὶ δίκαιον βίον.

[163] *Rep.*, 358, 359, 365; *Gorg.*, 483 ff. Cf. *Rep.*, 358 C, διατεθρυλημένος τὰ ὦτα; *Protag.*, 333 C, ἐπεὶ πολλοί γέ φασι; *Euthydem.*, 279 B, ἴσως γὰρ ἂν τις ἡμῖν ἀμφισβητήσειε; *Phileb.*, 66 E; *Gorg.*, 511 B; *Laws*, 889 D E, with *Theœtet.*, 177 C D.

[164] *Rep.*, 365 B; *Gorg.*, 510 D; *Laws*, 662 E.

[165] *Theœtet.*, 176 C D; 177 B, καὶ ἡ ῥητορικὴ ἐκείνη πως ἀπομαραίνεται. The whole passage is a description of the *Gorgias*. Cf., 527 A, νῦν δὲ ὁρᾷς, ὅτι τρεῖς ὄντες ὑμεῖς, οἵπερ σοφώτατοί ἐστε τῶν νῦν Ἑλλήνων . . . . οὐκ ἔχετε ἀποδεῖξαι, etc. *Laws*, 907 C, μή ποτε λόγοις ἡγῶνται κρατοῦντες, etc.

[166] E. g., the argument in *Rep.*, 349, 350, is a mere illustration of the game of question and answer. Thrasymachus sets up the thesis, οἱ ἄδικοι φρόνιμοι καὶ ἀγαθοί, and Socrates forces him to contradict himself. Zeller (p. 752) lists it among Plato's fallacies.

[167] Strictly speaking, Socrates's dialectic is employed merely to force from Callicles the admission that some pleasures are bad (449 B C; cf. *Rep.*, 505 C). From this point the argument, abandoning ethical theory, discusses social and political ideals at Athens. "Good" is treated as distinct from "pleasure," as it is in *Phœdr.*, 239 C. But the question whether it may not ultimately prove to be the favorable balance of pleasure (*Protag.*) is not raised. The crude identification of the terms is rejected for reasons still held valid in the *Philebus*. Cf. *Phileb.*, 55 B, with *Gorg.*, 498 C. There is no contradiction. The three dialogues, differing in mood, are logically consistent and supplement one another.

by noble eloquence. In the *Republic*, however, Plato undertakes not only to confute and silence, but to convince.[168] The real ground of conviction is the total underlying conception of the true nature, harmony, health, and consequent happiness of the soul.

But the formal proof is summed up in the ninth book in three arguments which, as Plato repeatedly tells us, constitute the framework of the whole design.[169] To these, in form at least, all other interests of the book are subordinate—the construction of the ideal state, the higher philosophical education, the idea of good, the character-sketches of degenerate types. The first argument is based on the comparison of the individual and the state which runs through the entire work from the second to the ninth book. It takes two forms: (1) That of a mere external analogy. As the happiness of the ideal state is to the misery of the ochlocracy or the tyranny, so is the happiness of the well-governed just soul to the wretchedness of the man whose soul is the prey of a mob of appetites, or the slave of a ruling passion.[170] (2) The force of this external analogy is derived wholly from the psychological truth that it embodies. Unity or factious division, the sovereignty of reason, or the usurpations of passion and appetite, harmony or discord, health or disease, as used of the soul, are more than mere figures of speech; they are the exact expression of inevitable alternatives resting on indisputable psychological facts. The dominance of the higher reason over disciplined emotion and controlled appetite is the sole and effective condition at once of the unity, harmony, and health of spiritual life which is happiness, and of the unswerving fulfilment of obligation which is the external manifestation of justice and virtue.[171] To ask whether happiness is compatible with a diseased soul is still more absurd than to expect it to dwell in a diseased body.[172]

The second argument is very brief, and Plato is probably aware that at the best it commands assent rather than inspires conviction.[173] The three faculties of the soul, taken abstractly, yield three types of pleasure—the pleasures of pure intelligence, of ambition, and of appetite. Plato assumes that the pleasures of intelligence belong to the man in whom the intellect directed toward the good controls the other faculties. In other words, he takes for granted the coincidence on the highest plane of intellect and virtue which he found in Socrates and which the education of the *Republic* secures in the guardians.[174] Now, the advocate of the intellectual and virtuous life has necessarily had some experience of the pleasures associated with gratified ambition and appetite. The ambitious man and the sensuous man know little or nothing of the higher order of pleasure. The preference of the "intellectual" for his own type of pleasure must be ratified as based on a completer experience. It would be a waste of time to cavil on minor fallacies or rhetorical exaggerations with which Plato burdens the argument in his eagerness to make a strong case.[175] The argument itself is familiar

---

[168] *Rep.*, 357 A B, 358 B, 367 A B, 367 E.

[169] 369 A B, 392 A B, 427 D, 445 A, 544 A.

[170] 576 C ff.   [171] 442 E.

[172] 445 A, 591 B, 589 E; *Gorg.*, 512 A, 479 B; "already" in *Crito*, 47 D E.

[173] *Rep.*, 580 D ff.   [174] *Cf. supra*, p. 11.

[175] Grote and Mill object that this argument, even if conclusive, is addressed to the wrong point, because the life supposed is not that of the simple, just man, but that of the philosopher But the case of the simple just man is met by the main arguments drawn from the order, har-

enough through its acceptance in substance by John Stuart Mill; who, however, seems to think Plato's use of it fallacious. It has been rejected as a fallacy on the ground that pleasure is not an objective measurable entity, but a relative individual feeling. Again at the limits of human thought we are confronted by an alternative the terms of which it is impossible to realize distinctly. Is it better to be a completely contented pig than a man? But if we waive the claim that the argument is an absolute proof, and turn from these unreal abstractions to the facts of life, what Plato affirms is simply that it is more pleasurable in the end to develop and foster the capacity for the "higher" pleasures than that for the lower, as is shown by the judgment of those who have experienced both. In this less absolute form the argument leans for support on that which precedes, and still more on that which follows it.

In the third place, the lower pleasures as compared with the higher are illusory, unreal, and impermanent, and they tend to destroy the healthy balance of faculties which is the condition of all true pleasure.[176] This is a repetition or anticipation [177] of the theory of the negativity of pleasure which we have already met in the polemic against hedonism.

This completes our sketch of the Platonic ethics. The rest is exhortation, inspiration, myth, things οὐκ ἀηδέστερα ἀκούειν, but not within the scope of the present study, nor indeed reproducible in any study. For the ethical and religious spirit that informs every page of Plato we must go to the master himself.

II. THEORY OF IDEAS

Plato's theory of ideas is (1) primarily a realistic way of speaking of the universal; (2) a poetic and mythical extension of this realistic language, by which the universal is treated, not only as a thing, but as a thing of beauty and object of desire and aspiration; (3) in relation to metaphysics, it is the definite and positive assertion that the substantive essences, or rather the objective correlates, of general notions constitute the ultimate ontological units of reality to which psychological and logical analysis refer us as the only escape from a Heraclitean or Protagorean philosophy of pure relativity. In the first sense the ideas occur throughout the dialogues. It is irrational to look for the other forms of the doctrine except when the argument naturally leads up to them. A Kantian does not expatiate upon the *Ding-an-sich* in an

---

mony, and health of the soul, and from the analysis of pleasure. Here Plato is renewing the debate between the "philosopher," the sensualist, and the politician begun in the *Gorgias*. He is indulging his feelings in a demonstration that in the Athens of his day the "philosophic" life is a higher and happier type than the life of the politician or the sensualist; and he holds that no real reform is possible until men can be found who approach political life as a necessary, not a desirable, thing, condescending to it from a life which they feel to be higher and more pleasurable (*cf. Rep.*, 521 B). The form of the argument of the *Republic* is determined by the purpose of contrasting the extreme types of the virtuous philosopher and the finished tyrant. But it applies to other men in proportion as they ap-

proximate to these types. And the statement of the argument in the *Laws* applies to the simple just man, 663 C, τὰ ἄδικα . . . . ἐκ μὲν ἀδίκου καὶ κακοῦ ἑαυτοῦ θεωρούμενα ἡδέα, etc., ... τὴν δ' ἀλήθειαν τῆς κρίσεως ποτέραν κυριωτέραν εἶναι φῶμεν; πότερα τὴν τῆς χείρονος ψυχῆς ἢ τὴν τῆς βελτίονος.

[176] *Rep.*, 583 B–586 C.

[177] Zeller thinks it a résumé of the fuller treatment of the *Philebus*. Those who put the *Philebus* late regard it as a preliminary sketch. The *Philebus* is probably late, as Mill affirmed before *Sprachstatistik* was conceived. But the psychology of pleasure in the two dialogues supplies no evidence. *Cf. infra*, "Plato's Psychology," and Part II.

essay on universal peace. Plato discussed many topics that did not require embellishment by the mythical description of the idea as type, or the explicit reaffirmation of
the idea as *noumenon*. And the apparent absence of either from a given dialogue
proves nothing.

Plato's fearless and consistent realism is so repugnant to "common sense" that
modern critics either take it as proof of the naïveté, not to say childishness, of his
thought, or extenuate the paradox by arguing that he could not have meant it
seriously and must have abandoned or modified the doctrine in his maturer works.
All such interpretations spring from a failure to grasp the real character of the metaphysical problem and the historical conditions that made Plato adopt and cling to this
solution. From Heraclitus to John Stuart Mill human thought has always faced the
alternative of positing an inexplicable and paradoxical *noumenon*, or accepting the
"flowing philosophy." No system can escape the dilemma. Plato from his youth up
was alternately fascinated and repelled by the philosophy of Heraclitus. No other
writer has described so vividly as he the reign of relativity and change in the world
of phenomena.[178] Only by affirming a *noumenon* could he escape Heracliteanism as
the ultimate account of (1) being, and (2) cognition.[179] He chose or found this *noumenon* in the hypostatized concepts of the human mind, the objects of Socratic inquiry,
the postulates of the logic he was trying to evolve from the muddle of contemporary
dialectic, the realities of the world of thought so much more vivid to him than the
world of sense.[180] This is the account of the matter given by Aristotle[181] and confirmed by the dialogues. Except in purely mythical passages, Plato does not attempt
to describe the ideas any more than Kant describes the *Ding-an-sich* or Spencer the
"Unknowable." He does not tell us what they are, but that they are. And the difficulties, clearly recognized by Plato, which attach to the doctrine thus rightly limited,
are precisely those that confront any philosophy that assumes an absolute.

Plato's particular selection of the hypostatized concept for his absolute seems
more paradoxical only because, from the common-sense point of view of a convenient
but inconsistent conceptualism, we ignore the real philosophical alternative of consistent nominalism or consistent realism, and forget the historical conditions that forced
Plato to make his choice. Realism was for Plato not merely the only metaphysical
alternative to Protagorean relativity; it was the only practicable way of affirming the
validity of universals and abstract thought. The psychology and logic of modern
nominalism as gradually worked out by Locke, Berkeley, John Stuart Mill, and
Taine, did not exist. The modern flowing philosopher can give a plausible account of

---

[178] *Symp.*, 207 D E; *Tim.*, 43 B C, 44 A B, 52 E, 69 C D;
Theœtet., 156 ff.

[179] *Cratyl.*, 439, 440; *Theœtet.*, 179 ff., 185, 186; *Tim.*, 27 D,
28 A, 49 D ff., 51 B C. Less directly pertinent are *Soph.*,
249 B; *Cratyl.*, 386; *Phileb.*, 58 E, with *Rep.*, 533 B.

[180] I do not mean that Plato said: "Go to, I need a
noumenon, I will hypostatize the Socratic concepts,"
which a malicious critic might infer from APELT's argument (*Beiträge*, pp. 81-3), that Plato would have made all

concepts ideas (which he did!) if his starting-point had
been the hypostatization of the concept, and (which is
partly true) that he would not have put forth the paradox
at all if he had not felt the necessity of positing some
reality beyond the world of sense. This last Apelt confirms
by *Met.*, 1040b, 27, which, however, proves nothing for Plato,
as it merely states a favorite thought of Aristotle.

[181] *Met.*, 1, 6, 987a, 29 ff., 1086b.

the universal, recognizes the general term as a convenient algebraic symbol, and so accepts the old logic as a practical working instrument of thought. But in Plato's time the old logic was still to be created, and the cruder forms of nominalism and relativity which he combated blocked the way by captious objections to the normal and necessary use of general terms.[182] The theory of ideas, then, often appears to be mainly, if not merely, an affirmation of the concept apart from explicit insistence on any theory of its psychological or ontological nature.[183] But the main issue is unaffected by this fact. Even if he had been acquainted with the analysis of Mill and Taine,[184] Plato would have continued to ask: Are the good and the beautiful and similar essences something or nothing?[185] Can everything in the idea be explained as the natural product of remembered and associated sensations?[186] Is not man's power of abstraction something different in kind from any faculty possessed by the brute?[187] Not all the refinements of the new psychology can disguise the fact that the one alternative commits us to the "flowing philosophers," the other to some form of Platonism. For the answer that the "good" and the "beautiful" are only concepts of the mind is an evasion which commends itself to common-sense, but which will satisfy no serious thinker. If these concepts are the subjective correlates of objective realities, we return to the Platonic idea — for Plato, it must be remembered, does not say what the ideas are, but only that they are in some sense objective and real.[188] If the concepts are the natural products of casual associations, accidental eddies in the stream of sense, the "flowing philosophy" receives us again.[189] Moreover, though this

---

[182] *Phileb.*, 14 D, σφόδρα τοῖς λόγοις ἐμπόδια; 15 A, 13 D E; *Parmen.*, 135 C; *Soph.*, 251 B C; *Theætet.*, 157 A B, 167 A, 180 D; *Euthydem.*, 301 A and *passim*.

[183] *Repub.*, 596 A; *Phædr.*, 249 B, though immediately followed by ἀνάμνησις; *Philebus*, 16 D, and all passages that describe the true method of generalization and division — *Phædr.*, 265, 266, 270 D; *Soph.*, 226 C, 235 C, 253; *Polit.*, 285 A; *Cratyl.*, 424 C; *Laws*, 894 A, 965 C.

[184] To MILL (*Diss. and Discuss.*, IV, p. 300) the Platonic ideas " are only interesting as the first efforts of original and inventive minds to let in light on a dark subject." They belong to the "theories which have arisen in ingenious minds from an imperfect conception of the processes of abstraction and generalization." But it is not really thinkable that the author of the *Sophist*, *Politicus*, and *Phædrus* (249 B) did not "understand" the common-sense explanation of the universal through abstraction and generalization. He rejected it, on the contrary, precisely because he foresaw that, if consistently carried out' and accepted as the final account of the matter, it leads straight to Mill's ultimate philosophy, which he would not have on any terms.

[185] *Protag.*, 330 C, ἡ δικαιοσύνη πρᾶγμά τι ἐστιν ἢ οὐδὲν πρᾶγμα; *Phædo*, 65 D, φαμέν τι εἶναι δίκαιον αὐτὸ ἢ οὐδέν; 76 E, 77 A, καλόν τε καὶ ἀγαθόν, 100 B, καλὸν αὐτὸ καθ' αὑτὸ καὶ ἀγαθόν. *Theætet*, 157 D, εἴ σοι ἀρέσκει τὸ μή τι εἶναι ἀλλὰ γίγνεσθαι ἀεὶ ἀγαθὸν καὶ καλόν. *Cratyl.*, 440 A, εἰ δὲ . . . . ἔστι δὲ τὸ καλόν, ἔστι δὲ τὸ ἀγαθόν. *Sophist*, 247 A–B, τό γε δυνατόν τῳ παραγίγνεσθαι καὶ ἀπογίγνεσθαι πάντως εἶναί τι φήσουσιν . . . . οὔσης οὖν δικαιοσύνης, etc. *Phileb.*, 55 B, πῶς οὐκ ἀλόγον ἐστι

[186] *Phædo*, 96 B; *Theætet.*, 156, 157, 184 D, εἰ πολλαί τινες ἐν ἡμῖν ὥσπερ ἐν δουρείοις ἵπποις αἰσθήσεις ἐγκάθηνται, ἀλλὰ μὴ εἰς μίαν τινὰ ἰδέαν, εἴτε ψυχὴν εἴτε ὅ τι δεῖ καλεῖν πάντα ταῦτα ξυντείνει. *Tim.*, 51 C, ἢ ταῦτα ἅπερ καὶ βλέπομεν (*cf.* ἅπερ ὁρῷεν, *Rep.*, 515 B; *Parmen.*, 130 D), ὅσα τε ἄλλα διὰ τοῦ σώματος αἰσθανόμεθα, μόνα ἐστὶ τοιαύτην ἔχοντα ἀλήθειαν.

[187] *Phædr.*, 249 B, δεῖ γὰρ ἄνθρωπον ξυνιέναι κατ' εἶδος λεγόμενον, ἐκ πολλῶν ἰὸν αἰσθήσεων εἰς ἓν λογισμῷ ξυναιρούμενον. τοῦτο δέ ἐστιν ἀνάμνησις, etc. *Cratyl.*, 399 C, μόνον τῶν θηρίων ὀρθῶς ὁ ἄνθρωπος ἄνθρωπος ὠνομάσθη, ἀναθρῶν ἃ ὄπωπεν. *Phædo*, 75 B, ὅτι πάντα τὰ ἐν ταῖς αἰσθήσεσιν ἐκείνου τε ὀρέγεται τοῦ ὅ ἐστιν ἴσον, etc.

[188] *Parmen.*, 132, νόημα δὲ οὐδενός; . . . . ὄντος ἢ οὐκ ὄντος; . . . εἶτα οὐκ εἶδος ἔσται τοῦτο τὸ νοούμενον ἓν εἶναι, ἀεὶ ὂν τὸ αὐτὸ ἐπὶ πᾶσιν; LUTOSLAWSKI, p. 403, misquotes and misinterprets this passage. PROFESSOR RITCHIE, *Plato*, pp. 91, 112, 113, recognizes that it is conclusive against conceptualism. *Cf.* ZELLER, p. 668. The further objection that if the ideas are thoughts and things partake of them, things must think, is generally treated as a verbal equivocation. *Cf. Euthydem.*, 287 D E. But, for the underlying metaphysical problem, see my discussion of Aristotle *de Anima*, 429 *b* 26 in *A. J. P.*, Vol. XXII, pp. 161 ff.

[189] *Cf.* the characterization of positivism or phenomenalism in *Rep.*, 516 C D, καθορῶντι τὰ παριόντα καὶ μνημονεύοντι μάλιστα, ὅσα τε πρότερα αὐτῶν καὶ ὕστερα εἰώθει καὶ ἅμα πορεύεσθαι. *Cf.* also *Phædo*, 96 B C; *Gorg.*, 501 A B.

point is not explicitly made by Plato, a concept of the mind, even apart from objective reference, either is or is not an entity of another than the natural or sensuous order. If it is, we are driven back upon Platonism. For, though the Platonic ideas are more than thoughts if thoughts are only decaying sense, thoughts, if radically different from sensations, become entities that may assume the rôle of Platonic ideas, as they do in the ultimate philosophy of Aristotle, and in the interpretation of those Platonists, ancient and modern, who conceive the ideas as thoughts of God. This is not Plato's doctrine, but only a plausible development of it by those who cannot acquiesce in his wise renunciation of systematic dogmatism.[190] In these matters Plato affirms no more than is necessary for his fixed faiths and purposes.[191] The objective reality in some sense of ideas (but no more) was so necessary. That it was a hard saying is as well known to him as it is to his critics.[192] And he has anticipated their objections. But this doctrine, or something equally and similarly paradoxical, was and is the sole alternative to a philosophy which he and the majority of his modern critics cannot and will not accept. The burden of proof rests heavily, then, on those who affirm that at any time he did or could abandon or seriously modify it. A survey of the dialogues discovers no evidence in support of such a contention.

For this purpose the dialogues fall into three (or four) groups: (1) Those that are supposed to precede the doctrine; or (2) to lead up to it; (3) those in which it is most specifically affirmed or mythically embellished; (4) those in which it is criticised or, as some say, abandoned or modified. In the case of the first and fourth group the argument is often made to turn upon the meaning to be assigned to εἶδος, ἰδέα, and other terms elsewhere distinctly appropriated to the transcendental idea. We are repeatedly warned that the mere use of the words εἶδος and ἰδέα is no evidence of the transcendental doctrine. This is obvious; but it is equally true that the possibility of taking these words in a conceptual sense raises no presumption that they must be taken in that sense exclusively and that the doctrine was absent from Plato's mind at the time. Such an assumption is made by modern critics in the interest of theories of development, or to free as many dialogues as possible from the distasteful paradox. But Plato was always at liberty to use the terminology of the ideas conceptually for the practical logical uses of definition and classification—even in the transcendental *Phædrus*.[193] All Platonic ideas are concepts. It does not follow that they are ever in Plato's intention no more than concepts. And, in any case, the absence of the theory from any given dialogue proves no more than does the virtual absence from the *Laws* of all metaphysics, including the "later" theory of ideas.

[190] *Cf. infra*, Part II, *Philebus*.

[191] *Meno*, 86 B, καὶ τὰ μέν γε ἄλλα οὐκ ἂν πάνυ ὑπὲρ τοῦ λόγου διισχυρισαίμην, etc.

[192] *Rep.*, 532 D, 476 A; *Parmen.*, 135 B C; *Phileb.*, 15 A B; *Tim.*, 51 C D; *infra*, p. 36.

[193] 237 C, 249 B, 263 E. *Cf.* also the loose popular use of εἶδος and ἰδέα 237 D, 238 A, 253 C D. NATORP, *Hermes*, Vol. XXXV, p. 409, infers that the *Phædrus*, "must" be earlier than the *Phædo* and *Republic*; LUTOSŁAWSKI (pp. 340, 341), that it must be later, because, if we interpret rightly, we "soon get quit of the riddle of self-existing ideas" and perceive that "ἰδέα and εἶδος are used in a meaning which is identical with the idea as conceived by Kant, a necessary concept of reason." Of course, Kant's ideas of reason are misapplied here and all Lutoslawski means is "Begriff," "concept."

Premising thus much, we turn to the first group. In the *Apology, Crito, Laches, Lysis, Charmides, Menexenus,* first four books of the *Republic,*[194] *Protagoras,*[195] and (some affirm) the *Euthyphro, Gorgias,* and *Euthydemus* there is no distinct mention of the (Platonic) ideas. There was no occasion for it in the *Apology, Crito,* and *Menexenus,* and little, if any, in the others. The relation of the *Lysis, Charmides,* and *Laches* to Plato's mature ethical theories and the subtlety of the *Charmides* and *Lysis*[196] make it improbable that they antedate the main tenet of his philosophy. This is still more obvious in the case of the *Menexenus* (387 (?), æt. 40).[197] The realistic language used of the definition in the *Euthyphro* must be presumed to imply what a similar terminology does elsewhere.[198] The joke about παρουσία in the *Euthydemus* is a distinct and familiar allusion to the Platonic idea of beauty.[199] Had Plato omitted that jest, the absence of the doctrine would prove no more than it does in the case of the *Protagoras.*

More interesting than this balancing of probabilities is the evidence presented by the *Gorgias.* This magnificent composition may or may not be earlier than the *Meno, Phædo, Euthydemus,* and *Cratylus.* It is certainly not appreciably less mature. It distinguishes and classifies "ideas" in the manner rather of the "later" dialogues,[200] and although it contains no explicit and obvious mention of the transcendental idea,[201] the doctrine is clearly suggested for all readers who look below the surface. It is worth while to dwell upon the point. In the *Cratylus,* 389 C, employing the terminology of the ideas in the manner of *Republic,* 596 A B, 597 B,[202] Socrates says that the workman who makes a tool puts into the material, the iron, the idea of the tool that exists in nature.[203] Similarly in *Republic,* 500 D, the philosopher statesman puts

[194] 402 C and 437, 438, presumably imply the ideas, but could be taken merely of concepts, classes or species. Not so 585 in Book IX. Pfleiderer therefore, in order to eliminate the ideas from Books VIII and IX, pronounces 580 B–588 A a later addition.

[195] But *cf.* 330 C, ἡ δικαιοσύνη πρᾶγμά τι ἐστιν ἢ οὐδὲν πρᾶγμα; 349 B, ἢ ἑκάστῳ τῶν ὀνομάτων τούτων ὑπόκειταί τις ἴδιος οὐσία καὶ πρᾶγμα ἔχον ἑαυτοῦ δύναμιν ἕκαστον; 330 E, αὐτὴ ἡ ὁσιότης.

[196] *Cf. supra,* n. 108.

[197] Wilamowitz has somewhere denied the Platonic authorship of the *Menexenus,* but he may have a "*peccavi*" in reserve. Life is short to debate such paradoxes; but if any athetizer will stake his reputation on the point, μαχοίμην ἂν πάντων ἥδιστα ἐνὶ τούτων.

[198] 5 D, ταὐτόν .... αὐτὸ αὑτῷ, etc.; 6 D E, τῶν πολλῶν ὁσίων (*cf. Phædo,* 78 D, τί δὲ τῶν πολλῶν καλῶν; *Rep.,* 596 A, εἶδος .... ἐν .... περὶ ἕκαστα τὰ πολλὰ) — αὐτὸ τὸ εἶδος ᾦ, etc. (*Phædo,* 100 D, τῷ καλῷ; *Meno,* 72 C, ἕν γέ τι εἶδος .... δι' ὅ), ἀποβλέπων .... παραδείγματι.

[199] 301 A. It is not the word πάρεστι that proves this, but the entire context ἕτερα αὐτοῦ γε τοῦ καλοῦ, etc. LUTOS-LAWSKI (p. 212) affirms that Plato "would have said later πάρεστι τὸ κάλλος (αὐτὸ καθ' αὑτό)." He never did say, nor could he have said, anything of the kind. Πάρεστι .... αὐτὸ καθ' αὑτὸ he would have felt as a contradiction in terms. (On the correct and incorrect use of αὐτὰ καθ' αὑτά,

etc., see my remarks in *A. J. P.,* Vol. IX, No. 3, p. 287.) Moreover, Plato never affirmed the presence absolutely of the idea with or in the particular (*Parmen.,* 131 A B; *Phileb.,* 15 B), but only its presence or communication somehow. The τι of κάλλος τι expresses this and Socrates's embarrassment very well. *Cf. Phædo,* 100 D, εἴτε παρουσία εἴτε κοινωνία εἴτε ὅπῃ δὴ καὶ ὅπως προσγενομένη. So *Symp.,* 211 B, μετέχοντα τρόπον τινὰ τοιοῦτον, etc.

[200] JOWETT, Vol. IV, p. 436: "The same love of divisions is apparent in the *Gorgias.*" *Cf.* 454 E, 455 A, in manner of the *Sophist. Cf.* 464, 465. It could be plausibly argued that the definition of rhetoric πολιτικῆς μορίου εἴδωλον (463 D) as explained in 464, 465, is a fuller and more explicit statement of the doctrine of *Politicus,* 291 B and 303 E–304 A, as to the difficulty of distinguishing the statesman from his imitators and the true relation of ῥητορεία to δικαστική and βασιλική.

[201] But *cf.* 474 D, ἀποβλέπων; 488 D, τὰ τῶν πόλλων νόμιμα, with *Rep.,* 479 D, τὰ τῶν πόλλων πολλὰ νόμιμα, etc.; *Gorg.,* 497 E, παρουσίᾳ .... οἷς ἂν κάλλος παρῇ.

[202] ὁ δημιουργὸς .... πρὸς τὴν ἰδέαν βλέπων .... ἡ ἐν τῇ φύσει οὖσα (κλίνη).

[203] On this passage as the chief Platonic source of the Aristotelian doctrine of matter and form see my remarks in *A. J. P.,* Vol. XXII, No. 2, p. 158. Campbell, overlooking this passage, finds in *Polit.,* 288 D, the earliest approach to the distinction of matter and form.

into the plastic stuff of human nature the forms or ideas of justice and temperance which he contemplates as existing in the transcendental world (ἐκεῖ), and so becomes an artisan of political and popular virtue.[204]   Expressed in slightly different imagery, this is the function of the statesman in the *Politicus*, 309 C (*cf.* 308 C D).   He is to implant in those rightly prepared by education, fixed, true opinions concerning the honorable, the just, and the good.[205]   The thought and the imagery belong to Plato's permanent stock.   We find them in the *Gorgias*, 503 E–504 D.[206]   Here, too, Plato conceives the true teacher, artist, or statesman as contemplating ideas or forms, which he strives to embody in the material with which he works, even as the Demiurgus of the *Timæus* stamps the ideas upon the matter of generation.

The origin, first suggestion, exposition, or proof of the theory of ideas is variously sought by different critics in the *Meno*, the *Cratylus*, the *Theætetus*, or even in the *Phædrus*, *Parmenides*, and *Symposium*.   Obviously Plato could at any time argue indirectly in support of the ideas as necessary postulates of ontology and epistemology. Our chief concern is with the hypothesis that the exposition of some particular dialogue marks a date in the development of his own thought.   The doctrine of reminiscence is introduced in the *Meno* to meet an eristic use of a puzzle allied to the psychological problem of "recognition."[207]   How, if we do not already know, shall we recognize a truth or a definition when we have found it?[208]   Socrates replies that the soul has seen all things in its voyagings through eternity, and that all our learning here is but recollection.[209]   This theory is confirmed in the case of mathematical ideas by Socrates's success in eliciting by prudent questions a demonstration of the Pythagorean proposition from Meno's ignorant slave.[210]   The *Phædo* distinctly refers to this argument as a proof of the reality of ideas,[211] and the myth in the *Phædrus* describes the ante-natal vision of the pure, colorless, formless, essences of true being.[212]   It follows that, though the ideas are not there explicitly mentioned, the reminiscence spoken of in the *Meno* must refer to them.[213]   But it is extremely improbable that this represents Plato's first apprehension of the doctrine.   Psychologically and historically the origin of the theory is to be looked for in the hypostatization of the Socratic concept and the reaction against Heracliteanism.[214]   Its association with Pythagoreanism and

204 ἃ ἐκεῖ ὁρᾷ μελετῆσαι εἰς ἀνθρώπων ἤθη . . . . τιθέναι . . . . δημιουργόν . . . . σωφροσύνης τε καὶ δικαιοσύνης. *Cf.* 501 B, πυκνὰ ἂν ἑκατέρωσε ἀποβλέποιεν . . . . καὶ πρὸς ἐκεῖνο αὖ ὃ ἐν τοῖς ἀνθρώποις ἐμποιοῖεν. *Cf. Polit.*, 309 D, τοῦτο αὐτὸ ἐμποιεῖν.

205 This does not refer exclusively to the higher education, as Zeller affirms.

206 ἀποβλέπων πρός τι . . . . ὅπως ἂν εἶδός τι αὐτῷ σχῇ τοῦτο ὃ ἐργάζεται. This is applied first to the body, then to the soul. The τάξις and κόσμος of the soul is δικαιοσύνη and σωφροσύνη. . . . . πρὸς ταῦτα βλέπων, etc. The ῥήτωρ ἀγαθὸς καὶ τεχνικός here = the true πολιτικός. And we may note in passing that the *Gorgias* "already" recognizes that rhetoric might be an art. The popular rhetoric is none because it ignores the ideas (1) as ethical ideals (*Gorgias*), (2) as the basis of scientific dialectic (*Phædrus*).

207 *Meno*, 80 D ff. *Cf.* my dissertation *De Platonis idearum doctrina*, pp. 15 ff.

208 οὔτε ζητεῖν οὔτε ἀπορεῖν ἄνευ προλήψεως, *Sext. Empir. Math.*, 1, 57.

209 " L'univers peut dire comme le Dieu de Pascal: 'Tu ne me chercherais pas, si tu ne m'avais déjà trouvé.' " — FOUILLÉE. *Cf. Polit.*, 278 D; *Tim.*, 41 E, τὴν τοῦ παντὸς φύσιν ἔδειξε. *Cf. infra*, p. 43.

210 82 ff.

211 73 A.

212 247 ff., 249 C, τοῦτο δέ ἐστιν ἀνάμνησις ἐκείνων, etc.

213 The realistic terminology of the definition would justify the same inference. *Cf.* 74, 75.

214 *Cf. supra*, p. 28.

the ante-natal life of the soul is mythical embellishment; and its application to the problem of the *a priori* element in human knowledge is a secondary confirmation of its truth.[215]   Nevertheless the *Meno*, which John Stuart Mill pronounces "a little gem," is admirably adapted to serve as an introduction to the Platonic philosophy.   It exemplifies in brief compass the Socratic method and the logic of the definition in terminology that suggests the ideas, touches on higher things in the theory of recollection and the problem of *a priori* knowledge, and clearly resumes the dramatic, ethical, and political puzzles that prepare for the teaching of the *Republic*.   Socrates's mention of the ideas at the close of the *Cratylus* as something of which he dreams as an alternative to Heracliteanism is taken by some critics to indicate that we have here an introduction to or a first presentment of the doctrine.[216]   They overlook two considerations: (1) the theory is taken for granted at the beginning of the dialogue, as we have already seen;[217] (2) there are no traces of immaturity in the thought of the *Cratylus*.   The polemic against the flowing philosophers and the forms of eristic associated with them is, in a jesting form, as sharp, and the apprehension of the real issues as distinct as it is in the *Theœtetus* and *Sophist*.[218]

Some scholars look upon the *Theœtetus* as a propædeutic introduction to the ideas,[219] while others take it as marking the transition to the later theory.   Strictly speaking, neither view can be correct, since, though the ideas are not often or very explicitly mentioned, there is enough to show the presence of the doctrine in its normal form.   The ἀγαθὸν and καλόν, claimed for being as against becoming in 157 D, is almost technical for the affirmation of the ideas.[220]   The παραδείγματα of 176 E can hardly refer to anything else.   And the close parallel between 186 A B and *Republic*, 523, 524, admits no other interpretation.   Among the νοητά which the soul grasps by

---

[215] PROFESSOR RITCHIE'S suggestion (*Plato*, pp. 86, 87) that the Platonic idea is a generalization of the Pythagorean treatment of mathematics is unsupported by evidence. See, however, ZELLER, pp. 654–6, for suggestions of other pre-Socratic influences on the theory.

[216] So once SUSEMIHL in his *Genetische Entwickelung*, Vol. I, p. 161. LUTOSLAWSKI, pp. 224, 225, thinks the ideas are not formulated even here, but only a something which in later dialogues proves to be the ideas! The terminology is complete — εἶδος, αὐτὸ ὃ ἔστι, τὸ φύσει, ποῖ βλέπων 389, εἰ δὲ . . . . ἔστι δὲ τὸ καλόν, ἔστι δὲ τὸ ἀγαθόν, ἔστι δὲ ἐν ἕκαστον τῶν ὄντων (440 B). All these phrases might conceivably be used of notions, conceptual ideas. But this proves too much. For, according to L., it holds of all dialogues except the *Symposium*, *Phœdo*, and parts of the *Republic*, and he is not quite sure of them. His real object is to eliminate the self-existent idea altogether.

[217] *Cf. supra*, p. 31. The doctrine of *Cratyl.*, 389, is furthermore identical with that of *Repub.*, 596 A ff.

[218] 386, 439, 440. On the μὴ ὄν and ψευδής δόξα fallacy, 429 ff., *cf. infra*, p. 53. On the ῥέοντες *cf.* 411 B C with *Phœd.*, 90 C; *Phileb.*, 43 A. LUTOSLAWSKI affirms (pp. 366, 367) that the subdivision of κίνησις into φορά and ἀλλοίωσις is a new and important discovery of the *Theœtetus*, 181, C. He fails to note that the argument of *Cratylus*, 339, 340, dis-

tinctly implies that πάντα ῥεῖ includes qualitative change. *Cf.* 439 D, ὅτι τοιοῦτον, 440 A, ἄλλο καὶ ἀλλοῖον γίγνοιτο . . . . ὁποῖόν γέ τί ἐστιν. 439 E, μηδὲν ἐξιστάμενον τῆς αὐτοῦ ἰδέας (*cf. Tim.*, 50 B, and *Rep.*, 380 D). *Cf.* the whole context of the argument and the use of ὑπεξέρχεται, *Cratyl.*, 439 D; *Theœtet.*, 182 D. In fact, the association of motion and qualitative change was always a commonplace with Plato. Both "before" and "after" the *Theœtetus* μεταβολή and ῥεῖν, etc., are used freely in both meanings. *Cf. Repub.*, 380 E ff., which alone refutes L.'s "discovery." οὐκοῦν ὑπὸ μὲν ἄλλου τὰ ἄριστα ἔχοντα ἥκιστα ἀλλοιοῦταί τε καὶ κινεῖται. The fact that the *Theœtetus* is slightly more explicit in formal classification proves nothing. The whole argument of the *Cratylus* passage hinges on the distinction precisely as does the argument of the *Theœtetus*. It appears explicitly again only in the *Parmenides*, and not in the "late" *Philebus* and *Timœus*. It is not included in the ten kinds of motion in the *Laws*, 893, 894, and L. finds it only by implication in 894 E, ἀλλ' ὅταν ἄρα αὐτὸ αὑτὸ κινῆσαν ἕτερον ἀλλοιώσῃ, which is no more explicit than the *Cratylus* or *Republic*.

[219] W. J. ALEXANDER in *Studies Dedicated to Gildersleeve*, p. 179, thinks its teaching to be: knowledge is of the ideas, error arises from imperfect ἀνάμνησις.

[220] *Supra*, n. 185.

herself,[221] and whose essence is apprehended through their relation of opposition,[222] are mentioned, after οὐσία, the ὅμοιον and ἀνόμοιον, the ταὐτὸν and the ἕτερον of the *Sophist*. But also, as in the *Parmenides*, the ethical ideas, καλόν, αἰσχρόν, ἀγαθόν, and κακόν;[223] and lastly, as in the *Republic*, the qualities of sense, σκληρὸν and μαλακόν.[224] The actual sensation of these opposites comes of course through sense. But the οὐσία and the ὅ τι ἐστόν, as in the *Republic*, is apprehended by the mind as an idea. There is no argument for holding these ideas to be mere concepts that would not prove the same for the *Republic*, which of course is impossible.[225] This point established, we may concede that the *Theœtetus* may be, not an introduction to the ideas, but an indirect argument in support of the familiar doctrine. The polemic against Heraclitus is always that.[226] And, though Plato himself may not be aware of it, the statement that the syllable is not the sum of its elements, but μία ἰδέα ἀμέριστος, embodies the principle and justification of a realistic logic.[227] The conceptual whole is not the sum of its parts, but a new entity and unity.[228]

What has been said of the *Theœtetus* applies to Zeller's theory[229] that the second part of the *Parmenides* is an indirect argument for the ideas. That this is not the main purpose of the *Parmenides* will appear in the sequel. And Zeller was mistaken in stating that only relative contradictions followed from the being of the one, while absolute contradictions resulted from its not being. But the Platonic idea is always suggested by the antithesis of the one and the many. And in the eighth hypothesis, 164 B ff., the "one" and "others" are no longer treated with dialectical impartiality, but there is a hint that the one may be regarded as the symbol of the idea. Symmetry leads us to expect the argument that, if the one is not (relative μὴ ὄν), other things both are and are not all contradictory predicates. Instead of "are" we find "appear" or "seem." Other things are indefinite bulks that break up under inspection and only seem to partake of unity and other predicates that derive from unity. These ὄγκοι certainly suggest the world of matter uninformed by ideas, the "being" of the materialists which the friends of ideas in the *Sophist* call "becoming" and break up into little bits.[230] And the statement that, as they cannot be other than the (non-existent) one, they are the other of one another, reminds us of ἀλλήλοις . . . . συν-

[221] αὐτὴ ἡ ψυχή 186 B. Cf. 187 A; Phœdo, 65 C; Rep., 524 B C, 526 B.

[222] τὴν ἐναντιότητα πρὸς ἀλλήλω. Cf. Rep., 524 D, ἃ μὲν εἰς τὴν αἴσθησιν ἅμα τοῖς ἐναντίοις ἑαυτοῖς ἐμπίπτει. Mr. Henry Jackson and others confound this special use of πρὸς ἄλληλα with τὰ πρός τι, relative terms generally, by the aid of Parmen., 133 C. The Theœtetus passage is the source of Hermodorus's distinction of πρὸς ἕτερα into πρὸς ἐναντία and πρός τι, which ZELLER (p. 706) says is not found in Plato.

[223] 130 B after ὁμοιότης.

[224] 186 B with Rep., 524 A.

[225] THOMPSON on Meno, 74 D, says that problems which in Phileb., 14 D, are δεδημευμένα are made the bases of a dialectical course in Rep., 523–6. This is a misapprehension. The Republic mentions (525 A) that the same object is perceived as one and many. It does not sport with the

paradox, but passes on to show how mathematics leads the mind to the apprehension of abstract and ideal unity. Philebus, 14 D ff., is concerned with logical method; Rep., 523–6, with psychology and education. But the thought of the Republic is not less mature, and is, indeed, repeated in Phileb., 56 E = Rep., 525 D E.

[226] οὐδὲν εἶναι ἓν αὐτὸ καθ᾽ αὑτό, etc. 157 A is the diametrical opposite of the ideas — εἶναί τι καλὸν αὐτὸ καθ᾽ αὑτό, Phœdo, 100 B.

[227] 205 C, 203 E.

[228] Cf. Parmen., 157 D, οὐκ ἄρα τῶν πολλῶν οὐδὲ πάντων τὸ μόριον μόριον, ἀλλὰ μιᾶς τινὸς ἰδέας καὶ ἑνός τινος ὅ καλοῦμεν ὅλον. See also A. J. P., Vol. XXII, No. 2, p. 158.

[229] Set forth in his Platonic Studies and the earlier editions of his History, but now virtually withdrawn.

[230] Soph., 246 B.C.

δεδέσθαι in the theory of pure relativity in *Theætetus*, 160 B. Similar hints occur in the fourth hypothesis, 157 B, which deals with ἄλλα on the supposition that the one is.[231] The main conclusion that ἄλλα, then, admit all contradictory predicates is indicated very briefly (159 A). What is emphasized is the fact that ἄλλα *per se* are πλήθη .... ἐν οἷς τὸ ἓν οὐκ ἔνι, that they are ἄπειρα (*cf. Phileb.*); that it is the one which introduces πέρας πρὸς ἄλληλα; and that, having parts, these parts must relate to μιᾶς τινὸς ἰδέας καὶ ἑνός τινος, ὃ καλοῦμεν ὅλον.[232] While the main object of the *Parmenides*, then, is to illustrate the communion of ideas and the doctrine of relative ὄν and μὴ ὄν set forth in the *Sophist*, there is a suggestion of polemic here and there directed against the infinite and indefinite world without unity of the materialists, relativists, and deniers of the ideas. But obviously the first origin and exposition of the ideas is not to be sought in a work that deals with problems and difficulties arising from the doctrine.[233]

The *Phædo, Phædrus, Republic,* and *Symposium,* the dialogues that are fullest in explicit affirmation or mythical embellishment of the transcendental idea, need not here detain us long. In his exaltation of pure thought and the dialectical method Plato clothes the ideas in all the contradictory attributes of a sensuous, æsthetic type, an ethical ideal, and a metaphysical *noumenon.* He is perfectly aware of this, and the inconsistency is common to all philosophies of the absolute.[234] In the *Phædrus* as elsewhere he warns us not to take the myth too seriously.[235] In the *Phædo* he describes the doctrine as familiar,[236] and reminds us that he does not insist upon the precise terminology, but only on the central fact.[237] In the *Republic* every terminology is employed from the most naïve to the most severely logical or the most transcendental.[238] Despite these facts, attempts have been made to extract evidences of contradiction or development from the varying imagery and terminology of these dialogues. The unity of the *Republic* has been broken up and its books variously dated according to the absence of the theory, or its presence in an "earlier" or "later" form. It has even been gravely argued in defiance of all psychological and historical probability that the *Symposium,* which in consonance with its theme mentions the idea of beauty only, represents a stage of development in which the Platonic

[231] Relative ὄν admitting κοινωνία.

[232] *Theætet.*, 203, 204.

[233] *Cf. infra*, Part II.

[234] JOWETT's common-sense and literary tact have answered literal-minded objectors once for all: "When the charioteers and their steeds stand upon the dome of heaven they behold the intangible, invisible essences which are not objects of sight. This is because the force of language can no further go."—Vol. I, p. 412.

[235] 265 C, τὰ μὲν ἄλλα τῷ ὄντι παιδιᾷ πεπαῖσθαι.

[236] Those who think that the ideas have been mentioned in only one preceding dialogue, as the *Meno* or *Symposium,* are much exercised by the θαμὰ λέγειν of 72 E, the ἃ θρυλοῦμεν ἀεί of 76 D, and the πολυθρύλητα of 100 B. LUTOS-LAWSKI's statement (p. 292) that these terms may refer to

Socratic ethical concepts, not Platonic ideas, is refuted by the context (ἡ τοιαύτη οὐσία .... ἀναφέρειν τὰ ἐν ταῖς αἰσθήσεσι, etc.). The suggestion that the reference is to conversations abandons the whole case, unless they are limited to the interval between the *Meno* and the *Phædo!* The simple truth is that Plato may at any time refer to any part of his permanent beliefs as familiar doctrine. On the theory of development, to what discussions is reference made in *Crito*, 46 D, and 49 A B? To the *Gorgias* and *Republic* I? Where has Plato often said that τὸ τὰ αὑτοῦ πράττειν is δικαιοσύνη? (*Rep.*, 433 A). Where has Glaucon heard οὐκ ὀλιγάκις that the idea of good is the μέγιστον μάθημα? (*Rep.*, 504 E).

[237] 100 D.

[238] 596, 597, 585, 534, 532, 514–17, 505–11, 500 D–501 B, 490 B, 485 B, 476–80.

philosophy contained but one transcendental idea, as if the problems of psychology and ontology which the theory of ideas sought to meet or evade could have been in any wise advanced by the hypostatization of one concept! We have glanced at such methods of reasoning already, and shall meet them again. At present we pass on to the hypothesis that the *Parmenides* contains a criticism of the ideas which leads to the abandonment or transformation of the theory in the fourth and latest group of dialogues. This hypothesis rests on the assumption that the criticism of the *Parmenides* is new, that Plato was bound either to answer it or give up the ideas, and that, as a matter of fact, the transcendental idea is not found in the later dialogues. These assumptions will not bear critical examination.

The objections brought forth against the ideas in the *Parmenides* are obvious enough, and, as Jowett says, are unanswerable by anybody who separates the phenomenal from the real. How can we bring the absolute into intelligible relation with the relative? How can the absolute ("the Gods") take cognizance of us or we apprehend what is adapted to their thought?[239] How can we without self-contradiction apply to it unity or plurality, or any other predicate of human knowledge?[240] More specifically, if the ideas are transcendental unities, how can we predicate multiplicity or parts of them as we must to connect them with one another and with phenomena?[241] How shall we interpret the figurative expressions that the ideas are present in things, or that things participate in or imitate the ideas?[242] If the idea is the postulated correlate of every *idem in multis*, why should we not assume an idea to explain the likeness of the idea and the particular, and so on in infinite regression?[243] To what extent the form of these objections is due to contemporary critics, or the misunderstanding of students, or the precocity of Aristotle, is an unprofitable inquiry. Their substance is in the *Republic*, not to speak of the *Phædo*, the *Euthydemus*, the *Timæus*, and *Philebus*.[244] Their presentation in the *Parmenides*, then, does not mark a crisis in Plato's thought calling for a review of his chief article of philosophic faith. Plato does not and cannot answer them, but he evidently does not take them very seriously,[245] though he admits that it would require a marvelous man to sift and analyze them all.[246] They arise from the limitations of our finite minds.[247] Here as in the *Philebus* he bids us disregard them, and proceed on the assumption of ideas to find the one idea

[239] *Parmen.*, 134.

[240] *Soph.*, 244, 245; *Parmen.*, 142 A; *Tim.*, 37 E, 38 A.

[241] *Parmen.*, 131; *Phileb.*, 15 B.

[242] *Parmen.*, 131 A, 132 D.   [243] 132 A, 132 E.

[244] *Rep.*, 476 A, αὐτὸ μὲν ἓν ἕκαστον εἶναι, τῇ δὲ τῶν πράξεων καὶ σωμάτων καὶ ἀλλήλων κοινωνίᾳ . . . . πολλὰ φαίνεσθαι ἕκαστον. *Cf. Phileb.*, 15 B; *Parmen.*, 144 E. Some ignore this passage. Others wantonly emend it, as BADHAM, who reads ἄλλῃ ἄλλων, and BYWATER, who reads ἀλλ' ἄλλων (*Journal of Phil.*, Vol. V, p. 122). RITCHIE (*Plato*, 96) takes it in a Pickwickian sense in order to avoid "anticipating the *Sophist*." PFLEIDERER uses it to prove that the fifth book of the *Republic* is later than the tenth. Anything rather than admit the obvious fact that Plato always recognized the "communion" of ideas, and argued it at length in the

Sophist, only because pedants were obstructing the way of logic by denying it. Similarly the τρίτος ἄνθρωπος is distinctly implied in *Republic*, 597 C, and *Tim.*, 31 A, as the difficulty of giving a precise meaning to παρουσία is in *Euthydemus*, 301 A, and *Phædo*, 100 D.

[245] *Phileb.*, 15 D E. In *Sophist* 251 B C, the reference is to the one and many in things, but the application to the communion of ideas immediately follows.

[246] *Parmen.*, 135 A B.

[247] *Tim.*, 52 B C, 34 C; *Phileb.*, 15 D, τῶν λόγων . . . πάθος ἐν ἡμῖν. The *Sophist* does not really contradict *Tim.*, 38 A B. Absolutely ὄν and μὴ ὄν remain a mystery (251 A, 251 D, 254 C). The *Sophist* merely fixes the practically necessary conventions of logical discourse about them — τὸν λόγον, ἐν τοῖς παρ' ἡμῖν λόγοις, etc., 251 A, 251 D.

and enumerate all its species.[248] The hypothesis must be judged by its total consequences.[249]

The text of the *Parmenides* does not bear out the assertion that the objections apply to any special form of the theory or can be met by a change of terminology. The suggestion that there may be some classes of concepts to which no idea corresponds is repudiated for good Platonic reasons.[250] The interpretation that the ideas are to be henceforth merely concepts is distinctly rejected, was *a priori* impossible for Plato, and is refuted by the positive affirmation of their objectivity in the *Timæus*.[251] Socrates's explanation that the ideas are παραδείγματα, patterns of which phenomena are likenesses, is nothing new. The terminology of pattern, copy, and artist looking off to his model is familiar throughout the "early" dialogues, whether used of the definition or the idea. There is no hint in the corresponding passages of the *Philebus* that such a variation of terminology could in any way affect the problem. It is not proposed in the *Parmenides* as a new doctrine, but merely as a different metaphor to evade the difficulty found in the literal interpretation of μετέχειν—it is a mere gloss upon the meaning of μετέχειν. But equally formidable difficulties confront this way of putting it.[252] And there is no systematic change of terminology in the "later" dialogues, which, like the earlier, employ in a purely natural and non-technical way the various synonyms and metaphors which Plato used to express the inexpressible.[253]

The challenge to find the ideas in dialogues "later" than the *Parmenides* is easily met. Nothing can be more explicit than the *Timæus*.[254] The alternative is distinctly proposed: are the objects of sense the only realities and is the supposition of ideas mere talk?[255] And it is affirmed that their reality is as certain as the distinction between opinion and science. They are νοούμενα and exist καθ' αὑτά.[256] There is no hint that

---

[248] 135 B C, *Phileb.*, 16 D. *Cf. Phædr.*, 270 D, ἐὰν δὲ πλείω εἴδη ἔχῃ ταῦτα ἀριθμησαμένους. *Laws*, 894 A, ἐν εἴδεσι λαβεῖν μετ' ἀριθμοῦ.

[249] *Parmen.*, 136; *Phædo*, 101 D.

[250] 130 D. See ZELLER, 700, 701, for lists of ideas. But, as we have seen, to admit that there is any conceptual unity not referable to an idea is to make the theory a mere play of fancy, and deprive it of all psychological and ontological meaning.

[251] 51 C. *Cf. supra*, n. 188.

[252] The τρίτος ἄνθρωπος is repeated in 132 D E. Other difficulties follow, and the final summing up, 135 A, is couched in the most general terminology: εἰ εἰσὶν αὗται αἱ ἰδέαι τῶν ὄντων καὶ ὁριεῖταί τις αὐτό τι ἕκαστον εἶδος. There is no suggestion that a new form or terminology makes any difference. The much misunderstood passage, 133 C D, is merely a special application of the general difficulty to relative terms. Ideal slavery is related only to ideal ownership, the slavery in us only to the ownership in us. There is no discrimination here of a class of αὐτὰ καθ' αὑτὰ εἴδη. (*Cf. A. J. P.*, Vol. IX, p. 287). Nor are there, as JOWETT and CAMPBELL affirm (*Republic*, Vol. II, p. 313, n. 1) two stages (1) ὁμοίωσις and (2) μέθεξις τοῦ ὁμοιώματος in the descent from the ideas to the individuals. ὁμοιώματα and μετέχοντες are merely two sides of the same fact—the participation somehow (εἴτε ὅπῃ δή τις αὐτὰ τίθεται) of the particu-

lar in the idea. The ὁμοιώματα are no more separable as an intermediate stage than are τὰ εἰσιόντα καὶ ἐξιόντα τῶν ὄντων ἀεὶ μιμήματα of *Timæus*, 50 C. In both cases we have only the idea and the particular and the metaphorical expression of their relation.

[253] See my note in *A. J. P.*, Vol. X, No. 1, p. 66. ZELLER, *Sitzungsber. d. Berl. Akad.*, 1887, No. 13.

[254] 51, 52.

[255] 51 C, τὸ δὲ οὐδὲν ἄρ' ἦν πλὴν λόγος. For the impossibility of taking λόγος as "Socratic concept" see my note in *A. J. P.*, Vol. X, p. 65.

[256] MR. ARCHER-HIND's attempt (*Jour. of Phil.*, Vol. XXIV, pp. 49 ff.) to "circumvent" this passage is based on a misinterpretation of 39 E. Since an idea of fire is not mentioned in the exhaustive enumeration there given of the ideas contained in the supreme idea, an idea of fire he argues, cannot be meant seriously here. But 39 E does not speak of the "supreme idea," which is a figment of modern Platonists. The ζῷον is simply the universal of animal or living thing, and as such the paradigm of the world which is a living thing. (*Cf. A.J. P.*, Vol. IX, p. 294.) It includes all subordinate νοητὰ ζῷα. There is no reason to look for other ideas in it. J. HOROWITZ (*Das Platonische νοητὸν ζῷον und der Philonische κοσμός νοητός*, Marburg, 1900) fails to prove his assertion that the νοητὸν ζῷον is "die Welt-Idee." Mr. Archer-Hind's further arguments merely pre-

they are mere concepts, or thoughts of God. On the contrary, God uses them as patterns, and as elements in the creation of the soul.[257] They are characterized in terms applicable only to pure absolute Being, and the familiar terminology is freely employed.[258] Three things, Plato repeats, must have existed from all eternity: the pure Being of the ideas, the generated copies, and space, the medium or receptacle.[259] The attempts of modern scholars to eliminate these elements or identify them with other categories found in other dialogues contradict Plato's explicit statements. We are often told that space is the θάτερον or μὴ ὄν.[260] For this there is not a scintilla of evidence.[261] Plato even says of space: ταὐτὸν αὐτὴν ἀεὶ προσρητέον (50 B), and calls it a τρίτον αὖ γένος ὂν τὸ τῆς χώρας ἀεί. The "same" and the "other" appear in a wholly different connection in the creation of the soul, and are obviously the categories of the *Sophist* attributed to the soul to explain its cognition of sameness and difference.[262] The occurrence of these categories in a dialogue that reaffirms the transcendental idea proves that to Plato's mind the two points of view were not incompatible, which, for the rest, is obvious enough from the *Phædrus*. We must interpret the *Sophist, Politicus,* and *Philebus* in the light of this presumption, and treat the terminology of the ideas as *prima facie* evidence of the doctrine. The *Republic* (476) "already" states that the transcendental unity of the ideas is somehow compatible with their communion. The *Sophist* formulates all the concessions which a "working logic" must demand from all philosophies of the absolute, be it absolute relativity, absolute Being, or absolute Platonic ideas. Plato minimized the inevitable inconsistency, and a sound interpretation will not exaggerate it. A working logic does not emphasize the transcendental character of the idea. But the language of 248 A, 247 A B, distinctly implies it.[263] The statement that δικαιοσύνη and φρόνησις are engendered in the soul (ἐγγίγνεται) obviously does not mean that they are *per se* concepts of the mind. Nor can we infer that the ideas are mere concepts from passages in

sent the usual objections of common-sense conceptualism—which are not competent to anyone who himself believes in any metaphysics or attributes metaphysics to Plato.

[257] 28 A, 29 A, 30 B C, 35 A. ZELLER, p. 665, n. 2, adds *Phædr.*, 247, which is irrelevant, and *Rep.*, 596 A ff., where God is the maker of the ideas. Lutoslawski's argument from νοήσει μετὰ λόγου περιληπτόν (27 E, 29 A, pp. 474, 477) interpreted as "included in thought" is a simple mistranslation.

[258] 52 A, 27 D, 28 A B, 29 B, 30 C. *Cf.* 39 E, ὃ ἔστι; 37 B, τὰ κατὰ ταὐτὰ ἔχοντα ἀεί; 48 E, παραδείγματος, to which correspond 50 C, μιμήματα, and 52 A, ὁμώνυμον ὅμοιον; 31 A, the τρίτος ἄνθρωπος.

[259] 52 D.

[260] *E. g.*, by RITCHIE, p. 116.

[261] ZELLER, pp. 719 ff., 733, produces none. Aristotle's obscure allusions prove nothing. The identification of the ἄπειρον of the *Philebus* with μὴ ὄν and matter breaks down. There remains the argument that, since in the *Republic* the ideas are ὄν and *phænomena* are μεταξύ — ὄντος and μὴ ὄντος, matter must be μὴ ὄν apprehended neither by νοῦς nor

αἴσθησις, but λογισμῷ τινι νόθῳ (52 B). But Plato's terminology cannot be used out of its context in this way. The μὴ ὄν problem belongs to logic. *Phænomena* are intermediate between ὄν and μὴ ὄν because they change, and are and are not the same predicates, not because they are the offspring of ideas and matter. In physics Plato was forced, however reluctantly, to assign a kind of eternity to matter or space. (*Cf.* BERKELEY, *Principles*, sec. 117: "either that real space is God, or that there is something beside God which is eternal, uncreated.") So far is it from being true that space or matter imparts μὴ ὄν to *phænomena* that, on the contrary, Plato explicitly says that *phænomena*, being unreal images, cling to essence (οὐσίας) somehow through their existence in space. *Tim.*, 52 C.

[262] 37 A B C is plainly a psychological myth or allegory expressing the results of the analysis of the *Sophist*. *Cf.* also *Theætet.*, 194 B.

[263] διὰ λογισμοῦ δὲ ψυχῇ πρὸς τὴν ὄντως οὐσίαν, ἣν ἀεὶ κατὰ ταὐτὰ ὡσαύτως ἔχειν φατέ. . . . . οὔσης οὖν δικαιοσύνης καὶ φρονήσεως . . . . πότερον ὁρατὸν καὶ ἁπτὸν (cf. *Tim.*, 28 B) εἶναί φασι τι αὐτῶν ἢ πάντα ἀόρατα.

which we are required to apprehend them in thought or in the soul.[264]   It is often said that souls take the place of ideas in Plato's later period.   This is a complete misconception of Plato's thought and style.   It is quite true that he could not confine the predicates of true or absolute Being to the ideas.   God is, of course, true Being, and in religious and metaphysical passages need not always be distinguished from the ideas taken collectively.   Both are invisible, eternal, intelligible.   In the *Timæus* space also is reluctantly treated as a kind of eternal being.   The *Sophist* tries to show that " being " is amenable to human logic and cognizable by finite minds.   This involves a contradiction for all except consistent relativists who renounce pure Being altogether. This Plato could not do, for, not only in the *Parmenides*, but in the late *Timæus*, he retains absolute Being for metaphysics and religion.   In the *Sophist* he shows that for human logic it is as impracticable as absolute not-Being.   To be known and talked about it must come out of its isolation and enter into relations—act and be acted upon. Being is therefore temporarily defined against the extremists of all schools as the power and potentiality[265] of action or passion, and the contradiction is smoothed over by the equivocal use of "true being" to denote both the metaphysical and the religious *noumenon*—the ideas and God.   True Being as God obviously possesses life, thought, motion, soul, and true Being as the ideas borrows so much life and motion as will explain their intercommunion in finite thought.[266]   But the definition, its purpose served, is never repeated, and pure transcendental being reappears in the *Timæus*. That the ideas still take precedence of souls appears distinctly from *Polit.*, 309 C, where it is said that fixed opinions in souls are a divine thing in a dæmonic thing. The same follows from the creation of the soul in the *Timæus*, and the hierarchy of elements in the good (*Phileb.*, 66) where pure ideas precede νοῦς.[267]   *Politicus*, 269 D, presumably implies the ideas;[268] 285 E ff. unmistakably affirms them.   What other possible interpretation can be put upon the statement ὅτι τοῖς μὲν τῶν ὄντων ῥαδίοις καταμαθεῖν αἰσθηταί τινες ὁμοιότητες πεφύκασιν?   These ὄντα are plainly ideas of material things, of which material things are likenesses.   But τὰ τιμιώτατα (justice, good, etc., *Phædr.*,

[264] *Sophist*, 250 B, τρίτον ἄρα τι παρὰ ταῦτα τὸ ὂν ἐν τῇ ψυχῇ τιθείς.   Cf. 243 C, οὐχ ἧττον κατὰ τὸ ὂν ταὐτὸν τοῦτο πάθος εἰληφότες ἐν τῇ ψυχῇ.   Cf. ὁμολογήματα . . . . ἐν τῇ ἡμετέρᾳ ψυχῇ, *Theœtet.*, 155 A, from which LUTOSLAWSKI, p. 383, infers that the ideas are subjective notions!

[265] 247 E, δύναμις probably includes both.

[266] The entire passage betrays embarrassment. To adapt "Being" to the necessities of logic, Plato is obliged to deny of it (248 D E) what in *Tim.*, 38 A B, his feelings require him to affirm.   He treats γιγνώσκεσθαι as a πάσχειν which ZELLER (p. 652), as a true Aristotelian, thinks a verbal fallacy.   In the crucial passage, 249 A, he uses αὐτὸ (μηδὲ ζῆν αὐτὸ) which draws our attention away from the ideas. And having attributed soul and mind to "it," he merely infers that, since these involve κίνησις, κίνησις must be included among ὄντα (which Campbell, *ad loc.*, regards as a formal fallacy).   Plainly, whatever implications we force upon Plato's words, his purpose here is not to attribute soul to the ideas, but to remove from the path of logic the

ἐν ἐστός of Parmenides (or his followers at Megara or in the school — οὐδὲν γὰρ ταύτῃ διαφέρει) as well as the πάντα ῥεῖ of Heraclitus for which he felt less sympathy.   Cf. *Theœtet.*, 180, 181, 183 E, 184 A.

[267] See ZELLER, pp. 689, 690, who seems to deny the contradiction altogether, and pp. 696–8, where he argues that the *Sophist* is early because life and causality are never again attributed to the ideas, and do not belong to them in Aristotle's representation.   Space fails to enumerate all points of agreement with or difference from APELT'S subtle study of the *Sophist* (*Beiträge*).   He points out that the definition of ὄν is directed mainly against the materialists, and calls attention to ἴσως εἰς ὕστερον ἕτερον ἂν φανείη.   He is right in denying that Plato's views changed, and in minimizing the significance of the apparent attribution of life to the ideas.   But he errs when he seeks an explicit statement of it in other dialogues and for this purpose presses ἄυπνον φύσιν, *Tim.*, 52 B.

[268] τὸ κατὰ ταὐτὰ καὶ ὡσαύτως ἔχειν, etc.

250 B, ὅσα ἄλλα τίμια ψυχαῖς), have no copies in the world of sense, and must be apprehended by reason.   This is precisely the doctrine of *Phædrus*, 250 B C D and 263 A B,
and ought to end controversy.[269]   We have already seen that the *Philebus* bids us
assume ideas and disregard the difficulties of the *Parmenides*.[270]   There is no hint
that they are only concepts.[271]   We may assume, then, that the language of 58 A, 59 C,
and 61 E implies the ideas.[272]

III. PSYCHOLOGY

Supposed variations in Plato's psychology have been used to determine the evolution of his thought and the relative dates of the dialogues.   The chief topics are:
(1) the immortality of the soul; (2) the unity of the soul, or its subdivision into
faculties; (3) the general argument that the psychology of the "later" dialogues is
richer and more precise than that of the earlier.

1. The immortality of the individual soul is for Plato a pious hope,[273] and an ethical
postulate,[274] rather than a demonstrable certainty.[275]   He essays various demonstrations,
but nearly always in connection with a myth, and of all the proofs attempted but one is
repeated.   In the *Apology* Socrates, addressing his judges, affects to leave the question
open.[276]   But we cannot infer from this that the *Apology* antedates Plato's belief in
immortality.   For, to say nothing of Pythagorean sources of inspiration, he had presumably read Pindar's second Olympian with approval; and Socrates's language in
Crito, 54 B, is precisely in the tone of the *Gorgias* and the *Phædo*.[277]   The *Meno*[278]
assumes the immortality and the prior existence of the soul to account for *a priori*
knowledge.   The *Phædo* presents a complicated proof or series of proofs.   The *Symposium* seems to recognize only the subjective immortality of fame, and the racial immortality of offspring.[279]   The "early" *Phædrus* and the late *Laws* alone agree in a proof
based on the conception of the soul as the self-moving.[280]   It is easy to foresee the
hypotheses which an ingenious philology will construct from these facts.   Krohn, Pfleiderer, and Rohde gravely argue that Book I of the *Republic* must be very early because
the aged Cephalus neglects the opportunity to supplement his citation from Pindar with
a scientific proof of immortality.   Horn tells us that the *Phædrus* represents the first

269 For ἀνάμνησις in the *Politicus cf. infra*, p. 44.

270 See *A. J. P.*, Vol. IX, p. 279.

271 LUTOSLAWSKI, p. 467, mistranslates, or, if he prefers,
misinterprets, 15 D: "the nature of thought requires the
union of notions into higher units, and this constitutes an
eternal necessity of the human mind." *Cf. supra*, p. 36.

272 τὴν γὰρ περὶ τὸ ὂν καὶ τὸ ὄντως καὶ τὸ κατὰ ταὐτὸν ἀεὶ
πεφυκὸς . . . . μακρῷ ἀληθεστάτην εἶναι γνῶσιν.— περὶ τὰ ἀεὶ κατὰ
τὰ αὐτὰ ὡσαύτως ἀμικτότατα ἔχοντα.—ἡ δὲ ἐπὶ τὰ μήτε γιγνόμενα
μήτε ἀπολλύμενα, κατὰ ταὐτὰ δὲ καὶ ὡσαύτως ὄντα ἀεί.   Cf. 62 A,
αὐτῆς περὶ δικαιοσύνης ὅ τι ἐστι. 66 A, τὴν ἀΐδιον . . . . φύσιν.

For the ideas in relation to the method κατ' εἴδη τέμνειν,
and a fuller discussion of the μὴ ὂν fallacy, see *infra*,
Part II.

273 *Phædo*, 114 D, χρὴ τὰ τοιαῦτα ὥσπερ ἐπᾴδειν ἑαυτῷ.

274 *Rep.*, 608 C ff.; *Laws*, 881 A, 967 D E, 959 A B; with
τὸν δὲ ὄντα ἡμῶν ἕκαστον ὄντως ἀθάνατον [εἶναι] ψυχήν, *cf.*

Phædo, 115 D E; and with the idea, 959 B, that the only
βοήθεια at the bar of Hades is a just life in this world, *cf.*
Gorg., 522 C D, 526 E; *Crito*, 54 B.

275 *Phædo*, 85 C, τὸ μὲν σαφὲς εἰδέναι ἐν τῷ νῦν βίῳ ἢ ἀδύνατον εἶναι ἢ παγχαλεπόν τι. Cf. 107 A B; *Tim.*, 72 D; *Meno*,
86 A B; *Phædr.*, 265 C.

276 40 C.   Cf. also *Phædo*, 91 B.

277 *Cratylus*, 403 D E, implies the doctrine of *Phædo*,
67, 68.

278 81 C.

279 207 D, 208 B.   Too much is made of this, for the same
inference could be drawn from *Laws*, 721 and 773 B.   The
popular belief in Hades is implied, 192 E, and there is even
a hint, 212 A, that the philosopher may be immortal: εἴπερ
τῷ ἄλλῳ ἀνθρώπων ἀθανάτῳ καὶ ἐκείνῳ.

280 *Phædr.*, 245 C; *Laws*, 894, 895.

youthful enthusiastic apprehension of immortality, the *Symposium* expresses the mood of sober manhood content with this life, while in the *Phœdo* old age, waiting for death, craves a real immortality. According to Thompson, the *Meno* reserves the proof of what it merely asserts; the *Phœdrus* outlines a general proof, the *Republic* later attempts another; the *Symposium*, dissatisfied with all so far achieved, ignores the subject; and finally the problem is taken up seriously in the *Phœdo*. Zeller, on the other hand, while holding that all the proofs are substantially identical, thinks, as we have seen, that the *Republic* refers to the *Phœdo*, and is also later than the *Phœdrus*. But to Lutoslawski it is evident that the proof given in the *Phœdrus* and repeated in the *Laws* is the latest. And he also can discern that the *Symposium*, in the first flush of idealism, could dispense with the personal immortality of the *Gorgias*, but that later, when the theory of ideas had grown familiar, Plato undertook in the *Phœdo* to affiliate upon it the old doctrine of immortality.

Hardly more profitable than these arbitrary speculations is the analysis of the separate arguments. Broadly speaking, Zeller is right in saying that they all amount to this, that it is the nature or essence of the soul to live. But this general truth becomes a fallacy when employed to identify absolutely the distinct arguments of the *Phœdo*, the *Republic*, and the *Phœdrus*. The gist of the argument in the tenth book of the *Republic* is a fallacy employed also in the first book (353 D E), the equivocal use of the ἀρετή or specific excellence of the soul in relation to its ἔργον, its function and essence. In both cases the ἔργον is defined in terms of mere life-vitality, while the ἀρετή is referred to the moral life. But in so far as the ἔργον or essence of the soul is mere life, its ἀρετή is intensity and persistency of life—not justice.[281] Similarly the *Phœdrus* and *Laws*, identifying life with self-movement, prove the eternity of the principle of motion, and assume it to include moral and intellectual qualities.[282] But there is a certain pedantry in thus scrutinizing these arguments. Plato's belief in immortality was a conviction of the psychological and moral impossibility of sheer materialism,[283] and a broad faith in the unseen, the spiritual, the ideal. The logical obstacles to a positive demonstration of personal immortality were as obvious to him as they are to his critics. If we must analyze the arguments of the *Phœdo*, the analysis of Bonitz is, on the whole, the most plausible.[284] They prove, at the most,

---

[281] *Cf.* the equivocal use of ἁρμονία in *Phœdo*, 93, 94, to denote the composition of physical elements that. on the hypothesis under examination, is life, and the harmony of spiritual qualities that is virtue.

[282] *Laws*, 896 C D.

[283] *Laws*, 891 C, κινδυνεύει γὰρ ὁ λέγων ταῦτα πῦρ καὶ ὕδωρ καὶ γῆν καὶ ἀέρα πρῶτα ἡγεῖσθαι τῶν πάντων εἶναι. *Cf. Phileb.*, 30 A; *Theœtet.*, 155 E, 184 D; *Sophist*, 246 A; *Tim.*, 51 C, ἢ ταῦτα, ἅπερ καὶ βλέπομεν . . . . μόνα ἐστὶ τοιαύτην ἔχοντα ἀλήθειαν.

[284] *I. e.*, the argument ἐκ τῶν ἐναντίων τὰ ἐναντία, 70 E ff., proves merely that the state of the soul after death is the same as that before birth. The argument from ἀνάμνησις, 73 ff., supplements this by the proof that before birth the soul possessed intelligence. The final argument meets all

objections by establishing the inherent immortality of the soul as a form that always involves the idea of life. I may add that the fallacy in this ingenious argument may be analyzed in various ways. In 103 B it is said that αὐτὸ τὸ ἐναντίον, as distinguished from τὰ ἔχοντα τὰ ἐναντία could never admit its opposite. Αὐτὸ τὸ ἐναντίον is then subdivided into τὸ ἐν ἡμῖν and τὸ ἐν τῇ φύσει. This seems to yield three things: the idea *per se*, the idea in the particular, and the particular as affected by the idea. (*Cf. supra*, n. 252.) But there are really only two things: the idea, and the particular affected by the "presence" of or "participation" in the idea. How the idea can be at once in itself and in the particular may be, as we have seen, a mystery. But it does not justify the duplication of the idea, which is a device employed here only, and presumably with full consciousness, for the purpose of the argument. For by its

the immortality of soul, not of the individual. This Plato presumably knew, but we cannot expect him to say so by the death-bed of Socrates or in the ethical myths, which obviously assume individual immortality.[285] But neither this unavoidable fundamental ambiguity nor the fanciful variations of the eschatological myths convict Plato of serious inconsistency, or supply any evidence for the dating of the dialogues.

2. In the *Republic* Plato bases the definitions of the virtues and the three classes of the population on a tripartite division of the soul, which he warns us is not demonstrated absolutely, but sufficiently for the purpose in hand.[286] A poetical passage of the tenth book hints that in its true nature the soul is one and simple, but that we cannot perceive this so long as, like the sea-god Glaucus, it is disguised by the accretions of its earthly life.[287] The tripartite division is embodied in the myth of the *Phædrus*, which, if we pedantically press the poetical imagery,[288] implies the preexistence even of the appetites.[289] In the *Timæus* the immortal soul is created by the Demiurgus, the mortal, which falls into two parts, spirit and appetite, by his ministers.[290] Here the tripartite division is subordinated to a bipartite, as Aristotle would have it.[291] But we are explicitly warned that the revelation of a god would be required to affirm the absolute scientific truth of this division, and to distinguish precisely the mortal from the immortal part.[292] In the *Laws* the question whether the θυμός is an affection or a distinct part of the soul is left open.[293] As Aristotle says, it makes no difference for ethical and political theory.[294] The *Phædo*, attempting to prove immortality, naturally dwells rather upon the unity of the soul, as does the tenth book of the *Republic*. But it distinguishes, quite in the manner of the *Republic*, the three types of character, the φιλόσοφος or φιλομαθής, the φίλαρχος or φιλότιμος, and the φιλοσώματος or φιλοχρήματος.[295] *Phædo*, 79 B C E, does not affirm that the soul is absolutely simple and uncompounded, but that the body is more akin to the composite, and the soul to the simple and unchanging. The contradictions found by Krohn and Pfleiderer in the psychology of the *Republic*, or between the *Republic* and *Phædo*, on this point, are sufficiently explained by Hirmer.[296] From all this it appears (1) that Plato affirmed nothing dogmatically with regard to the ultimate psychological problem. (2) That his primary classification was the distinction between the pure reason and the lower faculties subordinate to reason and dependent on the body. (3) That for ethical and political theory he found most helpful the tripartite classification—reason, spirit,

aid the life in the individual is posited as an intermediate entity between life *per se* and the living individual, and pronounced immortal because, like life *per se*, it will not admit its opposite. Another way of putting it is to say that, in 106 E ff., ἀθάνατον is equivocally used for (1) that which does not admit death (while life is present), (2) that which does not admit death at all.

[285] *Gorg.*, 524 ff.; *Rep.*, 614 ff. Cf. *Laws*, 904 B C; *Tim.*, 41 D, ψυχὰς ἰσαρίθμους τοῖς ἄστροις, etc.

[286] 435 C D ff.   [287] 611 C - 612 A.   [288] 246 A ff.

[289] NATORP, *Hermes*, Vol. XXXV, p. 430, objects that the souls of the gods are tripartite and that the horses, though in the procession, do not see the ideas! SUSEMIHL, *Neue*

Plat. Forsch., p. 33, says that *Rep.*, X, must be later than *Phædrus*, for in the *Phædrus* immortality belongs to all three parts of the soul!

[290] 34 B C, 69 C ff.

[291] *Eth. Nic.*, 1, 13, 9, οἷον τὸ μὲν ἄλογον αὐτῆς εἶναι, τὸ δὲ λόγον ἔχον.

[292] 72 D; cf. *Phædr.*, 246 A.

[293] 863 B, εἴτε τι πάθος εἴτε τι μέρος ὢν ὁ θυμός.

[294] *Eth. Nic.*, 1, 13, 10, οὐδὲν διαφέρει πρὸς τὸ παρόν.

[295] 68 C, 82 C.

[296] "Entstehung und Komposition der Plat. Politeia," *Jahrbücher für Phil.*, Suppl., N. F,. Vol. XXIII, pp. 642, 643.

appetite—which he also embodied in the myths of the *Phœdrus* and the *Timœus.*
(4) That, while this classification may be profitably compared with the modern intelligence, feeling, will, it is beside the mark to criticise it as if it were meant to be psychologically exact and exhaustive.[297] We cannot establish any fixed relation between the tripartite soul and the hierarchy of the cognitive faculties—νοῦς (νόησις, ἐπιστήμη), διάνοια, δόξα, πίστις, εἰκασία, etc.[298] Plato sometimes treats the inerrant reason as a distinct part of the soul from the fallible faculties of sense and opinion.[299] He sometimes associates sense-perception with sensuous appetite in common antithesis to the reason.[300] But he also, when it suits his purpose, virtually identifies (true) opinion with reason, in opposition to the impulses of instinct and appetite.[301] The θυμός, though associated with opinion,[302] cannot be assigned with it to a distinct part of the soul.[303] Nor can it be identified with the "feeling" of the modern psychologist. The will as a faculty distinct from the impulses of appetite and the judgments of the reason has no place in Plato's system. (5) That we cannot fix the time at which the notion of the tripartite soul first occurred to Plato, nor may we use apparent variations in the mythological dress of the doctrine in order to date the *Phœdo* and *Phœdrus* relatively to each other or to the *Republic.*

3. The chief changes alleged in Plato's "later" psychology are: (*a*) the abandonment of ἀνάμνησις; (*b*) a different conception of the relation of mind and body, more particularly as concerns the nature and seat of pleasure and pain; (*c*) a fuller and more precise terminology of the cognitive faculties and the degrees of knowledge. This later psychology must be sought chiefly in the *Philebus.* It is not enough to point out that the *Philebus* is especially rich in psychological detail. The subject called for it, and we cannot expect all the dialogues to be equally full in every topic. What is required is contradictions of earlier dialogues, or new thoughts not hinted at in them. And these are not to be found.

a) The explanation of the ordinary psychological meaning of ἀνάμνησις in *Philebus,* 34 B, no more proves the abandonment of the peculiar Platonic doctrine than does the occurrence of the word in that sense in the *Republic,* 604 D. The *Phœdo* itself treats the ἀνάμνησις of the ideas as a special case of recollection and association of ideas generally, and employs the consecrated phrase τοῦτο δ' ἐστὶν ἀνάμνησις of an example that fits the definition of the *Philebus.*[304] Plainly all recollection of the ideas is ἀνάμνησις, but all ἀνάμνησις need not be recollection of the ideas. Moreover, as the word occurs without the doctrine in the *Philebus,* so we find the doctrine without the word in the *Politicus.* As the point has been overlooked, it is worth while to dwell upon it. Every

---

[297] See JOWETT, Vol. I, p. 410; ZELLER, p. 846; LUTOS-LAWSKI, p. 278.

[298] The imagery and terminology of *Rep.,* 511 D, 534 A, belong to the literary machinery of the *Republic,* and are not to be pressed.

[299] *Rep.,* 478 A B, 602 E–603 A, τὸ παρὰ τὰ μέτρα ἄρα δοξάζον τῆς ψυχῆς τῷ κατὰ τὰ μέτρα οὐκ ἂν εἴη ταὐτόν.

[300] *Phœdo,* 65, 66.

[301] *Phileb.,* 60 D; *Phœdr.,* 237 D; *infra,* p. 48, n. 357.

[302] This is probably the meaning of ἀληθινῆς δόξης ἑταῖρος, *Phœdr.,* 253 D, despite the antithesis ἀλαζονείας ἑταῖρος. ἀληθινὴ is used of δόξα = opinion in *Theœtet.,* 187 C; *Phileb.,* 37 B.

[303] In *Tim.,* 37 B C, δόξαι and πίστεις belong to the circle of the θάτερον in the immortal soul.

[304] 73 D.

man, we are told, knows all things as in a dream, though he fails of waking knowl-edge.[305] This at once recalls the μεμαθηκυίας τῆς ψυχῆς ἄπαντα of the *locus classicus* on ἀνάμνησις, *Meno,* 81 D. In the *Meno,* too, it is said that this knowledge is at first dreamlike, but is converted by the elenchus into true science.[306] The *Politicus* goes on to show, by the use of Plato's favorite illustration of letters or "elements,"[307] how it is that, despite this antecedent knowledge, we go astray, and how in the study of complex and difficult things the right use of example and comparison will enable us to recognize the identity of the same form or idea everywhere, so that we shall have a waking and not a dreamlike knowledge.[308] Children, knowing their letters in some sort, distinguish them rightly in easy combinations, but blunder in long hard syllables, until by compari-son with the easy they learn to recognize the same letter everywhere. So our soul, similarly affected by nature toward the elements of all things (the ideas), sometimes and in some things is settled and fixed by truth concerning each one, but at other times and in other things is driven to and fro among them all, and of some it somehow forms right opinions among the combinations, but fails to apprehend these same things when transferred to the long and difficult syllables of facts. Not only the general drift, but the language and imagery of this passage must be understood of the recollections of the ideas. The phrase ταὐτὸν τοῦτο ἡμῶν ἡ ψυχὴ φύσει περὶ τὰ τῶν πάντων στοιχεῖα πεπονθυῖα does not refer mainly or solely to our liability to error, as might be sup-posed from Campbell's "is naturally liable to the same infirmity," or from Jowett's "has the same uncertainty." It refers to the whole preceding comparison of which the starting-point is that the soul knows all things in a sense, even as the children know all their letters imperfectly. That this is the meaning of φύσει . . . . πεπονθυῖα appears further by comparison with *Phædrus,* 249 E, πᾶσα μὲν ἀνθρώπου ψυχή φύσει τεθέαται τὰ ὄντα. The doctrine of ἀνάμνησις, then, repeated in the *Politicus,* is not abandoned in the *Philebus.* This conclusion might have been affirmed *a priori.* For "recollec-tion," once indissolubly associated with the ideas and the pre-existence of the soul, would not be given up while they were retained. But pre-existence is assumed in the *Laws,*[309] and the ideas, as we have seen, occur in the *Politicus*[310] and are reaffirmed in the *Timæus,* which also implies the soul's prior knowledge of all things, in language recalling the *Phædrus* and *Politicus.*[311]

    b) The general problem of the relation of mind and body is involved in that of immortality and the parts of the soul. As we have seen, the *Timæus,* though it assigns separate seats to the mortal and immortal soul, declines to dogmatize without the assur-

[305] 277 D, κινδυνεύει γὰρ ἡμῶν ἕκαστος οἷον ὄναρ εἰδὼς ἄπαντα αὖ πάλιν ὥσπερ ὕπαρ ἀγνοεῖν. RITCHIE, p. 143, misapprehends this passage when he associates it with the "lie of approxi-mation." We must use examples, not because in difficult matters it is permissible to fall back upon "picture-thinking and symbolism," but because only by beginning with easy examples can we learn how to convert our dream-like knowledge into real knowledge. The γὰρ introduces the whole parallel, of which the dreamlike knowledge of all things is only the first point.

[306] *Meno,* 85 C, ὥσπερ ὄναρ ἄρτι κεκίνηνται αἱ δόξαι αὗται.

[307] *Repub.,* 402 A B; *cf Soph.,* 253 A; *Phileb.,* 18 C; *Theæ-tet.,* 201 E; *Tim.,* 48 B, etc.

[308] 278 E, τέχνῃ γνωρίζειν, ἵνα ὕπαρ ἀντ' ὀνείρατος ἡμῖν γίγνηται.

[309] 904, 905.

[310] *Supra,* p. 39.

[311] 41 E, τὴν τοῦ παντὸς φύσιν ἔδειξε.

ance of a god, and the *Laws* leaves it an open question whether the parts of the soul are real parts or functions.[312] Of the dependence of our cognitive faculties on bodily organs Plato knew as much or as little as we know.[313] In the images of the wax tablet and aviary he anticipates all psychologies that explain memory, association, and recollection, and the distinction between latent and actual knowledge, by material analogies.[314] But sheer materialism and sensationalism he rejects, for many other reasons[315] and because it fails to account for the synthetic unity of thought.[316] The senses are the organs through which, not the faculties by which, we know.[317] Sometimes and for some purposes he exalts pure thought freed from all contaminations of sense.[318] In other moods, he recognizes that human thought takes its start from αἴσθησις or immediate perception.[319] He points out that the contradictions of sense give the first awakening stimulus to the generalizing activities of mind.[320] He admits that our minds are too weak to attain to knowledge without experience,[321] and require the aid of concrete examples in order to apprehend difficult abstractions.[322] We can recover the prenatal vision of the ideas only by association with their sensuous "copies," or by strenuous logical discipline.[323] And, though knowledge is not sense-perception, sense-perception is the best evidence that we have of some things.[324] Only a very literal-minded criticism will treat these concessions as a contradiction of the apotheosis of pure thought in the *Phœdo*.

Slightly more plausible is the claim that Plato contradicts himself in regard to the nature and seat of desire, pleasure, and pain.[325] The "early" *Gorgias* and the "late" *Philebus* explicitly affirm that the soul, not the body, is the seat of desire.[326] The *Philebus* adds the psychological reason that desire is dependent on memory.[327] The *Philebus* further explains pleasure and pain as mental states arising from changes in the body sudden enough or violent enough to affect the mind and pass the threshold of consciousness, in modern phrase.[328] Pain results from movements unfavorable to the "natural" condition of the body, pleasure from those that preserve or restore the natural

312 *Supra*, n. 293 ; *cf.* also *Rep.*, 612 A, εἴτε πολυειδὴς εἴτε μονοειδής, *Phædr.*, 271 A.

313 *Phœdo*, 96 B C, πότερον τὸ αἷμά ἐστιν ᾧ φρονοῦμεν, ἢ ὁ ἀὴρ ἢ τὸ πῦρ, etc. Note the irony of the whole passage.

314 *Theœtet.*, 191 D ff. (*cf. Phædr.*, 275 A, τύπων), 197 D, 197 B–200 B.

315 *Phœdo*, 80 B, 96 ; *Phileb.*, 30 ; *Tim.*, 51 C ; *Laws*, 889.

316 *Theœtet.*, 184 D.

317 *Theœtet.*, 184 C ; *Phœdo*, 65 D, 79 C ; *Tim.*, 67 B.

318 *Phœdo*, 65 C (*cf. Theœtet.*, 187 A), 66 A, εἰλικρινεῖ τῇ διανοίᾳ ; 67 C, τὸ χωρίζειν ὅ τι μάλιστα ἀπὸ τοῦ σώματος τὴν ψυχήν.

319 *Theœtet.*, 179 C, τὸ παρὸν ἑκάστῳ πάθος ἐξ ὧν αἱ αἰσθήσεις καὶ αἱ κατὰ ταύτας δόξαι. *Charm.*, 159 A, αἰσθησίν τινα παρέχειν, ἐξ ἧς δόξα ἄν τίς σοι περὶ αὐτῆς εἴη. *Phileb.*, 249 B, ἐκ πολλῶν ἰὸν αἰσθήσεων εἰς ἓν λογισμῷ ξυναιρούμενον.

320 *Rep.*, 524 B C ; *Theœtet.*, 186 A B.

321 *Theœtet.*, 149 C, ὅτι η ἀνθρωπίνη φύσις ἀσθενεστέρα ἢ λαβεῖν τέχνην ὧν ἂν ᾖ ἄπειρος.

322 *Polit.*, 277 D. *Cf. Phœdr.*, 262 C, ψιλῶς πως λέγομεν οὐκ ἔχοντες ἱκανὰ παραδείγματα.

323 *Phœdo*, 75 A ; *Polit.*, 286 A ; *Rep.*, 533 A, καὶ ὅτι ἡ τοῦ διαλέγεσθαι δύναμις μόνη ἂν φήνειεν ἐμπείρῳ ὄντι ὧν νῦν δὴ διῆλθομεν. *Tim.*, 47 A, τῶν νῦν λόγων περὶ τοῦ παντὸς λεγομένων οὐδεὶς ἄν ποτε ἐρρήθη μήτε ἄστρα μήτε ἥλιον μήτε οὐρανὸν ἰδόντων.

324 *Theœtet.*, 201 B, ὧν ἰδόντι μόνον ἔστιν εἰδέναι ἄλλως δὲ μή. *Sophist*, 234 D, καὶ διὰ παθημάτων ἀναγκαζομένους ἐναργῶς ἐφάπτεσθαι τῶν ὄντων. The whole passage is in seeming contradiction with the thought of *Phœdo*, 100 A, and *Rep.*, 473 A, that words (thought) come nearer to truth than deeds. See also *Meno*, 97 B.

325 Grote, Jowett, Mr. Henry Jackson, and others. HORN, who rejects the *Philebus*, says (p. 380) that it assigns desire to the soul, but pain and pleasure to the body.

326 *Gorg.*, 493 A, τῆς δὲ ψυχῆς τοῦτο ἐν ᾧ ἐπιθυμίαι εἰσί. So *Tim.*, 69 C.

327 35.

328 33, 34, 43 B C. *Cf. Rep.*, 462 C, 584 C, αἵ γε διὰ τοῦ σώματος ἐπὶ τὴν ψυχὴν τείνουσαι καὶ λεγόμεναι ἡδοναί. *Cf. Laws*, 673 A, μέχρι τῆς ψυχῆς ; *Tim.*, 45 D (of sensations).

state.[329] This is also the doctrine of the *Timæus*, and it is not contradicted anywhere. In ethical and religious discussion, however, it is natural to identify the "soul" with the higher intelligence, νοῦς or immortal soul, and to speak of the pleasures of the mortal soul which come through the body and are necessitated by the body as pleasures of the body. And Plato, though usually scrupulously precise,[330] occasionally permits himself this inexact way of speaking. The *Philebus* enumerates three kinds of mixed pleasures and pains: (1) merely mental, as in the pleasurable-painful emotions; (2) merely bodily; (3) those that arise when pleasure of mind accompanies pain of body, or the reverse.[331] In a few cases the "bodily" pleasures are spoken of as if they were literally in or of the body.[332] But Plato was justified in assuming that only a careless or captious reader would misunderstand him. For hardly three pages back he had explained that bodily states produce pleasure and pain only when they cross the threshold of consciousness.[333] There are also two or three cases in the *Phædo*. In the first the phrase "appetites of the body" is used in a highly wrought, ethical passage precisely as it might be employed by a modern preacher, with no implication of psychological doctrine.[334] The second occurs in the refutation of the hypothesis that the soul may be a "harmony" of material states or elements. To refute this objection Socrates employs the very argument used in the *Republic* to distinguish νοῦς from ἐπιθυμία and θυμός.[335] The soul cannot be identical with that which it rebukes and controls as a superior. The soul, instead of being controlled, ὑπὸ τῶν τοῦ σώματος παθῶν, is master of them. Therefore it cannot be a "harmony" composed of them. The appetites are treated as material παθήματα in order to refute, in its own terminology, the hypothesis that the soul is a composition of material παθήματα. The argument would lose its force if stated in the terminology of the *Republic*. If the tripartite soul were explicitly recognized, it would be necessary, first, to decide which parts are to be immortal; secondly, to prove directly, and not by the equivocal substitution of "bodily" appetites for states of matter, that the νοῦς or soul cannot be a harmony of material elements. For these reasons, in the *Phædo*, soul, tacitly identified with νοῦς, is opposed to body as a whole, including the appetites. But the literary and æsthetic necessity of this way of speaking having once been perceived, we cannot treat it as a contradiction of the psychological truth clearly stated in the "earlier"

[329] *Phileb.*, 31 D ff., 42 D; *Tim.*, 64 C D, 66 C, 68 A. Implied perhaps "already" in *Cratyl.*, 419 C, ἥ τε λύπη ἀπὸ τῆς διαλύσεως τοῦ σώματος. Aristotle, *Eth. Nic.*, 10, 3, 6, controverting the doctrine that pleasure is a γένεσις, says: εἰ δή ἐστι τοῦ κατὰ φύσιν ἀναπλήρωσις ἡδονή, ἐν ᾧ ἡ ἀναπλήρωσις, τοῦτ᾽ ἂν καὶ ἥδοιτο· τὸ σῶμα ἄρα· οὐ δοκεῖ δέ, where οὐ δοκεῖ expresses as often Plato's opinion.

[330] *Phileb.*, 39 D, τῶν διὰ τοῦ σώματος ἡδονῶν. So 45 B, *Phædo*, 65 A; *Tim.*, 64 A; *Rep.*, 584 C, 485 D; *Phileb.*, 45 A, αἱ περὶ τὸ σῶμα. So *Phædr.*, 258 E. Cf., *Cratyl.*, 404 A; *Rep.*, 442 A; *Tim.*, 64 A; *Phileb.*, 41 C, τὸ σῶμα ἦν τὸ παρεχόμενον; *Rep.*, 584 A, τό γε ἡδὺ ἐν ψυχῇ γιγνόμενον; 442 A.

[331] 47 E–50 D, 46 C, 47 C D.

[332] 46 B C, 50 D. So Prodicus in *Protag.*, 337 C. The statement, *Phileb.*, 31 B, that pleasure and pain originate

ἐν τῷ κοινῷ . . . . γένει is merely preparatory to the explanation that they are the psychic correlates of beneficial or harmful changes in the body. It is obviously no contradiction of the reference of ἡδονή to the ἄπειρον in 31 B. Cf. *A. J P.*, Vol. IX, No. 3, p. 284.

[333] 43 B C. Cf. 33 D, θὲς τῶν περὶ τὸ σῶμα . . . . παθημάτων τὰ μὲν ἐν τῷ σώματι κατασβεννύμενα πρὶν ἐπὶ τὴν ψυχὴν διεξελθεῖν. This is the doctrine of *Tim.*, 64 A B C, and it is "already" implied in *Theætet.*, 186 C, ὅσα διὰ τοῦ σώματος παθήματα ἐπὶ τὴν ψυχὴν τείνει. *Phileb.*, 55 B, explicitly affirms that pleasure is in the soul only: πῶς οὐκ ἄλογόν ἐστι μηδὲν ἀγαθὸν εἶναι . . . . πλὴν ἐν ψυχῇ καὶ ἐνταῦθα ἡδονὴν μόνον.

[334] 66 C, καὶ γὰρ πολέμους καὶ στάσεις καὶ μάχας οὐδὲν ἄλλο παρέχει ἢ τὸ σῶμα καὶ αἱ τούτου ἐπιθυμίαι.

[335] *Phædo*, 94 B ff.; *Rep.*, 441 B, 390 D.

Gorgias and "later" *Philebus*. One might as well argue that the tenth book of the *Republic* antedates or abandons the tripartite soul because the doctrine is ignored in the proof of immortality attempted there.

c) Lastly it is sometimes affirmed that the later dialogues show an increased precision in the use of psychological terminology. In fact, however, Plato's psychological vocabulary is nowhere technical. He is content to make his meaning plain by the context. Nor can we find in Spinoza or Kant or in any modern text-book the consistent precision that is sometimes demanded of Plato. There is no modern terminology which sharply discriminates mental states that are or are not supposed to involve the element of judgment and belief. There is none that shows independently of the context the precise line intended to be drawn between sensation and perception, or distinguishes revived and compounded "images" from "images" regarded as immediate impressions. We cannot, then, expect Plato to emphasize distinctions not needed for his immediate purpose, but if we bear this in mind, we shall find no serious inconsistencies or significant variations in his use of such terms as αἴσθησις δόξα and φαντασία.

Αἴσθησις is any immediate sensation or perception or consciousness including pleasure and pain and Locke's inner sense.[336] As sense-perception it is rightly said to involve judgment,[337] and so issues in δόξα, opinion or belief.[338] The word δόξα may be used in this neutral, psychological sense; it may be taken unfavorably to denote mere opinion as opposed to knowledge, or favorably when true opinions and beliefs are set in antithesis to the appetites and instincts.[339] These shades of meaning arise naturally out of Greek usage, and would call for no comment if they had not been cited to convict Plato of inconsistency or change. The mental process that terminates in the affirmation or negation that constitutes δόξα may be expressed in words, λόγος,[340] or take place in silent thought. In the second case it is διάνοια—a discourse in the soul.[341] Διάνοια, then, mere or silent thought, may be opposed to speech[342] or to thought accompanied or interrupted by sensation.[343] It is thus often a synonym of pure thought.[344] But the *Republic*, in default of a better term,[345] employs it to denote

---

[336] *Theætet.*, 156 B, 186 D E, 152 B C; *Phileb.*, 34 A; *Charm.*, 159 A.

[337] *Rep.*, 523 B, ὡς ἱκανῶς ὑπὸ τῆς αἰσθήσεως κρινόμενα. *Phileb.*, 38 C, πολλάκις ἰδόντι . . . . βούλεσθαι κρίνειν φαίης ἂν ταῦθ᾽ ἅπερ ὁρᾷ. This is not quite the modern psychologist's recognition of the judgment involved in perception, but it leads up to Aristotle's characterization of sensation as δύναμιν σύμφυτον κριτικήν. *Analyt. Post.*, *in fine*.

[338] *Phileb.*, 38 B, ἐκ μνήμης τε καὶ αἰσθήσεως δόξα. *Phædo*, ἐκ τούτων (sc. the senses) δὲ γίγνοιτο μνήμη καὶ δόξα. *Charm.*, 159 A, αἴσθησιν . . . . ἐξ ἧς δόξα. In *Theætet.*, 170 B, ἀληθῆ διάνοιαν . . . . ψευδῆ δόξαν, διάνοια and δόξα are virtually synonyms.

[339] *Phileb.*, 60 D, μνήμην καὶ φρόνησιν καὶ ἀληθῆ δόξαν τῆς αὐτῆς ἰδέας τιθέμενος. *Phædr.*, 237 D, ἔμφυτος ἐπιθυμία . . . . ἐπίκτητος δόξα. *Tim.*, 77 B. In *Theætet.*, 187 A, δοξάζειν is almost the pure thought of *Phædo*, 65 C.

[340] *Phileb.*, 38 E, καὶ λόγος δὴ γέγονεν οὕτως ὃ τότε δόξαν ἐκαλοῦμεν.

[341] *Phileb.*, 38 D; *Theætet.*, 189 E, 190 A. *Soph.*, 263 E, διάνοια μὲν καὶ λόγος ταὐτόν πλὴν ὁ μὲν ἐντὸς τῆς ψυχῆς πρὸς αὐτὴν διάλογος, etc.

[342] *Soph.*, 238 B, 264 A.

[343] *Theætet.*, 195 C D; *Rep.*, 511 C, διανοίᾳ μὲν . . . . ἀλλὰ μὴ αἰσθήσεσιν. In *Phædo*, 73 D, it is the (memory) imagination of modern psychology: καὶ ἐν τῇ διανοίᾳ ἔλαβον τὸ εἶδος τοῦ παιδός; in *Rep.*, 603 C, it is the mind, including higher and lower faculties.

[344] *Phædo*, 66 A, εἰλικρινεῖ τῇ διανοίᾳ; 65 E, αὐτὸ ἕκαστον διανοηθῆναι. In *Theætet.*, 195 D E, we pass from an image of a man, ὃν διανοούμεθα μόνον, ὁρῶμεν δ᾽ οὔ, to abstractions as τὰ ἕνδεκα ἃ μηδὲν ἄλλο᾽ῇ διανοεῖταί τις; cf. *Rep.*, 526 A, ὧν διανοηθῆναι μόνον ἐγχωρεῖ.

[345] 533 D, οὐ περὶ ὀνόματος ἀμφισβήτησις.

the processes of mathematics and the sciences, which are inferior to the pure thought, νοῦς, of dialectic, in that they depend on sensuous imagery and hypotheses.[346]

Plato describes memory images,[347] and images of "imagination."[348] But he has no term for imagination as a faculty intermediate between abstract or verbal thought, on the one hand, and sense-perception, on the other. For φαντασία takes its color from φαίνεται and φαντάζεται, which include all forms of opinion and illusion, and it is often merely a disparaging synonym of δόξα.[349] But φαίνεται, though applicable to any notion that appears true, is most naturally used of the appearances of sense, and so φαντασία is preferably the form of δόξα that accompanies sense-perception,[350] and may be defined as σύμμιξις αἰσθήσεως καὶ δόξας.[351] Pure infallible knowledge as an ideal must be sharply distinguished even from true opinion.[352] Strictly speaking, it cannot be defined,[353] and is unattainable in this life.[354] Poetically it may be described as the vision of the ideas, and we may be said to approximate to it in proportion as we "recollect" the ideas by severe dialectic.[355] Practically knowledge is true opinion, sifted and tested by dialectic, and fixed by causal reasoning.[356] "True opinion" may be disparaged in contrast with the ideal, or praised as a necessary stage toward its attainment.[357] It is a very mechanical criticism that finds contradiction or inconsistency here.

There is no limit to the contradictions or developments that a false subtlety can discover in Plato's psychology. Most of them are by implication explained away in the foregoing summary. I will close with two or three further examples which must stand for all.

Susemihl[358] argues that the *Theœtetus* marks an advance on the psychology of the *Phœdrus* because it includes *Wahrnehmungsurtheile* in δοκεῖν or δόξα.[359] But the *Theœtetus* itself elsewhere attributes them to αἴσθησις, for only so could it identify Protagoras's theory with the definition αἴσθησις = ἐπιστήμη. As we have seen, the distinction is futile, for αἴσθησις may at any time be the modern sense-perception,

---

346 *Rep.*, 511 D, 534 A. See *Idea of Good*, pp. 230 ff.

347 *Phileb.*, 39 C; *Phœdo*, 73 D; *Theœtet.*, 191 D, ἕως ἂν ἐνῇ τὸ εἴδωλον αὐτοῦ, etc.

348 *Phileb.*, 39 C, περι . . . . τῶν μελλόντων; 40 A B, and the fantastic account of the functions of the liver, *Tim.*, 71 A B. Grote, expecting the modern atomistic order: sensation, image, idea, judgment, is surprised that in *Phileb.*, 39, memory and sensation first write λόγοι in the soul, and that, secondly, a painter supervenes who paints images of these λόγοι and the corresponding δόξαι. But it is characteristic of Plato to put the image after the idea, the word, and the judgment everywhere. Moreover, the images here are not the primary images of perception, which are included in Plato's αἴσθησις, but imaginative visualizations of beliefs and hopes. In the mature human mind this is probably the real order: (1) sensation (perception), (2) faint verbal judgments, (3) vivifying of specially interesting judgments by imaginative visualization.

349 *Theœtet.*, 161 E, ἐλέγχειν τὰς ἀλλήλων φαντασίας τε καὶ δόξας.

350 *Theœtet.*, 152 C, φαντασία ἄρα καὶ αἴσθησις ταὐτὸν ἔν τε θερμοῖς καὶ πᾶσι τοῖς τοιούτοις. *Soph.*, 264 A, ὅταν μὴ καθ' αὑτὴν ἀλλὰ δι' αἰσθήσεως παρῇ τινι τὸ τοιοῦτον αὖ πάθος; *i. e.* it is here not a memory image, but a percept accompanied by belief.

351 *Soph.*, 264 B. Hence here 263 D, φαντασία, and *Phileb.*, 40 A, φαντάσματα (= imaginations or imaged expectations) are said to admit truth and falsehood. Modern atomistic psychology sometimes conceives "images" as mere pictures involving no affirmation or belief. Aristotle seems to express this view in *De Anima*, 432a, 10, ἔστι δ' ἡ φαντασία ἕτερον φάσεως καὶ ἀποφάσεως. But in 428a, 12, thinking of *Philebus*, 40 A B, he says, αἱ δὲ φαντασίαι γίνονται αἱ πλείους ψευδεῖς.

352 *Tim.*, 51 D E.   353 *Theœtetus*, *infra*; *supra*, p. 43.

354 *Phœdo*, 66, 67; *Laws*, 897 D, ὡς νοῦν ποτὲ θνητοῖς ὄμμασιν ὀψόμενοι.

355 *Supra*, n. 323.   356 *Infra*, on the *Theœtet.*

357 *Supra*, n. 301.

358 *Neue Plat. Forsch.*, p. 52.   359 209 ff.

including judgment, and δόξα may always be used either of the belief that accompanies αἴσθησις, or of the operation of the mind as opposed to sensation.

Campbell thinks the rejection in *Politicus*, 281 C D, of καλλίστην καὶ μεγίστην πασῶν as a satisfactory definition is an advance on *Theætet.*, 207 D, where the sun is defined as the brightest luminary, etc. But the point is simply that made "already" against Gorgias's μέγιστα τῶν ἀνθρωπείων πραγμάτων as a definition of the matter of rhetoric.[360] Again, Campbell thinks the mention of δόξαν and φαντασίαν in *Sophist*, 260 E, as distinct faculties implies an advance on the *Theætetus*. But the *Theætetus* does not identify the words by using them once or twice as virtual synonyms. The *Sophist*, 264 A, temporarily distinguishes φαντασία as a judgment present to the mind, δι' αἰσθήσεως,[361] while δόξα is a judgment, ἐν ψυχῇ κατὰ διάνοιαν . . . . μετὰ σιγῆς. But to press this would prove too much by distinguishing the *Sophist* from the late *Philebus* also.

Lastly, Lutoslawski argues[362] that the *Phædrus* and *Theætetus* are later than the *Republic*, because they familiarly employ δύναμις in a sense first explained in *Republic*, 477 C. He overlooks *Protag.*, 330 A, and the five occurrences of the word in *Charmides*, 168, in a passage fully as metaphysical and abstract as that cited from the *Republic*. Indeed, the case cited from the *Phædrus*, 246 D, πτεροῦ δύναμις, is a mere periphrasis like ἥ τε τοῦ πτεροῦ φύσις, 248 C, and of the two cases from the *Theætetus*, 158 E closely resembles the *Charmides*, using the word in the vague general sense of power or potentiality, and 185 C, ἥ γε διὰ τῆς γλώττης δύναμις, uses it of the senses, as do the *Charmides*, 168 D (ἀκοή, ὄψις), the *Republic*, 477 C (ὄψιν καὶ ἀκοήν), and the *Protagoras*, 330 A (ὀφθαλμός ὦτα). Of equal value are the developments which Lutoslawski finds in the use of διαλεκτική, φιλοσοφία μέθοδος, ἡ τῶν λόγων τέχνη, etc.[363]

PART II

The dialogues were composed in some order, and a study of their parallels, coincidences, or variations in thought will often seem to indicate the plausible, possibly the real, historic sequence. That is not the purpose of this paper. I wish to show (1) that our conception of Plato's philosophy is not appreciably affected by placing the dialectical dialogues — the *Sophist*, *Politicus*, *Philebus*, and possibly the *Parmenides* and *Theætetus* — after, rather than before, the *Republic;* (2) that the evidence is at present insufficient to date the dialogues of the "earlier" and "middle" Platonism, and that, again, from the point of view of the interpretation of the content, it does not greatly matter. The chief value of such negative results is that the way to them lies through a further positive interpretation of Plato's true meanings.

There are certain perennial puzzles of language or thought that present them-

---

[360] *Gorg.*, 451 D E.

[361] *Cf. Theætet.*, 158 C; *supra*, p. 48, n. 350.

[362] Pp. 331, 396.

[363] *Cf.* the statement, p. 373, *à propos* of the innocent phrase, *Theætet.*, 184 C, εἴτε ψυχὴν εἴτε ὅ τι δεῖ καλεῖν that:

"In earlier works Plato used the term soul as free from every ambiguity. Here we see already a trace of doubts about the existence of the soul." He might as well say that the existence of the soul is called in question by *Crito*, 48 A, ἐκεῖνο ὅ τι ποτ' ἐστί, etc., or by *Symp.*, 218 A, τὴν καρδίαν ἢ ψυχὴν γὰρ ἢ ὅ τι δεῖ ὀνομάσαι.

selves to Plato in three forms: as mere eristic sophisms; as hindrances to a sound logical method; as serious problems of epistemology and metaphysics. They may be roughly enumerated as the problem of Being and not-Being, or the true nature of predication and negation; the antithesis in thought and things of the one and the many, the whole and the part, permanency and change, rest and motion; the nature and possibility of real knowledge, and the meaning of consciousness of self. They are all directly or indirectly involved in the theory of ideas, but we may also study them in the group of dialogues in which they are most prominent.

The *Euthydemus* presents a broad burlesque of all the chief sophisms of eristic. The *Parmenides* systematically exposes all the antinomies concerning the one and the many, the whole and the part, rest and motion, that can be deduced from the abuse of the ambiguity of the copula. The *Theœtetus* covers with persiflage the forms of eristic associated with one-sided theories of knowledge, especially materialism and extreme Heracliteanism, and makes a serious effort to solve the epistemological problem. Here perhaps, and here only, does the Socratic avowal of perplexity express Plato's own state of mind. The *Sophist* makes explicit the lessons implied in the *Parmenides* and *Theœtetus*, and finally disposes of fourth-century eristic so far as it affects the presuppositions of practical logic and sound method. The *Politicus* applies the method of the *Sophist* to the definition of the true statesman, reaffirming from a different point of view, and perhaps with less confidence in the ideal, the chief doctrines of the *Republic*. The *Philebus* restates the true logical method that emerges from eristic or metaphysical debate and applies it to the ethical problem of the *summum bonum*.

We will begin with the *Sophist*, which contains the fullest exposition of method and the most explicit analysis of the fundamental eristic sophism. For our purpose there are three topics; (1) the method of definition by dichotomy; (2) the problem of Being and not-Being; (3) the logical and grammatical analysis of the sentence.

1. The formal dichotomies of the *Sophist* and *Politicus* lend these dialogues a very un-Platonic aspect. They may be said to be characteristic of Plato's "later" style, so far as this can be true of a feature that is less prominent in the *Laws* than it is in the *Gorgias* or *Phœdrus*. Their significance for Plato's later thought is very slight. To understand this we must distinguish the elaboration of a definition by successive dichotomies from the more general logical use of distinction, division, and classification. Aristotle is at great pains to prove that the method of dichotomy assumes and does not establish the definition.[364] His criticism may have been needed against literal-minded pupils of the Academy. Plato obviously is amusing himself by playing with the method.[365] He clearly recognizes that formally correct dichotomies may lead to half-a-dozen definitions of the same object.[366] All depends upon the tact with which the original "one," the concept to be divided, is chosen,[367] and the

[364] *Anal. Pr.*, 31; *Anal. Post.*, II, 5; *Part. An.*, 1, 2 ff.
[365] See BONITZ, pp. 180 ff.
[366] *Soph.*, 231.

[367] *Ibid.*, 232 B, ἀλλ' ἀναλάβωμεν ἐν πρῶτον τῶν περὶ τὸν σοφιστὴν εἰρημένων. ἐν γάρ τί μοι μάλιστα κατεφάνη αὐτὸν μηνῦον.

insight that selects at each turn[368] the most significant principle of subdivision. The process of dichotomy is only a mechanical aid to exhaustive search and the discovery of all relevant distinctions.[369] The elaboration of it as a method of definition in the *Sophist* and *Politicus* is a mere episode. It is not followed up in the *Philebus*, *Timæus*, or *Laws*, and is therefore of no importance for Plato's "later" thought.

A very different thing is the broader use of the method for the avoidance of eristic equivocation and the correction of hasty generalization or inarticulate empiricism. To distinguish and divide for these purposes is still the only way of clear thought and accurate speech, and Plato's insistence upon it as the one principle of logical salvation is worthy of the keenest dialectician that ever lived. But in this larger use the method κατ' εἴδη τέμνειν is by no means confined to the *Sophist* and *Politicus*. There are hints of it in the *Symposium*.[370] The *Gorgias* employs it with some ostentation.[371] It is found in the *Phædo*,[372] the *Cratylus*,[373] and the *Theœtetus*.[374] Its terminology and use are familiar to the *Republic*.[375] Most explicit is the *Phædrus*, which not only makes an ostentatious display of divisions and subdivisions,[376] but describes the entire procedure of true method in language that closely resembles the summing up of the whole matter found in the *Philebus*.[377] But side by side with

[368] Note κατιδεῖν, *Soph.*, 232 A; *Polit.*, 266 E, etc.

[369] The imagery of the *Sophist* and *Politicus* implies this throughout. *Cf. Soph.*, 235 C; *Polit.*, 258 C, 260 E, 262 A, τὸ ζητούμενον ἐν διπλασίοισι τὰ νῦν ἐν τοῖς ἡμίσεσιν εἰς τότε ποιήσει ζητεῖσθαι; *Soph.*, 229 D, εἰ ἄτομον ἤδη ἐστὶ πᾶν, ἤ τινα ἔχον διαίρεσιν ἀξίαν ἐπωνυμίας; *Phædr.*, 227 B, κατ' εἴδη μέχρι τοῦ ἀτμήτου τέμνειν; *Phileb.*, 13, 14 B, τὴν τοίνυν διαφορότητα; etc.

[370] *Symp.*, 205 B C D, ἀφελόντες . . . . τι εἶδος . . . . ἐν μόριον ἀφορισθὲν τὸ περὶ . . . . οἱ μὲν ἄλλη τρεπόμενοι . . . . οἱ δὲ κατὰ ἔν τι εἶδος ἰόντες. *Cf. Polit.*, 262 D, τὸ μὲν . . . . ὡς ἐν . . . . ἀφαιροῦντες . . . . καὶ γένος ἐν αὐτὸ εἶναι. *Soph.*, 222 A, ἐκτρέπεσθον; *Polit.*, 258 C; *Tim.*, 60 B, γένος ἐκ πάντων ἀφορισθέν; *Soph.*, 229 C, 257 C, 268 D.

[371] 454 E, δύο εἴδη θῶμεν. The two εἴδη are denoted, as in the *Sophist*, by adjectives in -κός, 455 A, frequent also in pp. 464, 465. Socrates's humorous definition of rhetoric, pp. 462 ff., is in the vein of the *Sophist*. It starts from the alternative art (science) or not-art, 462 B C, like *Soph.*, 219 A; *Polit.*, 258 B. It is found to be a branch of the pseudo-art κολακευτική, which is divided τέτραχα, corresponding to a four-fold division of art obtained by two successive sub-divisions. Similarly Sophistic is finally found to be a part, μόριον, *Soph.*, 268 D, of the quadripartite φανταστικόν.

[372] 79 A, θῶμεν . . . . δύο εἴδη, etc.; 90 B, ἄνευ τῆς περὶ τοὺς λόγους τέχνης; 75 D, οἷς ἐπισφραγιζόμεθα τοῦτο ὃ ἔστι. *Cf. Phileb.*, 26 D; *Polit.*, 258 C.

[373] In 424 C D, the division of letters κατὰ εἴδη and the subdivision of these εἴδη is the method of *Philebus*, 18 B C. We are further required to examine the things to be named by letters and see εἰ ἐν αὐτοῖς ἔνεστιν εἴδη, and then apply one set of εἴδη to the other, precisely as in *Phædrus*, 277 B.

[374] 147 D, ἐπειδὴ ἄπειροι τὸ πλῆθος . . . . ξυλλαβεῖν εἰς ἐν (cf. *Phileb.*, 18 B, ὅταν τις τὸ ἄπειρον ἀναγκασθῇ πρῶτον λαμβάνειν, etc.); 147 E, τὸν ἀριθμὸν παντα δίχα διελάβομεν, etc.

[375] 397 B, τὰ δύο εἴδη; 440 E, 445 C. In 454 A, eristic arises διὰ τὸ μὴ δύνασθαι κατ' εἴδη διαιρούμενοι τὸ λεγόμενον ἐπισκοπεῖν, precisely as in *Polit.*, 285 A. *Cf. Phileb.*, 17 A; *Soph.*, 253 D. Again, cf. *Rep.*, 470 B, δύο ταῦτα τὰ ὀνόματα . . . . ὄντα ἐπὶ δυοῖν τινοῖν διαφοραῖν; 532 E, κατὰ ποῖα δὴ εἴδη διέστηκεν; with which cf. 504 A; *Phileb.*, 23 D, and *Polit.*, 260 C, τὴν . . . . τέχνην . . . . θεατέον εἰ πῃ διέστηκεν with context. Compare further 544 C D, ἤ τις καὶ ἐν εἴδει διαφανεῖ τινι κεῖται with *Polit.*, 285 B, διαφορὰς . . . . ὁπόσαιπερ ἐν εἴδεσι κεῖνται; 580 D, διῄρηται κατὰ τρία εἴδη, οὕτω καὶ ψυχὴ . . . . τριχῇ.

[376] 244 E, 253 C, 270 B, 271 D.

[377] It is often affirmed (Jowett, Natorp, Jackson, Bury, etc.) that the method of the *Philebus*, *Politicus*, and *Sophist* is more advanced than that of the *Phædrus*, in which "the complementary methods of generalization and division are applied merely to the discovery of Socratic definitions with a view to consistency in the use of debatable terms." Well, the subject of the *Phædrus* being the necessity of basing rhetoric upon definitions and dialectic, that point is naturally emphasized there (265 D, ἵν' ἕκαστον ὁριζόμενος δῆλον ποιῇ, περὶ οὗ ἂν ἀεὶ διδάσκειν ἐθέλῃ). But all theories of a sharp distinction between the method of the *Phædrus* and that of the "later" dialogues will only injure the scholarship of their propounders. The *Phædrus* requires τὴν ὁμοιότητα τῶν ὄντων διειδέναι (262 A; cf. *Soph.*, 231 A, δεῖ πάντων μάλιστα περὶ τὰς ὁμοιότητας ποιεῖσθαι τὴν φυλακήν; *Phileb.*, 13 A B). To do this we must know ὁ ἔστιν ἕκαστον τῶν ὄντων (262 B). The method is twice described (265, 266, and 270 D). We must first reduce to unity τὰ πολλαχῇ διεσπαρμένα (265 D; cf. *Phileb.*, 16 D, ἀεὶ μίαν ἰδέαν περὶ παντὸς ἑκάστοτε θεμένους ζητεῖν; cf. 26 D). This unity we are to divide κατ' ἄρθρα ᾗ πέφυκε (265 E; cf. *Polit.*, 262, and with καταγνύναι cf. *Polit.*, 287 C, 265 D, καταθραύειν) and subdivide (266 A, τέμνων οὐκ ἐπανῆκε), distinguishing and following up separately the right- and left-hand paths (266 A, δεξιὰ . . . . ἀριστερὰ; cf. *Soph.*, 264 E, πορεύεσθαι κατὰ τοὐπὶ δεξιὰ ἀεὶ μέρος τοῦ τμηθέντος), till the object of our search and of our praise

what seems to us the purely logical treatment of the ideas as conceptual genera and species, the *Phædrus* pictures the prenatal vision of them; the *Republic* announces the most naïve realism with regard to any and every universal; and the *Timæus* solemnly reaffirms their objectivity.[378] In the face of these facts, it is impossible to maintain that the dichotomies of the *Sophist* are evidence of a later doctrine in which the transcendental or naïvely realistic idea is discarded for the genera and species of conceptual logic. The emphasis and center of interest may shift from dialogue to dialogue—the doctrine remains the same.

But the opposition between the two points of view cannot be denied or disguised. The noumenal idea is one. But not only as reflected in things, but as subdivided by logic, it is many. By a natural and inevitable metaphor both Plato and Aristotle speak of particulars and lower species as parts of the higher conceptual whole to which they are subordinated. By the theory of ideas, as we have said, each of these parts, every subordinate concept, is an idea, not only the *summum genus* and the lowest species, as animal and dog, but the intermediate groups, mammal and quadruped, etc. The Aristotelian objection that the one dog will thus embody a whole series of ideas we have dismissed with the metaphysics of the subject. The relation of the particular to the idea is a mystery. And once we have accepted the metaphors "presence," "participation," "pattern," a number of ideas can be reflected by or present in one thing as easily as can one idea.

But the elaboration of logical and scientific classification brings up the difficulty in a new and more specific form less easily evaded. For the theory of ideas any and every subordinate group apprehended as a conceptual unit by the mind is an idea.[379] For sound logical and scientific classification only true genera and species are ideas— not necessarily "true species" in the sense of the modern naturalist, but in the sense of the Platonic logic; that is, classes and groups based on significant and relevant distinctions. From the one point of view we expect every part to be an idea; from the other, Plato explicitly warns us against mistaking for true ideas what are mere fragments or parts.[380] His embarrassment shows that he felt the difficulty. Sound

and blame is found (266 A; *cf. Soph.*, 235 C, ξυνακολουθεῖν αὐτῷ διαιροῦντας . . . . ἔωσπερ ἂν ληφθῇ). He who can thus look εἰς ἓν καὶ ἐπὶ πολλά is a dialectician (266 B C; *cf. Parmen.*, 132 A, μία τις ἴσως δοκεῖ ἰδέα εἶναι ἐπὶ πάντα ἰδόντι; *Soph.*, 235 C, τὴν τῶν οὕτω δυναμένων μετιέναι καθ' ἕκαστά τε καὶ ἐπὶ πάντα μέθοδον). Again, looking at it from the point of view of science rather than of rhetoric and dialectic (270), the object of investigation is either simple or manifold. If it has many εἴδη, we must enumerate them (270 D, ταῦτα ἀριθμησαμένους; *cf. Phileb.*, 16 D, πρὶν ἂν τις τὸν ἀριθμὸν αὐτοῦ πάντα κατίδη τὸν μεταξὺ τοῦ ἀπείρου τε καὶ τοῦ ἑνός), and treat each subordinate ἕν (*cf. Phileb.*, 16 D, καὶ τῶν ἐν ἐκείνων ἕκαστον πάλιν ὡσαύτως) as we do the original unity—*i. e.*, study its potentialities (δύναμις, active or passive; *cf. Soph.*, 247 D E) in relation to other things. Rhetoric is a special psychological application of this general scientific method. It is one method which is described in *Phædr.*, 265, 266, 270 D; *Phileb.*, 16–18; *Cratyl.*, 424 C; *Soph.*, 226 C, 235 C, 253,

etc.; *Polit.*, 285 A, etc.; *Laws*, 894 A A, 963 D, 965 C. Each dialogue brings out some aspect of it less emphasized in the others. We cannot expect Plato to repeat himself verbatim. But these variations have little or no significance for the evolution of his thought.

[378] *Supra*, p. 35, n. 238; p. 37, n. 256.

[379] *Rep.*, 596 A., 479 D; *Soph.*, 225 C, ταῦτα θετέον μὲν εἶδος, ἐπείπερ αὐτὸ διέγνωκεν ὡς ἕτερον ὂν ὁ λόγος, ἀτὰρ ἐπωνυμίας . . . . οὔτε νῦν ὑφ' ἡμῶν τυχεῖν ἄξιον. *Phileb.*, 18 C D, the δεσμός of association in our minds makes a unity, and hence an idea of γραμματική.

[380] *Polit.*, 287 C, implied "already" in *Phædr.*, 265 E; *cf. Polit.*, 262 B, ἀλλὰ τὸ μέρος ἅμα εἶδος ἐχέτω. We are more likely to "meet with ideas" if we bisect the universal (μεσοτομεῖν) and proceed by successive dichotomies, than if we attempt to separate the ultimate species at once. *Cf.* the insistence on τὰ μέσα in *Phileb.*, 17 A.

method required him to emphasize the distinction. But he was quite unable to define its nature.[381] The nominalistic logic of the modern "flowing philosophy" of evolution would meet the problem by making both "true species," and the tentative species of imperfect or erroneous generalization alike relative to the purposes of man—working hypotheses, instruments of greater or less precision and range, employed by thought in the effort to shape in its own image or check for its own ends the ever-flowing stream of change.

Plato would have preferred mystery and self-contradiction to this as an ultimate philosophy. But his logical practice approaches nearer to it than does any intermediate compromise of common-sense from Aristotle to the nineteenth century. Psychologically and ontologically all universals, as opposed to sensations and images, are equally noumenal ideas, whether language provides a name for them or not.[382] In logical and scientific practice the only ideas worth recognizing, whether named or not, are those that embody significant distinctions relevant to the purpose in hand.[383] The recognition that words are mere counters[384] and do not always stand for (relevant) ideas[385] is an apparent, but not real, contradiction of the abbreviated formula of the *Republic* that we assume an idea for every word.[386] Similarly, as we have already seen, the occasional and inevitable use of conceptual language is no derogation from Plato's philosophic realism.[387] Practical logic and psychology must treat ideas as concepts, whatever else or more they may be.

2. The puzzle that false speech and erring opinion are impossible because we cannot say or opine that which is not, is nothing, must be translated into Greek to win even a semblance of seriousness. To appreciate Plato's achievement in disposing of it forever we must have studied it in the poem of Parmenides and in the eristic of the fourth century.[388] Our problem here is the seeming contradiction between the *Republic* and the *Sophist*. The *Republic* distinctly avers that it is impossible even to opine that which is not—thus apparently yielding to the fallacy.[389] The admirable analysis of the *Parmenides* and the *Sophist* explains it by pointing out that *is*, in its double function of copula and substantive verb, is ambiguous,[390] and that this ambiguity extends to the convenient Greek idiomatical use of the parti-

---

[381] *Polit.*, 263 A B, to distinguish genus (or species) and part would require a long discussion. He can only say that, while every species is a part, every part is not a species (εἶδος).

[382] *Supra*, p. 37, n. 250.

[383] *Rep.*, 445 C, 544 A D, ἢ τίνα ἄλλην ἔχεις ἰδέαν πολιτείας, ἥτις καὶ ἐν εἴδει διαφανεῖ τινὶ κεῖται; *Tim.*, 83 C, εἰς πολλὰ μὲν καὶ ἀνόμοια βλέπειν, ὁρᾶν δὲ ἐν αὐτοῖς ἓν γένος ἐνὸν ἄξιον ἐπωνυμίας; *Soph.*, 229 D, ἢ τινα ἔχον διαίρεσιν ἀξίαν ἐπωνυμίας; 223 A, 225 C, 267 D, names for ideas often fail because the ancients were neglectful of τῆς τῶν γενῶν κατ' εἴδη διαιρέσεως. *Polit.*, 260 E, ἀνώνυμον .... ὄνομα ἕτερον αὐτοῖς παραχωρήσαντες θέσθαι τινά; 261 E, τὸ μὴ σπουδάζειν ἐπὶ τοῖς ὀνόμασι, 263 C.

[384] "Already," *Charm.*, 163 D; *Polit.*, 261 E; *Theœtet.*, 168 B, 184 C; *Soph.*, 218 C; *Laws*, 627 D, and *passim*.

[385] *Soph.*, 217 A; *Polit.*, 263 C, ὅτι πᾶσι ταὐτὸν ἐπονομάζειν ἔσχες ὄνομα; *Rep.*, 454 A.

[386] 596 A. The common name of πολλά does imply a conceptual ἕν, which implies an idea, though it may not be relevant or worth while (ἄξιον ἐπωνυμίας) for the classification or purpose in hand.

[387] *E. g.*, *Phœdr.*, 263 D E, ἠνάγκασεν ἡμᾶς ὑπολαβεῖν .... ἕν τι τῶν ὄντων, etc.; *Polit.*, 258 C, δύο εἴδη διανοηθῆναι τὴν ψυχὴν ἡμῶν ποιῆσαι; *Phileb.*, 18 C D, 23 E, νοῆσαι, πῇ ποτε ἦν αὐτῶν ἓν καὶ πολλὰ ἑκάτερον. See *supra*, p. 39, n. 264.

[388] See *A. J. P.*, Vol. XII, pp. 349 ff., and Vol. XXI, pp. 205 ff.

[389] 478 B. *Cf. Parmen.*, 132 B C, 142 A, 164 A, 166 A; *Theœtet.*, 167 A, 188 D.

[390] *Parmen.*, 142 C, νῦν δὲ οὐκ αὕτη ἐστὶν ἡ ὑπόθεσις, εἰ ἓν ἕν .... ἀλλ' εἰ ἓν ἔστιν; 163 C, τὸ δὲ μὴ ἔστιν .... ἆρα μή τι ἄλλο σημαίνει ἢ οὐσίας ἀπουσίαν; 162 A B, with my interpretation, *A. J. P.*, Vol. XII, pp. 349 ff.; *Sophist.*, 256 D E ff.; *Tim.*, 38 B.

ciple—ὄν and μὴ ὄν, ὄντα and μὴ ὄντα; that μὴ ὄν is not nonentity, but otherness; not nothing, but some other thing.[391] If we can show that other dialogues, presumably earlier than, or contemporary with, the *Republic*, ridicule the fallacy, or imply the answer to it given in the *Sophist*, we have established a *prima facie* presumption for an interpretation of the *Republic* that will remove the contradiction.[392] This is the case. In the *Euthydemus* the μὴ ὄν puzzle is one of the stock fallacies of the eristics. To desire to make Kleinias wise is to wish to make him other than he is, what he is not—not to be. The suggestion enrages Ctesippus, but Socrates bids him μὴ ὀνόματι διαφέρεσθαι.[393] And when the quibble is further invoked in support of the paradox that ψευδῆ λέγειν and ψευδὴς δόξα are impossible, since we cannot opine or say what is not, Socrates observes that this opinion refutes itself as well as all others, and declines to take it seriously.[394] In the *Cratylus* Cratylus argues by a fallacy, elsewhere exemplified in Plato,[395] that a bad law is no law, an unapt name is no name, and a false statement is no statement, because it is τὸ μὴ τὰ ὄντα λέγειν.[396] Socrates dryly observes that this thesis, though it has many supporters, is too subtle for him,[397] and then proceeds to offer a perfectly sufficient practical explanation of the difficulty by means of an illustration analogous to the image employed in the *Theætetus*[398] to account for certain forms of mental confusion. As you may wrongly assign A's picture to B and B's to A, so in the use of terms it is possible to apply X to A and Y to B when the opposite distribution would be correct, and, in the case of words, true.[399] This explanation Cratylus is urged to accept in order to avoid (eristic) debate, ἵνα μὴ μαχώμεθα ἐν τοῖς λόγοις.[400] And when he yields, Socrates commends him on the ground that this is not the place to argue the question.[401] There is a further anticipation of the *Sophist* in the suggestion that those who insist on the quibble are ὀψιμαθεῖς.[402]

---

[391] It is true that Plato nowhere states the ambiguity of the copula with the explicitness of Aristotle and John Stuart Mill. But the passages cited in the preceding note prove that he understood it perfectly. Grote, in his criticism of the *Sophist*, objects (1) that Plato fails to distinguish ἔστιν in its function of pure and simple copula; (2) that the (absolute) other of Being is just as meaningless as absolute not-Being; (3) that negation is something different from otherness, and that to define it as otherness is to confuse the distinction between contrary and contradictory. These criticisms ignore the difference between Greek and English idiom, the necessity that Plato felt of meeting the μὴ ὄν fallacy in its own terminology, and the religious or ontological associations which half playfully, half seriously, he was resolved to preserve for εἶναι. τὸ μὴ ὄν, besides its ontological meaning, can be naturally used in Greek idiom as a mere category embracing all particular cases of (*a*) negative predication, (*b*) misstatement. Any particular μὴ ὄν is something other than the corresponding ὄν; and, generalizing, Plato may say that μὴ ὄν is the other of the ὄν without implying that it is the other of absolute Being. For the same reason, in explaining the nature of error and misstatement, he is justified in substituting for the general category μὴ ὄν a concrete (affirmative) misstatement, "Theætetus flies." It all sounds crude enough, if we think it only through English idiom. But it was the most effective analysis of the fallacy in the form in which Greek usage presented it. Plato is, for the rest, aware of the distinction between contradictory and contrary opposition (*Symp.*, 201 E; *Parmen.*, 160 B C; *Soph.*, 257 B, οὐκ ἄρ', ἐναντίον ὅταν ἀπόφασις λέγηται σημαίνειν συγχωρησόμεθα), and he understands the use of εἶναι as a copula, though the religious and metaphysical associations of "Being" cause him to stigmatize it as "inexact" (*Tim.*, 38 B).

[392] My task would be much simplified if I could accept NATORP'S view (*Hermes*, Vol. XXXV, p. 425), that the relative Being of the *Sophist* is distinctly anticipated in *Phædo*, 79 A, δύο εἴδη τῶν ὄντων τὸ μὲν ὁρατόν, τὸ δὲ ἀειδές. But ὄντων is not to be pressed here.

[393] *Euthyd.*, 283, 285 A.

[394] 286 C, where, as in the *Theætet.*, it is attributed to Protagoras with a malicious allusion to ἀλήθεια.

[395] 429 B; *cf. Hipp. major*, 284 E; *Minos*, 314 D ff.

[396] 429 D.

[397] κομψότερος μὲν ὁ λόγος ἢ κατ' ἐμὲ, etc.; *cf. Soph.*, 239 B.

[398] 194 B.

[399] 430 D, ἐπὶ δὲ τοῖς ὀνόμασι πρὸς τῷ ὀρθὴν καὶ ἀληθῆ.

[400] 430 D. [401] 431 A.

[402] 433 A, δόξωμεν αὐτῇ τῇ ἀληθείᾳ οὕτω πως ἐληλυθέναι ὀψιαίτερον τοῦ δέοντος. *Cf. Soph.*, 251 B, 259 D.

It is obvious (1) that the fallacy is none to Plato; (2) that he feels himself able to carry the analysis farther; (3) that he does not do so because he wishes to write the *Cratylus*, not the *Sophist*.

In the *Theætetus* the matter is somewhat more complicated. As we shall show more fully below, the object of the *Theætetus* is not to refute or analyze the logical fallacy that false opinion is impossible, but to explain the psychological nature of error, and with it of cognition: τί ποτ' ἐστὶ τοῦτο τὸ πάθος παρ' ἡμῖν καὶ τίνα τρόπον ἐγγιγνόμενον.[403] For this the μὴ ὄν quibble would have been wholly unfruitful. But it could not be altogether ignored. Hence it is perfunctorily dismissed in a page with the admission that the method of εἶναι and μὴ εἶναι offers no explanation of error, since ὁ δοξάζων ἕν τι δοξάζει, and ὁ μηδὲν δοξάζων τὸ παράπαν οὐδὲ δοξάζει.[404] We are thus left free to pursue the psychological analysis κατὰ τὸ εἰδέναι καὶ μή. But it is absurd to suppose that Socrates is really baffled in the *Theætetus* by a fallacy at which he laughs in the *Euthydemus* and *Cratylus*. And his real opinion of it is sufficiently indicated by his attribution of it to Protagoras in this very dialogue.[405]

The final analysis of the fallacy in the *Sophist* is introduced and accompanied by persiflage in the manner of the *Euthydemus* and *Cratylus*, and by hints that it is a mere eristic puzzle.[406] The final common-sense formula that true speech and opinion represent τὰ ὄντα ὡς ἔχει or ὡς ἔστι is not new.[407] It evades the psychological problems of the *Theætetus*, and it is reached by arguments purely logical and practical. If we do not admit that μὴ ὄν normally means otherness rather than non-existence, we shall make all rational speech and thought impossible.[408] The absolute ὄν (and μὴ ὄν) of the *Parmenides* to which no intelligible predicates attach is reserved for ontology and mysticism.[409] But ἐν τοῖς παρ ἡμῖν λόγοις (251 D) we must accept a doctrine of mixed and relative Being and not-Being.[410]

The result of the inquiry is that, if Plato in the *Republic* falls into this fallacy, the *Republic* must be earlier and less mature, not only than the *Sophist*, but than the *Euthydemus* and the *Cratylus*. But Plato does not yield to the fallacy in the *Republic*. He merely varies his terminology to suit his theme. He needs the transcendental absolute Being for the world of ideas as opposed to the world of sense, for the symbolism of the idea of Good, the image of the sun, the cave, and the conversion from the shadows to the realities. It would have been singularly tactless to preface these passages with an explanation that ὄν, like μὴ ὄν, is a relative term, and that all ὄντα with which human logic can deal are likewise μὴ ὄντα. There is no occasion for the ὄντα and μὴ ὄντα of practical logic here. Absolute not-Being is consigned to total

403 187 D.   404 188, 189 A.

405 In Socrates's ironical defense of ultra-Protagoreanism, 167 A, οὔτε γὰρ τὰ μὴ ὄντα δυνατὸν δοξάσαι, οὔτε ἄλλα παρ' ἃ ἂν πάσχῃ. Cf. Cratyl., 286 C.

406 236 E, ἐναντιολογίᾳ μὴ συνέχεσθαι, etc.; 237 B C; 239 B, ἐμέ . . . . πάλαι καὶ τὰ νῦν ἡττημένον ἂν εὕροι περὶ τὸν τοῦ μὴ ὄντος ἔλεγχον, etc.; cf. 242 A, 243 A B, 252 C. Note also the close parallelism of this part of the *Sophist* with the intentional fallacies of the *Parmenides*, infra, pp. 58, 59.

407 263 B, λέγει δὲ αὐτῶν ὁ μὲν ἀληθὴς τὰ ὄντα ὡς ἔστι περὶ σοῦ. Cf. Cratyl., 385 B, ὃς ἂν τὰ ὄντα λέγῃ ὡς ἔστιν ἀληθῆ; Euthydem., 284 C, ἀλλὰ τὰ ὄντα μὲν τρόπον τινὰ λέγει, οὐ μέντοι ὥς γε ἔχει.

408 238 C, 239 B, 249 B C, 252 C, 259 A, ὁ δὲ νῦν εἰρήκαμεν εἶναι τὸ μὴ ὄν, ἢ πεισάτω τις ὡς οὐ καλῶς λέγομεν ἐλέγξας ἢ μέχρι περ ἂν ἀδυνατῇ, λεκτέον καὶ ἐκείνῳ καθάπερ ἡμεῖς, etc., 260 A.

409 258 E; cf. supra, p. 39.

410 251 A, 254 C D, 259 A B.

ignorance as it is in the *Sophist*.[411] Pure Being is reserved for the ideas, as it is in the *Timæus*, which was written at a time when the results of the *Sophist* were certainly familiar to Plato. Its antithesis, the world of phenomena, is described as tumbling about between Being and not-Being—as a mixture of the two; the things of sense are always changing—they are and are not.[412] It is not necessary to dash the spirit of mystic contemplation and enthusiasm by the reminder that the ideas themselves, when drawn down into the process of human thought, move to and fro and partake of both Being and not-Being.[413] We are concerned here only with the broad contrast between the two worlds. To say that the objects of sense and the notions of the vulgar tumble about between Being and not-Being, is merely another way of saying that they belong to the domain of the mixed or relative Being and not-Being described in the *Sophist*.[414] Only a deplorably matter-of-fact criticism can find in this adaptation of the terminology to the immediate literary purpose a concession to a fallacy ridiculed throughout the dialogues. And the arguments that would prove the results of the *Sophist* unknown to the author of the *Republic* would apply almost equally to the *Timæus;* for there, too, Plato calmly reinstates the absolute ὄν which the *Sophist* banishes from human speech as no less contradictory than the absolute μὴ ὄν, and treats as an inaccuracy the expression τὸ μὴ ὂν μὴ ὂν εἶναι, the practical necessity of which the *Sophist* demonstrates.[415] Yet the treatment of the "same" and the "other" in the ψυχογονία (35) proves that the analysis of the *Sophist* was familiar to the author of the *Timæus*.

3. The explicit discrimination of ὀνόματα as names of agents and of ῥήματα as names of actions is peculiar to *Sophist*, 262. So the special definition of διάνοια is confined to the *Republic*,[416] and nearly every dialogue employs some definition or distinction which Plato does not happen to need again. Even if we concede that this greater explicitness of grammatical and logical analysis marks the *Sophist* as late, its significance for the development of Plato's thought is slight. It is not repeated in the *Politicus* or *Laws*,[417] and it is virtually anticipated in the *Cratylus*, where it is twice said that λόγος is composed of ῥήματα and ὀνόματα.[418] It is barely possible, but not necessary, to take ῥήματα here in the sense of "expression" or "phrase." Even then it must include the verb. For ὄνομα is plainly used in the sense of "name" or "noun." Lutoslawski's argument[419] that "it would be unjustifiable to apply to the *Cratylus* a definition given only in the *Sophist*," obviously begs the question. The expression (425 A), καὶ συλλαβὰς αὖ συντιθέντες ἐξ ὧν τά τε ὀνόματα καὶ τὰ ῥήματα συντίθενται, seems to put ὀνόματα and ῥήματα on the same plane and is unfavorable to

---

411 477 A, μὴ ὂν μηδαμῇ; 478 D E, τοῦ πάντως μὴ ὄντος. Not foreseeing modern philology, Plato did not think it necessary to add πάντως or μηδαμῇ a third time in 478 B, when he asks ἢ ἀδύνατον καὶ δοξάσαι τὸ μὴ ὄν, which LUTOSLAWSKI, p. 429, thinks would be unaccountable coming after the inquiry of the *Sophist*. Similarly APELT (*Beiträge*).

412 479 B C D.

413 Though it is hinted in the ἀλλήλων κοινωνίᾳ of 476 A; *cf. supra*, p. 36, n. 244.

414 *Cf. A. J. P.*, Vol. IX, p. 307.

415 *Tim.*, 38 A B.   416 *Supra*, n. 346.

417 Lutoslawski is mistaken in saying that ῥῆμα is used in the distinctive sense of predicate in *Polit.*, 303 C, and *Laws*, 838 B. In both places it means "saying," "statement."

418 425 A, 431 C, λόγοι γάρ που ὡς ἐγῷμαι, ἡ τούτων ξύνθεσίς ἐστιν.

419 P. 431.

the notion of a progression from syllables to words, and from words to phrases and sentences. In 431 B, if ῥήματα means "verbs" or "predicates," we understand the statement that they as well as ὀνόματα may be falsely applied. But what is a false application of phrases? And if we evade this difficulty by taking ῥήματα as "sentences," then λόγοι must mean, not "sentences," but "discourses," and what is a false attribution of discourses? In fact, it would be easy to argue that the *Cratylus* takes for granted the results of the *Sophist* and is therefore later. Our concern is not with such "arguments," but merely to show that, conceding the utmost that the texts will bear, the difference very slightly affects the relative maturity of the thought in the two dialogues.[420]

THE PARMENIDES

A great deal of ink has been spilled over the *Parmenides*, and the profoundest mystical meanings have been discovered in its symmetrical antinomies.[421] To rational criticism nothing can be more certain than that they are in the main a logical exercitation more nearly akin to the *Euthydemus* and the *Sophist* than to the *Timæus*, and that they are not meant to be taken seriously except in so far as they teach by indirection precisely the logic of common-sense expounded in the *Sophist*.[422] In style, however, the *Parmenides* presents few, if any, traces of the elaborate "late" manner of the *Sophist*,[423] and this fact makes the identity of doctrine the more significant. Both the *Theætetus* and the *Sophist* allude to a meeting between Socrates and Parmenides.[424] The method of argumentation employed is characterized in the *Phædrus* as a kind of rhetoric, and in the *Sophist* as mere eristic.[425] Many passages closely resemble arguments and expressions which are ridiculed in the *Theætetus* and *Sophist*, and which are presumably not serious here.[426] The dialogue itself abounds in hints

---

[420] *Cf. supra*, p. 33, n. 218. The further points made by Lutoslawski are nearly all misapprehensions. He says that the admission that philosophic teaching may be given by continuous lecture, as well as by the method of question and answer, is first found in 217 C. But *Theætet.*, 167 D, recognizes the same choice. The meaning of μέθοδος in *Soph.*, 227 A, is not more definite than that in *Phædr.*, 270 D, and *Rep.*, 533 C ff., except in so far as the method of the *Sophist* and *Politicus* lays more stress on the mere mechanism of definition by dichotomy. *Cf. supra*, n. 377. The notion of logical exercise is not new here, but is found in *Meno*, 75 A, ἵνα καὶ γένηταί σοι μελέτη, etc., and is implied in *Theætet.*, 147 A ff. Dialectic in the *Republic* is as clearly the science of the division of notions as it is in the *Phædrus* and *Sophist*. See 454 A, 535 B, *supra*, n. 365. See also on δύναμις, *supra*, p. 49; and on the ideas as souls, *supra*, p. 39.

[421] BURY on "Later Platonism," *Jour. of Phil.*, Vol. XXIII, pp. 161 ff., gives a useful summary of recent discussions.

[422] *Cf. supra*, p. 54. *De Plat. idearum doctrina*, pp. 41 ff.; *A. J. P.*, Vol. IX, pp. 185, 290 ff.

[423] NATORP, *Archiv*, Vol. XII.

[424] *Theætet.*, 183 E; *Soph.*, 217 C. Either allusion might precede or follow the actual composition of the *Parmenides*. NATORP, *Archiv*, Vol. XII, pp. 291, 163, supposes that

Plato at the time of *Theætet.*, 183 E, intended to discuss rest and motion, but, writing the *Parmenides* much later, changed his mind and devoted Part I to objections to the ideas, and Part II to metaphysical problems still debated.

[425] *Phædr.*, 261 D, τον οὖν Ἐλεατικὸν Παλαμήδην (Zeno?) λέγοντα οὐκ ἴσμεν τέχνῃ ὥστε φαίνεσθαι τοῖς ἀκούουσι τὰ αὐτὰ ὅμοια καὶ ἀνόμοια, καὶ ἓν καὶ πολλά, etc. *Soph.*, 259. It is equally foolish to deny or to take seriously the antinomies (ἐναντιώσεσιν) that arise from the communion of ideas and the relativity of ὄν, μὴ ὄν, and θάτερον. *Cf.* 259 D, τὸ δὲ ταὐτὸν ἕτερον ἀποφαίνειν ἀμῇ γέ πῃ . . . . καὶ τὸ μέγα σμικρὸν καὶ τὸ ὅμοιον ἀνόμοιον . . . . οὔτε τις ἔλεγχος οὗτος ἀληθινός, etc. Such contradictions are nothing difficult when one knows the trick. 259 C, εἴτε ὥς τι χαλεπὸν κατανενοηκώς. *Cf. Parmen.*, 159 A, καὶ πάντα τὰ ἐναντία πάθη οὐκέτι χαλεπῶς εὑρήσομεν, and Socrates's congratulations to the Sophists in the *Euthydemus* on the ease with which Ctesippus picked up their method (303 E).

[426] *E. g.*, the quibble, *Parmen.*, 147 D ff. (of which Alice's "jam every *other* day" is the only English analogue), that the "other" is the "same" because the word ἕτερον in Greek idiom applies to both, and the word must refer to the same essence. This is parodied by Socrates in *Euthydem.*, 301 B, and explained in *Theætet.*, 190 E, ἐπειδὴ τὸ ῥῆμα ἕτερον τῷ ἑτέρῳ κατὰ ῥῆμα ταὐτόν ἐστιν. The extension of this reasoning to the ἀνομοιότατον is deprecated as eristic in

to that effect. It is recited by one whose light has gone out more completely than that of Heraclitus's sun, and who now is devoted to horsemanship.[427] Parmenides himself characterizes it as a kind of intellectual gymnastics which it would be unseemly to practice in the presence of the uninitiated,[428] and explicitly terms it a πραγματειώδη παιδιάν.[429] He chooses as his respondent the youngest interlocutor, on the ground that he will be least likely πολυπραγμονεῖν — that is, to interrupt the flow of plausible ratiocination by distinctions like those with which Socrates checked the stream of fallacy in the *Euthydemus*.[430]

These are probabilities. The proof is that the fallacies are symmetrically deduced by a systematic abuse of the ambiguity of the copula, and that Plato gives us clear warning of this at each turn in the argument. The symmetry is of course not perfect, and there are various minor fallacies that arise from other equivocations. An analysis full enough to show this in detail would defeat its own object by wearying the reader and obscuring the main design, which is not open to debate.[431] The groups of contradictory conclusions deduced from the hypothesis that the One is and that the One is not derive almost wholly from the equivocal meaning of "is"—from taking "is" or "is not" to signify now the absolute uncommunicating Being or not-Being which the *Sophist* dismisses as impracticable, and now the relative Being and not-Being, or otherness, which the *Sophist* establishes as the only tenable use of the terms in human logic. And near the beginning of each hypothesis we are distinctly warned of the sense in which "is" and "is not" must be taken.[432] This is perhaps sufficient; but another way of putting it will bring out the parallelism with the *Sophist* still more clearly. The eristic combated in the *Sophist* may be resumed in two fallacies: (1) The noumenal unity of the idea is incompatible with any suggestion of change, relation, or multiplicity. The ideas will not communicate or mix. Predication is impossible. You cannot say, "Man is good," but only, "Man is man" and "Good is good."[433]

Phileb., 13 D. The *Parmen.*, 148 A, infers that κατ' αὐτὸ τοῦτο ἅπαν ἅπασι ὅμοιον ἂν εἴη. Now, it is precisely the function of deceptive rhetoric πᾶν παντὶ ὁμοιοῦν, *Phœdr.*, 261 E; and it is precisely this that the *Sophist*, 259 D, and the *Philebus*, 13 A, stigmatize as eristic. Similarly the antinomies of whole and part in 137 C D, 144 E, 145 E, 157 E, 159 C D, recall *Theœtet.*, 204, 205, and *Soph.*, 245. On rest and motion cf. 139 B with *Soph.*, 250 C, 146 A, 156 E, 162 E, with 255 E; *Theœtet.*, 181-3. In *Theœtet.*, 180 D, the words ἵνα καὶ οἱ σκυτοτόμοι . . . . παύσωνται ἠλιθίως οἰόμενοι τὰ μὲν ἑστάναι, τὰ δὲ κινεῖσθαι τῶν ὄντων, show Plato's real opinion of these absolute antinomies; cf. *Soph.*, 249 C D. For the negation of all intelligible predicates cf. 142 A, 164 B; *Soph.*, 248 C; *Theœtet.*, 157 D. In general the *Parmenides* exemplifies what the *Sophist* terms, 245 E, τοὺς . . . . διακριβολογουμένους ὄντος τε περὶ καὶ μή.

[427] 128 C.

[428] 135 D, 136 D E. The *Euthydemus* hints that listening to eristic may be a useful discipline. This is the meaning of the intervention of the δαιμόνιον, 272 E, and of 305 D, often misunderstood.

[429] 137 B.

[430] LUTOSLAWSKI, p. 418, misunderstands this, saying: "It is only in the *Parmenides* that discussion (πολυπραγμονεῖν) is declared useless."

[431] See APELT, *Beiträge*.

[432] (1) 137 D, εἰ ἓν ἔσται τὸ ἕν; (2) 142 C, νῦν δὲ οὐχ αὕτη ἐστὶν ἡ ὑπόθεσις εἰ ἓν ἕν . . . . ἀλλ' εἰ ἓν ἔστιν . . . . ; (4) 157 C, οὐδὲ μὴν στέρεταί γε παντάπασι τοῦ ἑνὸς τἆλλα, ἀλλὰ μετέχει πῃ . . . . ; contra (5), 159 B, Ἆρ' οὖν οὐ χωρὶς μὲν τὸ ἓν τῶν ἄλλων, χωρὶς δὲ τἆλλα τοῦ ἑνὸς εἶναι; (6) 160 C, ὅτι ἕτερόν τι λέγοι τὸ μὴ ὄν, ὅταν εἴπῃ ἓν εἰ μὴ ἔστι, καὶ ἴσμεν ὃ λέγει (cf. *Soph.*, 237 B) 160 E, εἶναι μὲν δὴ τῷ ἑνὶ οὐχ οἷόν τε . . . . μετέχειν δὲ πολλῶν οὐδὲν κωλύει. From this οὐσίας μετέχειν and then εἶναι μὴ ὄν are deduced; contra (7) 163 C, τὸ δὲ μὴ ἔστιν . . . . ἆρα μή τι ἄλλο σημαίνει ἢ οὐσίας ἀπουσίαν; (cf. AR., *Met.*, 1004a, 15).

[433] 251 E, 259 E, 251 C; *Theœtet.*, 201 E - 202 A. The εἰδῶν φίλοι, 248 A (cf. 246 B, 248 E), represent not so much a particular school as a generalized tendency of thought. They are literal-minded Platonists or Eleatics who introduce into logic Plato's (and Parmenides's) poetical absolutism. Plato's criticism is not a recantation of "earlier" Platonism, for their dogma in *Soph.*, 248 C, is precisely what Plato himself says in *Tim.*, 38 A; cf. *supra*, p. 39.

(2) The negative "is not" denotes absolute non-existence, which is unutterable and unthinkable.[434] Plato answers in substance: (1) We must admit the mixture of ideas, the seeming multiplication of one idea by communion with others, as a condition of intelligible speech. Without it we cannot even predicate existence, identity, and diversity.[435] (2) Absolute not-Being is no more nor less a problem than absolute Being.[436] The only not-Being that finds a place in intelligible speech is otherness — that which is not this, but is some other thing.[437] Now, in the eight or nine[438] hypotheses of the *Parmenides* these two principles are alternately and systematically violated and recognized — the consequences in each case being drawn out in exact parallelism to those indicated in the *Sophist*. In the absolute theses the ideas are taken in self-identity, in isolation, χωρίς.[439] The one has no parts, and the exclusion of parts is found to shut out all predicates that imply multiplicity, space, time, or number.[440] And since these are the forms in which Being appears,[441] we cannot even say that it is.[442] There is neither knowledge nor speech of it.[443] In the absolute negative theses μὴ ὄν is taken to exclude every sense of εἶναι, with a similar result.[444] In the hypotheses concerned with relative Being and not-Being the reasoning is reversed. If we speak of *unum* and *alia*, we imply existence in some sense. The existent one is two (unity and existence), has parts, and so by necessary implications is clothed in all the predicates of space, time, and relation.[445] Instead of abiding in isolation, the one everywhere united with essence, οὐσία, is divided up among the indefinite multiplicity of ὄντα.[446] And it is explicitly affirmed that this is true of the most abstract and ideal unity that we can conceive.[447] Similarly, starting from the assumption that μὴ ὄν (or μή ἕν) means something, and something different,[448] we deduce first "participation" in various predicates,[449] and finally the defiant paradox of the *Sophist* that μὴ ὄν ἐστι.[450] The doctrine of these relative hypotheses is that of the *Sophist*. The reasoning of the absolute hypotheses is that of the preliminary ἀπορίαι

[434] 238 C – 241 A, etc.

[435] 252 C, 256 A B, 259 E, etc.

[436] 250 D E, 258 E.

[437] 257 ff.

[438] The third ἔτι δὴ τὸ τρίτον λέγωμεν, 155 E, stands by itself. It is in some sort a reconciliation of the contradictions of the first two, and, by implication, of all.

[439] 137 C, 139 E, τοῦ δέ γε ἐνὸς χωρὶς ἐφάνη τὴν φύσιν τὸ ταὐτόν, 140 A, 159 B, Ἀρ οὖν οὐ χωρὶς μὲν τὸ ἓν τῶν ἄλλων, etc. Cf. *Euthyd.*, 284 A, ἐν μὴν κἀκεῖνό γ᾽ ἐστὶ τῶν ὄντων, ὃ λέγει χωρὶς τῶν ἄλλων. *Theætet.*, 205 C, διότι αὐτὸ καθ᾽ αὑτὸ ἕκαστον εἴη ἀσύνθετον, καὶ οὐδὲ τὸ εἶναι περὶ αὐτοῦ ὀρθῶς ἔχοι προσφέροντα εἰπεῖν. Another form of this fallacy, πᾶν ἀπὸ παντὸς χωρίζειν, appears in the Protagorean doctrine: *Cratyl.*, 385 E, ἰδίᾳ αὐτῶν ἡ οὐσία εἶναι ἑκάστῳ; *Theætet.*, 166 C, ἴδιαι αἰσθήσεις ἑκάστῳ ἡμῶν γίγνονται. Absolutism, whether sensational or verbal and ideal, destroys rational thought, and is refuted by pushing it to the extreme where this is apparent.

[440] 137 C – 142 A. Similar results follow for τἄλλα from taking ἓν χωρὶς and without parts 159 B – 160 A.

[441] *Tim.*, 52 B.

[442] 141 E, οὐδ᾽ ἄρα οὕτως ἐστιν ὥστε ἓν εἶναι. Damascius says that Plato does not negate ἓν of ἕν, but SIMPLICIUS, *Phys.*, 88, 32, contradicts him.

[443] 142 A; cf. *Soph.*, 248 C ff.

[444] 163 C, 164 B, οὕτω δὴ ἓν οὐκ ὂν οὐκ ἔχει πως οὐδαμῇ.

[445] 142 C, ὡς ἄλλο τι σημαίνον τὸ ἐστι τοῦ ἐν . . . . τοιοῦτον ὂν τὸ ἓν σημαίνειν οἷον μέρη ἔχειν, etc.; cf. *Soph.*, 244 D ff.

[446] 144 B, ἐπὶ πάντα ἄρα πολλὰ ὄντα ἡ οὐσία νενέμηται, etc.; 144 C, πρὸς ἅπαντι ἄρα ἑκάστῳ τῷ τῆς οὐσίας μέρει πρόσεστι τὸ ἕν. Cf. *Soph.*, 245, 256 D E, 258 D E.

[447] 144 E, οὐ μόνον ἄρα τὸ ὂν ἓν πολλά ἐστιν ἀλλὰ καὶ αὐτὸ τὸ ἓν ὑπὸ τοῦ ὄντος διανενεμημένον; cf. 143 A. *Republic*, 525 E, however, points out that thought must restore the abstract unity as fast as analysis divides it: ἀλλ᾽ ἐὰν σὺ κερματίζῃς αὐτὸ, ἐκεῖνοι πολλαπλασιοῦσιν, εὐλαβούμενοι μή ποτε φανῇ τὸ ἓν μὴ ἓν ἀλλὰ πολλὰ μόρια. For the use of κερματίζω here and in the *Parmenides*, cf. *Soph.*, 258 D.

[448] 160 C, ὅτι ἕτερον λέγει τὸ μὴ ὄν . . . . καὶ ἴσμεν ὃ λέγει.

[449] 161 A, 158 A, *Soph.*, 255 A B.

[450] 162 A, δεῖ ἄρα αὐτὸ δεσμὸν ἔχειν τοῦ μὴ εἶναι τὸ εἶναι μὴ ὄν. For the indispensable emendation of what follows, see my note in *A. J. P.*, Vol. XII, pp. 349 ff.

in *Sophist*, 237–46, and it is well described in Theætetus's language there (246 E): συνάπτεται γὰρ ἕτερον ἐξ ἄλλου, μείζω καὶ χαλεπωτέραν φέρον περὶ τῶν ἔμπροσθεν ἀεὶ ῥηθέντων πλάνην.

In view of these facts, it is idle to attempt to date the *Parmenides* and the *Sophist* by their philosophical content. The substantial identity of doctrine does not, of course, exclude many minor differences in the literary form and the secondary purposes of the two dialogues. One object of the *Parmenides*, for example, is to illustrate exhaustively the " both and neither " of the eristic caricatured in the *Euthydemus*. The absolute hypotheses issue in blank negation. In order to make the "both and neither" plausible, some reasoning from the absolute point of view is introduced into the relative hypotheses.[451] Again, it is not easy to say how much importance Plato attached to the third division of the argument in which the contradictions of the first two hypotheses, and, by implication, of all the others, are resolved. Contradictory predicates (the "both") can be true simultaneously—they belong to different times. The "neither" belongs to the instantaneous moment of transition, the "sudden" which is outside of time altogether.[452] It would be possible to read a plausible psychological meaning into this ingenious solution of the Zenonian problem of change.[453] But it cannot easily be translated into the terminology of the theory of ideas. Pure Being admits of neither of the contradictory predicates, and the ideas as *noumena* are outside of space and time. But the "one" which is here spoken of as out of time, and without predicates at the moment of transition, is apparently not the idea, but any one thing which may participate in the ideas. This consideration, and the fact that the ἐξαίφνης is never mentioned again, seem to indicate that it was only a passing fancy.

Lastly, though the main object of the dialogue is the illustration of the ambiguity of the copula, and the fallacy of isolating the ideas, the one is in some passages a representative of the Platonic idea, and in others of the absolute Being which ontology and mysticism recognize even after its banishment from logic. This explains and partly justifies the interpretations of the neo-Platonists and that of Zeller already considered; but does not necessitate any serious qualification of that here proposed.[454]

THE POLITICUS

The *Politicus* quotes the *Sophist*,[455] and is closely related to the *Timæus* and the *Laws*. Its style and its tone of "mixed pathos and satire"[456] in the reluctant abandonment of impracticable ideals[457] mark it as probably late. But there is nothing in the thought to necessitate or strongly confirm this view.[458] It cannot be shown that Zeller, Grote, or, more recently, Pöhlman[459] are led into error in the interpretation of the thought by their assumption that it precedes the *Republic*, and the attempts of

451 *E. g.*, in 149 E–150 the denial of communion between the ideas: οὐδέ τι ἔσται σμικρὸν πλὴν αὐτῆς σμικρότητος.

452 156 D, ἀλλ' ἡ ἐξαίφνης αὕτη φύσις ἄτοπός τις ἐγκάθηται μεταξὺ τῆς κινήσεως καὶ στάσεως, ἐν χρόνῳ οὐδενὶ οὖσα.

453 See *De Plat. idearum doc.*, pp. 44–6.

454 *Supra*, p. 34.

455 257 A, 266 D, 284 B, 286 B.

456 263 D, 266 B C.

457 272 C, 301, 302.

458 For the theory of ideas and ἀνάμνησις, *cf. supra*, p. 44.

459 *Geschichte des antiken Kommunismus.*

Lutoslawski and others to show that the doctrine must be late are either fallacious[460] or prove at the most that it is genuinely Platonic.[461]   Much of the dialogue is devoted to the illustration and perfection of the method of dichotomy set forth in the *Sophist*.[462] In form it is an attempt to define by this method the true statesman — to discriminate him sharply from other rulers and caretakers, and in particular from the politicians, sophists, rhetoricians, and generals, who usurp the name at Athens.[463]

This logical process is illustrated and its tedium relieved by a myth[464] and by elaborate analogies from the art of weaving which also separates, purifies, and re-combines.[465]   Remarks are made on the necessity of thus mingling jest with earnest, and of employing concrete imagery or patterns to illustrate abstract thought.[466]   The charge of undue prolixity is anticipated.[467]   Our object is the elucidation of sound method and for that no briefer treatment of the theme would suffice.[468]   In general, Plato tells us, the clever men who proclaim that all things are subject to number and measure have neglected to observe that there are two distinct types or ideas of measurement:[469] the purely relative mathematical measurement of one thing against another,[470] and the measurement in reference to fixed, absolute standards of the suitable, the just mean or measure in every art and procedure.   Long and short as terms of censure applied to a philosophical discussion have no meaning except in the latter sense.   That such absolute standards exist Plato cannot delay to prove except by a summary form of argument employed in the same way to cut short discussion in the *Phœdo* and *Timœus*.[471]   The proposition to be proved is indissolubly bound up with another proposition which the opponent can hardly reject.   In this case, as surely as the various arts and sciences exist, so surely is the μέτριον or absolute measure of fitness a reality.   For all arts and sciences postulate it.   This simple thought has often

---

[460] 309 C, ἀληθῆ δόξαν . . . . θείαν φημὶ ἐν δαιμονίῳ γίγνεσθαι γένει does not mean that truth, etc., is "to be seen only in divine souls," *cf. supra*, p. 39.   In 272 C, συναγυρμὸν φρονήσεως does not mean "an ideal totality of individual endeavors . . . . transmitted from generation to generation."   The word is used here not only for the first but for the last time.   CAMPBELL's citation of *Sophist*, 259 D, is irrelevant; *cf. supra*, n. 439.   The use of δύναμις proves nothing; *cf. supra*, p. 49.   308 C has nothing to do with the modern notion of building up a science by selection, "while useless observations and notions are rejected;" nor with *Cratyl.*, 438 E.   The statement, 308 E, that the royal art puts to death, τοὺς μὴ δυναμένους κοινωνεῖν, is not an admission of the "impossibility of proof in moral questions," and in any case is virtually identical with *Protag.*, 322 D, τὸν μὴ δυνάμενον αἰδοῦς καὶ δίκης μετέχειν κτείνειν.   "The unity of universal science" is not affirmed in 258 E, or *Sophist*, 257 C, except as the concept or idea (like any other concept) is one "already" in *Rep.*, 438 C D.   The question is merely: Shall our dichotomies start from the concept "science" or from some other concept as, *e. g.*, ἐμπειρία?   *Cf. Soph.*, 219 A, with *Gorg.*, 462 B C.

[461] The employment of a periphrasis in *Phœdo*, 99 B, for the technical term συναίτιον used in the *Politicus*, 281 D, 287 C, 281 C E, etc., and in the *Timœus*, 46 C, and nowhere else, proves nothing.   A periphrasis is used for the idea in the "late" *Philebus*, 27 A, τὸ δουλεῦον εἰς γένεσιν αἰτίᾳ.   The word in an allied sense occurs in *Gorgias*, 519 B.   It is possible that it did not occur to Plato's mind in writing *Phœdo*, 99 B, but more probable that he deliberately preferred the periphrasis which is far more impressive in the context: ἄλλο μέν τί ἐστι τὸ αἴτιον τῷ ὄντι, ἄλλο δ' ἐκεῖνο ἄνευ οὗ τὸ αἴτιον οὐκ ἄν ποτ' εἴη αἴτιον.

[462] See CAMPBELL on 263 D.

[463] In 267 successive dichotomies have distinguished the statesman only as the caretaker of the biped human flock. It remains to define his specific service to this flock, 287 B, 291 B, 303 C ff.

[464] 269 ff.

[465] For the characteristic Platonic generalization of διακριτική *cf.* 282 B C with *Soph.*, 226 D, and "already" *Cratyl.*, 388 B C.   *Cf. Phileb.*, 23 D.

[466] 268 D, 277 ff.   [467] 283 ff.

[468] 285 D, 286.

[469] 283-5.   The κομψοί are apparently the Pythagoreans.

[470] πρὸς ἄλληλα, 284 B.   The parallel with *Rep.*, 531 A, ἀλλήλοις ἀναμετροῦντες, seems to have been overlooked.

[471] 284 D, ὡς ἄρα ἡγητέον ὁμοίως, etc.   *Phœdo*, 77 A, εἰς τὸ ὁμοίως εἶναι, etc.   *Tim.*, 51 D.

been misunderstood.[472]   It is implied in the doctrine of ideas,[473] in Plato's polemic against mere relativity,[474] and even in the remark attributed to Prodicus in *Phædrus*, 267 B, αὐτὸς . . . . ὧν δεῖ λόγων τέχνην· δεῖν δὲ οὔτε μακρῶν οὔτε βραχέων, ἀλλά μετρίων.   The fact that it is explicitly stated "for the first time" in the *Politicus* proves no more than does the fact that it is never stated again.   Plato happened to formulate it only once, but it is clearly involved in *Republic*, 531 A, ἀλλήλοις ἀναμετροῦντες, etc.

The myth may be profitably compared with the *Timæus*, *Philebus*, and *Laws*, but cannot be pressed to yield developments or contradictions of doctrine.   Its service to the argument is merely to distinguish the mythical ideal of a shepherd of the people, who plays providence to his flock, from the modern ruler who leaves other specialists to feed, clothe, and house them, and confines himself to his specific task of government.[475]   In other words, it emphasizes the demand often repeated in Plato for a precise definition of the specific function and service of the royal or kingly art; and, as Zeller says, rejects with a touch of irony ideals drawn from a supposed state of nature.   This ruler is further discriminated, as in the *Euthydemus* and *Gorgias*,[476] from the pretenders or subordinate ministers who usurp his name, the rhetorician,[477] the general,[478] the dicast.[479]   Lastly, his special task is defined.   As implied in the *Meno* and *Euthydemus*, and stated in the *Republic*, he is to teach virtue and inculcate right opinion.[480]   And that his teaching may be effective and the seed fall in good ground, he is, like the rulers of the *Republic* and the *Laws*, to control marriages and the propagation of the race—especially with a view to harmonizing and blending the oppositions of the energetic and sedate temperaments.[481]

The accompanying classification and criticism of forms of government imply no change of opinion unless we assume that Plato was bound to repeat himself verbatim. The classification of the *Republic* is first the ideal state governed by philosophic wisdom, whether βασιλεία or ἀριστοκρατία,[482] and then in progressive decadence timarchy, oligarchy, democracy, tyranny.   The *Politicus* apparently recognizes seven states: one, the right state (302 C), the only Polity deserving the name (293 C), in which the rulers are ἐπιστήμονες.   Six others are obtained by distinguishing the good and bad forms of the three types recognized in ordinary Greek usage.[483]   We thus get monarchy or royalty, and tyranny, aristocracy, and oligarchy, and democracy, lawful and lawless.[484]   The differences are due mainly to the necessity of presenting a continuous

---

[472] *E. g.*, by SIEBECK, *Untersuchungen zur Phil. d. Griechen*, pp. 92 ff., who over-emphasizes the analogies with the πέρας of the *Philebus*.

[473] The μετρίου γένεσις, 284 A B, to which every artist looks, is virtually the idea which he tries to realize, *Gorg.*, 503 E.

[474] *Cf.* πρὸς ἄλληλα four times in 283, 284 with *Theætet.*, 160 B, 182 B, *Parmen.*, 164 C.

[475] 274, 275.

[476] *Gorg.*, 517 B, 521 D.

[477] 304 D, *Euthydem.*, 289 D E.   *Cf. Gorg.*, 464–6, 502 E.

[478] 304 E, *Euthydem.*, 290 B.

[479] 305 B.

[480] 309 C D.

[481] 309, 310. The *Republic* recognizes the control of marriage, 460, and the importance and difficulty of reconciling the two temperaments. 503 C. It does not happen to bring the two ideas together. The *Laws*, 773 A B, does.

[482] 445 D. It cannot be a democracy, because φιλόσοφον . . . . πλῆθος ἀδύνατον εἶναι = *Polit.*, 292 E, μῶν οὖν δοκεῖ πλῆθός γε ἐν πόλει ταύτην τὴν ἐπιστήμην δυνατὸν εἶναι κτήσασθαι.

[483] *Rep.*, 338 D. Pindar., *Pyth.*, II, 87.

[484] *Polit.*, 291, 301, 302 C ff.

descending scale in the *Republic*. This leaves no place for a good form of democracy or a good monarchy apart from the ideal kingdom.[485] The fundamental distinction of the scientific state once noted, Plato plays freely with the conventional terminology, and no inferences can be drawn from his "contradictions." There are countless forms of government if one cares to look beyond the conspicuous εἴδη.[486] In the *Republic* the good oligarchy, the aristocracy of the *Politicus*, is a timarchy. In the *Menexenus* the good democracy of Athens is an aristocracy governed by kings![487] In the *Laws*,[488] from the historical point of view, all governments are regarded as variations of the two mother types, the Persian absolutism and the Athenian democracy. But in respect of the ease with which reform may be effected the tyranny ranks first, the kingdom second, a certain type of democracy third, and oligarchy last.[489] I have already discussed the significance of the opposition of the two temperaments for the definition of the virtues and the antinomies of the minor dialogues.[490] Grote strangely ignores this when he affirms that these difficulties are not touched in the *Politicus*.

THE PHILEBUS

The *Philebus* was selected by Dionysius of Halicarnassus as a type of Plato's simpler Socratic style. The majority of recent critics more plausibly see signs of Plato's later manner in the poverty of the dramatic setting, and the curious elaboration of phrasing and logical framework. The introduction presents again the objections to the theory of ideas advanced in the *Parmenides*, and, like the *Parmenides*, but more explicitly, hints that these puzzles are due to the limitations of human reason.[491] It bids us disregard them and, assuming ideas, to deal with them and our subject according to the true dialectical method set forth in the *Phædrus*.[492] It does not state that these metaphysical problems must be solved before we can so proceed.[493] It merely says that we must come to such an understanding about them as will prevent the puzzle of the one and many from confusing our inquiry.[494] We have no reason to look for a solution of them in the subsequent course of the argument. None is given. There was, as we have seen, none to offer.[495] The attempts of modern scholars to find one are very ingenious.[496] But they are not supported by Plato's words, and they proceed on the erroneous assumption that he thought it possible to give any other than a poetical and mythical account of the absolute, or to say more of the *noumenon* than

---

[485] The *Politicus* does not describe the development of one form from the other but merely states the order of preference among the lawful and lawless forms of the three types. CAMPBELL, *Intr.*, p. xliv, overlooks all this when he treats as proofs of lateness the addition of βασιλεία as one of the lower forms, and the depression of ὀλιγαρχία below δημοκρατία.

[486] *Rep.*, 544 D.   [487] 238 D.   [488] 693 D.

[489] 710 E. The paradox, τυραννουμένην μοι δότε τὴν πόλιν, 709 E, is literally incompatible with the associations of τύραννος in the *Republic*, but the notion of a revolution accomplished by arbitrary power is found in 501 A, 540 E.

[490] *Supra*, pp. 11, 13, 15, n. 59.   [491] *Supra*, pp. 36, 37.

[492] *Supra*, n. 70.   [493] 15 C, 16 A B.

[494] *Cf.* on this point my criticism of JACKSON, *A. J. P.*, Vol. IX, pp. 279, 280. Even SCHNEIDER (*Plat. Metaphysik*, p. 53), whose interpretation of this part of the *Philebus* is excellent, does not make it clear that the metaphysical problem is merely evaded by the assumption of ideas and the method κατ' εἴδη.

[495] *Supra*, p. 36.

[496] As types of all may be cited: SCHNEIDER, *Platonische Metaphysik;* SIEBECK, *Untersuchungen zur Philosophie der Griechen*, II; *Plato's Lehre von der Materie;* HENRY JACKSON, *Plato's Later Theory of Ideas*. See *A. J. P.*, Vol. IX, p. 282.

that it exists.[497]   The elaborate apparatus of classifications and categories employed to decide whether pleasure or intelligence is more nearly akin to the good is due, apart from Plato's interest in dialectical exercise, to his unwillingness to treat the problem of the good in isolation.   His imagination and religious feeling require him to associate the ethical good of man with the principles of order, harmony, measure, beauty, and good in the universe.   We thus get many interesting analogies with the *Timæus*, but no solution of the problem of ideas.   The direct classification and estimate of the different species of pleasure and intelligence, which was all the ethical problem required,[498] is subordinated to a larger classification of all things which, however, deepens and enriches our conception of the psychological and ontological relations of the elements of merely human good and happiness.[499]

The terms of this classification are the πέρας, the ἄπειρον, the μικτόν or mixture of the two, and the αἰτία or its cause.   These terms represent, for the purposes of the argument, characteristic Platonic generalizations[500] of the ideas naturally associated with these words.   Whatever else they may mean is at the most suggestion and analogy.   Πέρας is a generalization of the idea of limit—whether it be the limitation of matter by form, of chaos by the principle of order and measure, of appetite by reason, or of the indeterminate genus by a definite number of species and sub-species. It is the idea of the *Timæus*, so far as that is conceived as a principle of limit and form stamped upon chaos.   But it is not the Platonic idea—the hypostatization of the concept—for the purposes of metaphysical theory.[501]

The ἄπειρον denotes among other things (1) the indefinite multiplicity of particulars as opposed to the unity of the idea—a conception found elsewhere in Plato.[502] Plato generalizes the term σῶμα for "matter" in 29 D.   (2) Indeterminate matter as opposed to the form or limit that shapes it.   In this sense it may be "equated" with the space, matter, or mother of all generation in the *Timæus*, 50 D.[503] (3) Indeterminate

---

[497] *Cf.* EMERSON, *Representative Men*, "Plato," "No power of genius has ever yet had the smallest success in explaining existence. The perfect enigma remains. But there is an injustice in assuming this ambition for Plato."

[498] The net result of the introduction is (19 B) εἴδη γάρ μοι δοκεῖ νῦν ἐρωτᾶν ἡδονῆς ἡμᾶς Σωκράτης, etc.

[499] 23 C ff.

[500] So Plato generalizes μάχη, *Euthyd.*, 271, 272: κήλησις (ἐπῳδῶν τέχνη), *ibid.*, 289 E; θηρευτική, *ibid.*, 290 B; *Laws*, 823 B; *Polit.*, 299 D; *Rep.*, 373 B; *Soph.*, 221, 222; πλεονεξία, *Laws*, 906 C, *cf. Symp.*, 186 C, *Gorg.*, 508 A; κιβδηλεία, *Laws*, 916 D; ποίησις, *Symp.*, 205 B; ἔρως, *ibid.*, 205 D, and *passim; γένεσις, Polit.*, 261 B, etc.; διακριτική, *Soph.*, 226 C; πιθανουργική, *ibid.*, 222 C; κολακεία, *Gorg.*, 463 B ff.; the comparative degree, τὸ μᾶλλόν τε καὶ ἧττον, *Phileb.*, 24; and many minor examples, *Polit.*, 279, 280, 289.

[501] SCHNEIDER, p. 133, and SIEBECK, p. 73, make it a mediating principle between the idea and phenomena. But Plato never speaks of the "idea," but only of the ideas or the idea of something. Πέρας is itself an idea and is the cause of limit, in any given case, precisely as the idea of whiteness is the cause of white, or the idea of dog the cause of a dog.

[502] *Theætet.*, 147 D, ἐπειδὴ ἄπειροι τὸ πλῆθος . . . . ξυλλαβεῖν εἰς ἓν implies the method of *Phileb.*, 15, 16. *Cf. Rep.*, 525 A; *Polit.*, 262 D; *Soph.*, 256 E; *Parmen.*, 158 C. SCHNEIDER, p. 4, n. 1, notes this meaning, but still insists that the ἄπειρον of the *Philebus* primarily means indeterminate matter, which he rightly shows is not = μὴ ὄν, p. 5 (*cf. supra*, n. 261), but wrongly denies to be virtually identical with space. See SIEBECK, p. 84. The *Timæus* does not explicitly identify "matter" and "space" merely because it does not distinctly separate the two ideas. See *A. J. P.*, Vol. IX, p. 416. But whether we call it matter or space, the χώρα, the πανδεχές, the mother of generation is one.

[503] SIEBECK compares it as the antithesis of the idea to the μὴ ὄν, the ἕτερον of the *Sophist*, the matter or space of the *Timæus*, the principle of necessity or evil, and the μέγα καὶ μικρόν. More precisely (p. 89), the ἄπειρον is the mediating link between the θάτερον of the *Sophist* and the χώρα of the *Timæus*. Now these terms undoubtedly have this in common, that they are variously opposed to the ideas, but Plato employs them in different connections and we cannot equate them. SIEBECK argues (pp. 58 ff.) that the absolute μὴ ὄν abandoned in the *Sophist* (258 E) must mean something. He finds it in the absolute hypothesis of

physical and chemical "process," as opposed to ideally or mathematically defined "states."[504]   (4) The insatiate, limitless character of undisciplined desire and appetite—a conception which we have met in the *Gorgias*.[505]

The μικτὸν is the mixture or union of πέρας and ἄπειρον in any or all of these senses giving rise to various γενέσεις, both in the world of matter and in souls.[506]   As the union of matter and form it may be "equated" with the "offspring" of the idea and the "mother" in the *Timæus*.[507]   As the mixed life of pleasure and intelligence it obviously may not.[508]

Αἰτία is the principle of cause in general, and in particular the cause of the due mixture of pleasure and intelligence in the happy life.[509]   In the one sense it may be identified with the Demiurgus who embodies the principle of cause in the *Timæus*.[510] The ultimate cause is conceived by Plato as beneficial intelligence which is virtually synonymous with the good. He intentionally confounds the good in human life with the good in the universe. It is possible, then, to say that God, or the good, or beneficent intelligence is the cause alike of the cosmos or ordered world and of the well ordered life.[511] We may identify the supreme mind (νοῦς) with the Demiurgus of the *Timæus* and the Idea of Good in the *Republic*. We may conceive the ideas as thoughts of God, identify God with the sum of his thoughts (νόησις νοήσεως) and so bring the ideas under the principle of αἰτία as not only formal but efficient causes.[512] But in all this we are mechanically "equating" the terminology and imagery—the literary machinery, so to speak, of three distinct lines of thought in three different dialogues, for the sake of attributing to Plato a rigid and ingenious metaphysical system wholly foreign to his spirit.

We have already discussed the psychology and the main ethical argument of the

the *Parmenides* as the antithesis of the ἓν regarded as the symbol of the principle of the ideas. From this it is an easy step to identifying it with matter which is also the antithesis of the idea. But it is not true that the absolute μὴ ὄν must mean something. Plato's rejection of it in the *Sophist* is sincere, and is confirmed by the *Parmenides* which makes it unspeakable and unthinkable. The absolute ὄν, as we have seen, was reinstated for religious and metaphysical purposes, as it is by many philosophers of every age. There was no such motive for forcing a meaning upon the absolute μὴ ὄν, and the identification of it with matter is, as we have seen, quite impossible. (*Supra*, n. 261.)

SIEBECK then proceeds to associate the logical ἄπειρον and the θάτερον with space and to attribute to Plato an "intelligible" as well as a phenomenal space by pressing all passages in which the logical relations of concepts are expressed in spatial terms (p. 90). As the human mind naturally thinks logical determinations in spatial imagery, he has no difficulty in finding such passages. But plainly the method is vicious. We cannot infer an intelligible "space" or the identity of θάτερον and space because the ideas are spoken of as "living apart," or "included" in a larger idea, or because the method of dichotomy proceeds to the right and leaves on the left the other of the particular idea pursued. Still less can we infer it from the νοητὸς τόπος, or from the fact that move-

ment and measure are spoken of in connection with the ideas, and movement and measure imply space!

[504] *Phileb.*, 24 B, 25 C, 26 A.

[505] 27 E, 31 A, *Gorg.*, 492–4, *supra*, p. 24.

[506] 27 D, 25 E, 26 B, καὶ ἐν ψυχαῖς αὖ πάμπολλα, which alone refutes the equation, ἄπειρον = matter.

[507] 50 D.

[508] There is a slight equivocation in the assumption (27 D) that the "mixed" life of pleasure and intelligence belongs to the μικτόν of πέρας and ἄπειρον.

[509] 26 E, 23 D, 64 C.

[510] In 30 D the βασιλικὴν ψυχήν, etc., = the soul of the world, and the αἰτίας δύναμιν = the Demiurgus.

[511] *Cf. Idea of Good*, pp. 188, 189, n. 2.

[512] SCHNEIDER identifies God not with the Idea of Good, but with the ideas. The ideas, he argues, must be real and they must be thoughts. They are, therefore, thoughts of God. We have already considered this theory, *supra*, p. 38. It is for the modern systematic philosopher the most plausible escape from the difficulty of positing two distinct *noumena*, God and the Ideas. Perhaps Plato would have accepted it, if it had been presented to him. Unlike the majority of its advocates, SCHNEIDER does not misinterpret particular passages in order to support it. He merely combines and equates lines of thought which Plato left unfinished and distinct.

Philebus, and seen that neither contradicts or appreciably modifies the doctrine of the earlier dialogues.[513]   There remains only the question whether the demonstration of the unreality of pleasure presupposes, or, as Zeller still maintains, is presupposed by, the shorter proof of the *Republic*.   Believing that the *Philebus* is probably late, I am logically committed to the first branch of the alternative.   But this opinion is entirely compatible with the view that the differences between the two treatments of the theme are not in themselves sufficient to show which must be the earlier.   It is impossible to determine *a priori* whether the slighter treatment is an anticipation or a résumé of the fuller discussion.   The main doctrine was always a part of Plato's thought, as appears from the *Gorgias*, the *Phœdo*, and the *Phœdrus*.[514]   The differences between the *Republic* and the *Philebus* have been much exaggerated.   The abbreviation of the argument in the *Republic* is sufficiently explained by the subordinate place which it occupies in the scheme of the entire work.   It affords no proof of the date, and no presumption even of a change of doctrine.[515]

THE THEÆTETUS

The date of the *Theœtetus* has been much debated on external grounds.[516]   Its wealth of thought and dramatic vivacity of style make it one of the most difficult dialogues to classify.   In psychological depth and dialectical acuteness it ranks with the *Sophist, Philebus*, and *Parmenides*, many of the thoughts of which it anticipates or suggests.[517]   But it has nothing of their dogmatic finality of manner.   Socrates is still the midwife delivering ingenuous youth of opinions which fail to stand the test of the elenchus.   And the conclusion is an avowal of Socratic ignorance.[518]

Before losing ourselves in details we must recall why this is so.   There are two reasons: (1) The formal quest for an absolute definition always fails in Plato.[519]   (2) It is not possible to define knowledge or explain error.   We can only describe and classify different stages of cognition and various forms of error.   All seemingly intelligible explanation rests on material images, like Plato's figure of the wax tablets and the aviary.   But these analogies either commit us to sheer materialism and the flowing philosophy, or they explain nothing.   No spatial image can represent the synthetic

---

[513] *Supra*, pp. 24, 43, 45 ff.

[514] *Supra*, p. 24.

[515] See ZELLER, p. 548. The question whether pleasure or φρόνησις is the good (*Rep.*, 505 B) need not be a specific reference to the *Philebus*.   It is virtually raised in the *Protagoras* and *Gorgias*. Zeller's table of agreements between the *Rep.* and *Phileb.* merely proves the unity of Plato's thought.   *Rep.*, 584 D – 585 A – E, 586 A – C, which he cites, present, at the most, different imagery.   The thoughts are in the *Philebus*.   That the *Philebus* does not refer specifically to the Idea of Good is no stranger than is the fact that no other dialogue does.   On the other hand LUTOS-LAWSKI's objection (p. 470) that the difficulty, *Rep.*, 505 B, that the sought-for φρόνησις is φρόνησις τοῦ ἀγαθοῦ is disposed of by our observation that the reference, if reference there must be, is to the *Charmides*, *supra*, n. 61.   JACKSON argues

that the *Republic* is not yet acquainted with the thought that the neutral state implies not absolute quiet in the body, but slight motions which do not cross the threshold of consciousness.   But the thought is implied in *Rep.*   Cf. *supra*, n. 328.

[516] See ZELLER, p. 406, n. 1; CAMPBELL's Introduction; LUTOSLAWSKI, p. 385.   It is on the whole more probable that the battle in which Theætetus was wounded belongs to the Corinthian war, 394–387, than to the year 368.

[517] Cf. *supra*, pp. 33, 34, 55, nn. 179, 182, 389.

[518] 149 ff., 161 AB, 209 E, 210 C.

[519] Cf. *supra*, p. 13, p. 16, n. 86.   JOWETT says, Vol. V, p. 119: "We cannot suppose that Plato thought a definition of knowledge to be impossible."   But it is impossible, and that for the very reasons suggested by Plato.

unity of consciousness and memory. None can explain the comparison of past and present impressions in an unextended focal point of consciousness. None can represent except in the vaguest poetic figure[520] a psychical mechanism that now operates correctly, yielding right opinion, and now incorrectly, resulting in error.[521] On the other hand, if we invoke the absolute unity of mind behind our imagined mechanism, we are merely moving in a circle. We reaffirm our faith in the immaterial soul, but we can offer no intelligible explanation of degrees in cognition or of the psychological process of error.[522]

The quest for a definition, then, fails, as Plato expected it to do. But the analysis is carried far enough (1) to refute to Plato's satisfaction all psychologies of pure materialism or relativism;[523] (2) to justify a purely logical and practical treatment of the μὴ ὄν, ψευδὴς δόξα, and similar fallacies in the *Sophist*.[524] This and the immense wealth of psychological suggestion scattered by the way are the chief positive results of the dialogue.[525]

It has been repeatedly analyzed in detail.[526] As in the *Gorgias* and *Philebus*,[527] much of the argument is purely dramatic, directed only against the cruder forms of the theory combated.[528] The ingenious attempts to reconstruct the doctrines of contemporary thinkers from Plato's polemic are more apt to confuse our understanding of Plato than to add to our knowledge of Protagoras, Aristippus, or Antisthenes.[529] As Professor Campbell says: "Whoever the contemporaries were to whom Plato refers as the disciples of Protagoras, he aims beyond them at the whole relative side of Greek thought of which Heraclitus was the most prominent exponent."

The identification of the ἄνθρωπος μέτρον, the πάντα ῥεῖ, and the definition that knowledge is sensible perception, is a part of Plato's literary machinery which we must accept untroubled by nice historic scruples. The ἄνθρωπος μέτρον is not a scientific or philosophic principle, but a rhetorical paradox or truism embodying a

---

[520] *Cf. Tim.*, 37 AB, with *Theœtet.*, 194 B.

[521] ZELLER, p. 590, thinks that the section on ψευδὴς δόξα is an indirect refutation of the definition that knowledge is ἀληθὴς δόξα. He says that the difficulty of explaining false opinion arises only from the assumption that knowledge is "right opinion." That is not so, either absolutely or in Plato. The ultimate difficulty is: if the mind *apprehends* as a psychic unit, how is *mis-apprehension*, as distinguished from non-apprehension, possible? BONITZ is undoubtedly right in affirming that the question for Plato is not so much the fact or possibility of error as the psychological explanation. (Pp. 83, 89. *Cf.* my paper, *De Platonis idearum doctrina*, pp. 17–19.) The length of the "digression" is justified by the interest attached to the problem of ψευδὴς δόξα and the psychological analysis that it provokes. It is a "digression" and a negative result only for those who naïvely assume that Plato himself expected to reach a positive definition.

[522] 184 CD, 200 AB.

[523] *Supra*, p. 34, n. 283. *Cf. Theœtet.*, 184 C ff. Up to 183 C the identity of ἐπιστήμη and αἴσθησις is refuted only so far as it depends on extreme Protagorean relativity or Heracliteanism, which makes all thought and speech impossible. κατά γε τὴν τοῦ πάντα κινεῖσθαι μέθοδον.

[524] *Cf. supra*, p. 55.

[525] On its relation to the theory of ideas *cf. supra*, p. 33.

[526] By BONITZ, NATORP, CAMPBELL, JOWETT, GROTE, etc.

[527] *Supra*, n. 137.

[528] *Supra*, n. 7. Note especially the tone of 163–6, where avowedly eristic arguments are employed against the literal identification of ἐπιστήμη and αἴσθησις. Observe the persiflage of 156, 157, 167 A, 179, 180. NATORP, *Philol.*, Vol. L, p. 263, thinks 161 B–165 E a parody of Antisthenes's attack on Protagoras, 166–8 C being Protagoras's defense. Any allusion to eristic may be in a sense a parody of Antisthenes or of any other eristic contemporary. Protagoras himself is represented as employing the μὴ ὄν quibble, 167 A. *Cf. supra*, n. 405, and *Euthydem.*, 286 C.

[529] See NATORP's acute *Forschungen zur Geschichte des Erkenntnissproblems im Alterthum*, and his "Protagoras und sein Doppelgänger," *Philologus*, Vol. L, pp. 262 ff. NATORP's analyses retain their value, even if we doubt the possibility of reconstructing Protagoras. For Antisthenes and the *Theœtetus* see the phantastic conjectures of JOEL, *Der echte und der xenophontische Sokrates*, Vol. II, pp. 839 ff.

practical tendency of the age repugnant to Plato's taste and feeling. This seems to be overlooked in the controversy between Natorp (*Philologus*, 50) and Gomperz, as to the meaning of the formula. Plato, as Natorp shows, explicitly affirms the thought to be: things are to (each and every) man as they appear to him. If sugar tastes bitter to the sick man, it is bitter to him—there is no other test. But there is no evidence and no probability that Protagoras had systematically drawn out the consequences of generalizing this proposition in its application to ethical and logical truths. He did not need to ask himself whether he meant by ἄνθρωπος this, that and the other man, or human cognitive faculties in general. He took ὄντα, as he found it in Greek idiom, without distinguishing things, qualities, and truths—though his simplest examples would naturally be qualities. By ὡς he presumably meant "that," but "that" and "how" are closely associated in Greek idiom and are often confounded in popular not to say in Platonic usage. If he used φαίνεται and φαντασία he probably did not distinguish the "it seems to me" of actual sensation from the "it seems to me" of any opinion,[530] and Plato avails himself of the ambiguity for the half serious περιτροπὴ that since Protagoras's "truth" does not seem true to the majority, it is admitted by Protagoras himself to be oftener false than true.[531]

Πάντα ῥεῖ Plato himself accepts for the phenomenal world.[532] As a metaphysical dogma it is tantamount to materialism in that all materialists are more or less consciously Heracliteans, though all Heracliteans need not be materialists.[533] As a neo-Heraclitean paradox it is the negation of the ideas, of the universal, of rational logic and speech.[534] As a rhetorical formula it is the symbol of the restless spirit of innovation which Plato detested.[535] Before generalizing and restating for serious refutation what he conceives to be the common psychological presuppositions of these catchwords, Plato covers them with persiflage and assails them with arguments which he admits to be rhetorical and eristic. There is no probability that the representatives of these doctrines could have explained their meaning or defended themselves as well as Plato has done it for them. So far as we know, he is the first thinker who was capable of distinguishing, dividing, classifying, and generalizing ideas, of noting the affinities and differences of philosophic doctrines, and of translating them freely into different terminologies. All other early thinkers, like the majority of thinkers always, are the prisoners of their formulas and can only abound in their own sense. Plato, as Emerson says, "needs no barbaric war paint, for he can define and divide," and he delights to prick with the keen point of his dialectic the bubbles of imagery, rhetoric, and antithesis blown by his predecessors. Heraclitus means well when he says that the one is united by disunion,[536] or that the hands at once draw and repel the bow.[537] But the epigram vanishes under logical analysis. The pre-Socratics discourse, in a

[530] Cf. *supra*, p. 48.

[531] 170, 171. Cf. *Euthyd.*, 286 C, καὶ τούς τε ἄλλους ἀνατρέπων καὶ αὐτὸς αὑτόν.

[532] *Cratyl.*, 439 D; *Symp.*, 207 D; *Timæus, passim.*

[533] *Theœtet.*, 155 E, 156 A.

[534] *Cratyl.*, 439, 440; *Theœtet.*, 179, 180; *Soph.*, 249 D.

[535] PATER, *Plato and Platonism*, pp. 16-20.

[536] *Symp.*, 187 A.

[537] *Rep.*, 439 B. The saying is Heraclitean in tone.

fine imaged style, about Being, but a plain man can not be sure of their meaning.[538] Absolute formulas, like πάντα ῥεῖ, πᾶν ἕν, πάντων μέτρον ἄνθρωπος, have an imposing sound, but if we press for their interpretation, prove to be either truisms or paradoxes, destructive of intelligible speech.[539]

It is an ingenious sport to construct for Protagoras some subtle and nicely guarded modern system of phenomenalism. But we must then pass over the purely dramatic parts of Plato's discussion, and limit ourselves to his final and seriously meant arguments against the psychology of materialism and the logic of relativism. There are two such arguments which neither Plato nor his critics are careful to distinguish sharply: (1) The first is that the senses are organs of mind and that sense perception itself implies the "soul" or some central "synthetic unity."[540] This, if fully understood, is conclusive against the sensationist materialism of Condillac's statue. But Plato's chief interest is in the second argument derived from this. (2) The objects of each sense we can perceive only through the specific organ of that sense.[541] But the general common categories of Being, not-Being, number, likeness, difference, the same, and the other,[542] as also ethical universals, and the abstract definitions of sensuous qualities[543] are apprehended without subsidiary organs solely through the action of the mind, and its reflections on the contradictions of sense. Availing himself of the double meaning of οὐσία (1) logical essence, (2) reality, truth, Plato argues, as in the Phædo,[544] that truth and reality are attained only by the "pure" thought of the soul acting independently of the body.

A modern Theætetus, of course, might deny that abstract thought has no bodily organ, or that its objects are more "real" than the perceptions of sense. But the absolute identification of αἴσθησις and ἐπιστήμη is sufficiently refuted, and the suggestiveness of this definition having been exhausted, a fresh start is made with the definition "knowledge is true opinion." But this implies that we understand erroneous opinion, and error proves to be inexplicable. The attempt to explain it calls forth many interesting analogies and distinctions.[545] One large class of errors is accounted for as arising from the wrong reference of present sensations to stored up memory images.[546] The distinction between latent or potential and actual knowledge postpones the final difficulty.[547] But in the end it must be faced: error as a matter of fact occurs in "pure" thought. How can pure thought misapprehend its object? A bodiless intelligence either touches or does not touch the object of thought. We can understand

[538] Soph., 242, 243.

[539] Cratyl., 439, 440; Theætet., 183 A B, 179 D E; Soph., 249 C D.

[540] 184 D, δεινὸν γάρ που, ὦ παῖ, εἰ πολλαί τινες ἐν ἡμῖν, ὥσπερ ἐν δουρείοις ἵπποις, αἰσθήσεις ἐγκάθηνται, ἀλλὰ μὴ εἰς μίαν τινὰ ἰδέαν, εἴτε ψυχὴν εἴτε ὅ τι δεῖ καλεῖν, πάντα ταῦτα ξυντείνει, etc.

[541] 185 A C. LUTOSLAWSKI, pp. 276, 372, fancies that this is an anticipation of the modern "law of specific energies of the senses," "already" glanced at in Rep., 352 E, but showing progress in the formulation here. The modern law could not be anticipated without knowledge of the nerves, but Empedocles "already" remarked of the senses, οὐ δύνασθαι τὰ ἀλλήλων κρίνειν, Theophr. sens., 7, Dox. 500.

[542] 185 C D. [543] 186 A B. Cf. supra, nn. 221 and 222.

[544] Theætet., 187 A; Phædo, 65 C.

[545] Cf. supra, p. 55; n. 520 with text.

[546] 193, 194. The memory image is treated as knowledge, εἰδέναι.

[547] 197. This is the distinction invoked in Euthyd., 277, 278, to meet the eristic fallacy of the alternative εἰδέναι ἢ μὴ εἰδέναι.

the confusion of one object with another, the misplacement of cognitions, only in terms of spatial imagery which, if accepted literally, is materialism again, and if taken as a symbol implies the synthetic unity of mind behind it, and so renews the puzzle in infinite regress.[548] Modern metaphysicians evade the difficulty by assuming an infinite thought of which our erring thought is a part. Their task then is to preserve the individuality of a consciousness that is part of another mind. This problem disappears in a mist of theistic language enveloping pantheistic doctrine. Plato does not soar to these heights, but having carried the psychological analysis to the limit, he disposes of the equation, ἐπιστήμη = λόγος ἀληθής, by pointing out a sharp practical distinction between knowledge and right opinion. True opinions may be imparted by persuasion and hearsay about things which we can know only if we have seen them.[549]

The third and final suggestion is that knowledge is right opinion coupled with λόγος.[550] This is for practical purposes substantially Plato's own view.[551] Transcendentally knowledge is the apprehension of the idea. In human life it is the dialectician's reasoned mastery of his opinions implying stability, consistency, and the power to render exact account of beliefs. Plato reserves the terms knowledge, intelligence, pure reason, for the man who co-ordinates his opinions, unifies them by systematic reference to higher principles, ideals, and "ideas," and who can defend them in fair argument against all comers.[552] This is not a definition, but it is quite as good a description as the most modern of his critics can produce. This view is set forth in the *Republic* in the context necessary to make it intelligible. It would not have suited Plato's design to repeat or anticipate that description in the *Theœtetus* which is cast in the form of a dialogue of search. Moreover, it is one thing to give a general definition of knowledge and another thing to describe the state of mind to which the term science or knowledge κατ' ἐξοχὴν is applicable. Sensible perception is not a synonym or definition of knowledge, nor, according to Plato, knowledge in the highest sense. But it is the most certain and the only knowledge we possess of some kinds of objects. And the recognition of this fact in various passages of the *Theœtetus* would in itself make a satisfactory all-inclusive definition of knowledge impossible.[553]

Accordingly Plato brings the dialogue to a plausible conclusion by discussing (and rejecting) various possible meanings of λόγος, none of which yields a good defini-

---

[548] 200 A B. The original ἀπορία arose from the unmediated antithesis εἰδέναι ἢ μὴ εἰδέναι – a conscious fallacy, as the language of 188 A and *Euthyd.*, 277, 278, shows. Psychology is enriched, and the practical fallacy is disposed of, by the distinction of grades and kinds of cognition, but in the end our analysis brings us to an indivisible act of psychic apprehension which either is or is not.

[549] 201 B; Grote triumphs in the admission that sense-perception is, after all, sometimes knowledge; cf. *supra*, n. 324.

[550] 201 C D.

[551] The *Timœus* (51 D) sharply distinguishes νοῦς and ἀληθὴς δόξα, but adds τὸ μὲν ἀεὶ μετ' ἀληθοῦς λόγου, τὸ δὲ ἄλογον. In the *Meno*, 98 A, right opinions became knowledge when bound αἰτίας λογισμῷ. In *Symp.*, 202 A, ὀρθὰ δοξάζειν — ἄνευ τοῦ

ἔχειν λόγον δοῦναι is opposed to ἐπιστήμη. In ethics fixed, stable, true opinion is virtually a synonym of φρόνησις: *Laws*, 653 A, φρόνησιν δὲ καὶ ἀληθεῖς δόξας βεβαίους. Strictly speaking, there are three grades: (1) casual right opinion; (2) right opinion fixed by judicious education from youth; (3) right opinion fixed and confirmed by the higher education and accompanied by the ability δοῦναι λόγον. But Plato is not careful to distinguish the last two. They are both μόνιμοι (*Meno*, 98 A; *Rep.*, 430 B, reading μόνιμον). In *Polit.*, 309 C, ἀληθῆ δόξαν μετὰ βεβαιώσεως cannot be referred exclusively to the philosophic virtue with ZELLER (p. 596). It includes the virtues of fixed habit guided from above, as appears, e. g., from the reservation ὥς γε ἐν πολιτείᾳ, 309 E, which is precisely equivalent to πολιτικήν γε in *Rep.*, 430 E.

[552] *Supra*, p. 17; n. 91 with text.   [553] *Supra*, n. 549.

tion.[554] Socrates has heard a theory that the first elements of things are simple and not objects of knowledge. For knowledge implies giving and taking an account, and no account can be given of elements beyond naming them. They will not admit any other predicate.[555] In this paragraph we may discover allusions to Antisthenes's paradox about predication and definition, to current philosophies of materialism, and to mechanical interpretations of Plato's own formula δοῦναί τε καὶ δέξασθαι λόγον. But whatever Plato's secondary literary intentions, his main purpose is to present a serious psychological and metaphysical problem. Is the whole the sum of its parts except in mathematics? Can the world be explained as a mechanical summation of elements? The problem presents itself to us in psychology and cosmogony.[556] Plato treats it in dialectical abstraction, taking the syllable and its letters ("elements," στοιχεῖα) as representatives of elements and compounds. He decides (1) that the syllable is not the mere equivalent of its elements, but a new emergent form and distinct idea; (2) that, whether this be so or not, the elements and the syllable are equally knowable and unknowable. For if the syllable is the sum of the elements it cannot be known if they are not. And if it is a new unity it is as elemental as they and cannot be explained by resolution into its parts.

The second conclusion disposes of the proposed definition. The first, as we have already seen, is a suggestion of the doctrine of ideas as against philosophies of mechanical materialism.[557] But we are not therefore justified in making this episode the chief purpose of the dialogue. Two other possible meanings of λόγος are shown to yield no result, and the dialogue closes with the Socratic moral that we are at least wiser for knowing that we do not know.

THE PHÆDRUS

The *Phædrus*, with its profusion of ideas, its rich technical and poetical vocabulary, and its singular coincidences with the *Laws*[558] and *Timæus*,[559] makes the impression of a mature work. This impression is confirmed by *Sprach-Statistik*, and by the fact that it directly parodies a sentence of Isocrates's *Panegyricus* published in 380.[560] It is possible to say that the thoughts are merely sketched in a "program" of future work; that the dithyrambic vocabulary is due to the theme; and that the phrase of Isocrates is taken from an older, common source.[561] Anything may be said in debate.

[554]LUTOSLAWSKI (p. 371) argues that the *Theœtetus* rejecting λόγος, etc., contradicts the opinion "provisionally" received in *Meno*, 98 A, *Symp.*, 202 A, and *Phœdo*, 96 B. He fails to note (1) that this "provisional" view recurs in the *Timœus*, (2) that *Phœdo*, 96.B, is an ironical summary of materialism and is irrelevant here, (3) that the omission of αἰτία which surprises him (p. 378) is presumably intentional and minimizes the contradiction. Plato does not intend to "define" knowledge, but he is careful not to contradict the practical description of it given in the *Republic*. The phrase δοῦναί τε καὶ δέξασθαι λόγον is mentioned as a *conditio sine qua non* of knowledge (202 C), but only in connection with the rejected theory of elements, and its full dialectical significance is not developed.

[555] 202.

[556] *E. g.*, WUNDT's psychology differs from that of the pure associationists chiefly in that he insists that the whole is not the sum of its parts — ἀλλ' ἐξ ἐκείνων ἕν τι γεγονὸς εἶδος ἰδέαν μίαν αὐτὸ αὑτοῦ ἔχον, *Theœtetus*, 203 E.

[557] *Supra*, nn. 227, 228 with text.

[558] 245 D, ἀρχὴ κινήσεως, etc.

[559] In the style of the myths.

[560] 267 A, τά τε αὖ σμικρὰ μεγάλα καὶ τὰ μεγάλα σμικρὰ . . . . καινά τε ἀρχαίως, etc. *Isoc. Pan.*, 8, καὶ τά τε μεγάλα ταπεινὰ ποιῆσαι καὶ τοῖς μικροῖς μέγεθος περιθεῖναι, καὶ τά τε παλαιὰ καινῶς διελθεῖν, etc.

[561] GOMPERZ, *Ueber neuere Plato-Forschung*.

But there is an end to all use of Isocratean parallels if we cannot infer that the *Phœdrus* is later than a work which it explicitly parodies.

If we assume Lysias, who died in 378, to be still living, the date may be still more precisely determined to about the year 379. The strongest confirmation of this date is the weakness of the arguments for an earlier date, which it is hard to take seriously. The politician who recently called Lysias a λογογράφος need not have been Archinos, and, if he was, Plato's use of ἔναγχος may be merely dramatic.[562] The patronizing commendation of Socrates at the end[563] is not incompatible with a sly parody of his Gorgian style, nor even with the sharp rap on the knuckles administered to him (if it is Isocrates) at the close of the *Euthydemus*. Still less can we say that Plato and Isocrates could never have been friends after the declaration at the close of the tract against the Sophists that virtue cannot be taught, or, for that matter, after any other polemical innuendo in their works. Huxley, Matthew Arnold, Frederick Harrison, Herbert Spencer, and other knights of nineteenth-century polemics, combined much sharper thrusts than these with the interchange of courteous or slightly ironical compliments.

Our chief concern, however, is with arguments drawn from the thought. We have already seen that the dialectical method of the *Phœdrus* is not appreciably less mature than that of the *Philebus* or the *Sophist*,[564] and that, on the other hand, there is nothing in the psychology or ethics of the *Phœdrus* that necessarily fixes its relation to the *Republic*, the *Phœdo*, or the *Symposium*.[565] What can be said, then, of the attempts of distinguished scholars to show that the thought of the *Phœdrus* dates it *circa* 392, or even ten years earlier? The only one that calls for serious consideration is Natorp's argument[566] that the immaturity of the *Phœdrus* is proved by the absence of the notion of a supreme science, or of ultimate categories found in the *Symposium*, *Republic*, *Sophist*, and even in the *Euthydemus*. The answer is that such a notion never appears in Plato except in some special form adapted to a particular argument. Natorp includes very different things under this rubric. The supreme science of the *Symposium* is merely the knowledge of the idea—of the idea of beauty as distinguished from particular beauties. That of the *Republic* is knowledge of the idea—of the idea of good as the σκοπός or aim of true statesmanship. That of the *Euthydemus* is in one place by implication dialectic (290 C), in another the "political art" (291 C). In other passages the unity of science is merely the unity of the concept or idea, ἐπιστήμη.[567] The ontological categories of the *Theœtetus*, *Sophist*, and *Parmenides* belong to a different line of thought and have a mainly logical significance. They are connected with the notion of a universal science only in so far as they are apprehended and discriminated by dialectic. Now the subject of the *Phœdrus* did not call for the explicit assumption either of supreme categories or a universal science. The chief point in the myth, ignored by Natorp and the majority of commentators, is that

---

[562] 257 C.

[563] 279 A, τοὺς λόγους οἷς νῦν ἐπιχειρεῖ may well be the *Panegyricus*, but might be anything.

[564] *Supra*, n. 377.

[565] *Supra*, pp. 19, 43; n. 152.

[566] HERMES, Vol. XXXV, pp. 405 ff.

[567] *Supra*, n. 460.

the ecstasy of love is due to a speciality of the idea of beauty. Unlike other ideas, it is represented in this world by a not wholly inadequate copy, the sight of which recalls the beatific vision of the original.[568] The proof of immortality requires only the categories of the self-moved and that moved by another.[569] The absence of other abstract logical categories proves no more here than it does in the *Laws*. The method of dialectic is described in its relation to rhetoric, which is regarded as an art of deceptive dialectic or almost eristic.[570] There is no occasion for going back to ultimate categories or hypothesis beyond hypothesis. The subject about which it is desired to effect persuasion is the starting-point.[571] The rhetorician's art is to bring this under a definition or category from which there is a plausible transition to praise or blame.[572] So even in the *Philebus* the account of the true dialectical method starts from the concrete ἄπειρον to be investigated, or the idea, the ἕν, that it reveals to inspection, and says nothing there of ontological categories, ultimate hypothesis, or a supreme science.[573] The *Philebus* is not for that reason less mature than the *Phædo*.[574] Plato cannot always delay to tabulate ultimate categories or to reaffirm the unity of science, whether it be (1) as dialectic, (2) as the vision of the idea, or (3) as the "political art."

Natorp's other arguments merely confirm our main position by illustrating once more, and typically, the desperate straits to which an acute scholar is reduced in the attempt to date the dialogues by their thought. For example, there is obviously no connection between the remark that those who affirm that φρόνησις is the chief good are unable to define what φρόνησις (*Rep.*, 505 B), and the enthusiastic declaration that if wisdom (φρόνησις) could be seen by mortal eyes (as beauty in some measure can) it would enkindle δεινοὺς . . . . ἔρωτας (*Phædr.*, 250 D). Yet Natorp regards the first passage as a distinct criticism of and advance upon the latter. But the *Phædrus* passage merely says that φρόνησις, if we could only see it, would be still more lovable than beauty. It does not affirm it to be the chief of goods, and, if it did, need not for that reason precede the *Republic*, unless we are to say the same of *Laws*, 631 C.[575]

Again, in 245 C the unctuous phrase δεινοῖς μὲν ἄπιστος, σοφοῖς δὲ πιστή is said to mark Plato's early, unscientific mood, because mature Platonism ranks knowledge above πίστις. But plainly a religious thinker may affirm the superiority of knowledge to belief and yet indulge himself in the ironical declaration that the "clever" will disbelieve, but the wise believe, his proof of immortality. Similarly in 247 C the statement that no poet has ever worthily sung the region above the heavens is taken to prove that the passage is Plato's first exposition of the theory of ideas. But such

---

[568] 250 B C D.   [569] 245 C.

[570] 261 D with *Sophist*, 259 D. Rhetoric is generalized to include dialectic and eristic, just as in *Sophist*, 222, 223, πιθανουργική embraces all forms of rhetoric, the higgling of the market, the Lucianic art of the parasite, and the whole teaching and eristic of the Sophists.

[571] 263 D E.   [572] 265, 266 A.   [573] 16 C D E.

[574] The division of all things into πέρας, ἄπειρον, μικτόν, and αἰτία is given in a different connection, and has nothing in common with the five categories of the *Sophist*, the supreme science of the *Symposium*, or the ὑπόθεσις of the *Phædo* and the *Republic*.

[575] *Phædr.*, 250 D, seems destined to misinterpretation. LUTOSLAWSKI, p. 339, misses the meaning altogether, and HORN, pp. 212, 213, actually takes δεινοὺς ἔρωτας (understanding δεινούς in a bad sense) as Plato's reason why we have no vivid images of other ideas than beauty, and objects that the passionate love of justice would be a good, since it would not be exposed to sensual excess!

a prelude is a mere commonplace of rhetoric, as in *Phædo*, 108 C; *Meno*, 239 C; *Polit.*, 269 C.

The argument that dialectic is first introduced as a new term in 266 C will not bear scrutiny. In *Philebus*, 53 E, ἕνεκά του is introduced still more circumstantially. The ideas are a dream in *Cratyl.*, 439 C; dialectic is dramatically led up to in *Cratyl.*, 390; and in *Sophist*, 265, 266, an elaborate explanation has to be given of what is taken for granted in the phrase φαντάσματα θεῖα, *Rep.*, 532 C.[576] Natorp says "der Begriff Dialektik ist im *Gorgias* noch nicht geprägt, sondern erst im *Phædrus*." But διαλέγεσθαι is contrasted with ῥητορικὴ in the *Gorgias*, 448 D, and the term διαλεκτικός–ή, if I may trust my memory and Ast, does not happen to occur in the *Symposium*, *Theætetus*, *Timæus*, *Parmenides*, *Phædo*, *Philebus*, or *Laws*. It is begging the question, then, to assume that διαλέγεσθαι in the *Gorgias* does not connote true Platonic διαλεκτική, but only Socratic conversation. There is not a word about "dämonischen διάλεκτος" in *Symp.*, 202 E, 203 A, and the notion of philosophy as the seeking rather than the attainment of knowledge occurs not only in *Symp.*, 203 D–204 B, "after" the *Phædrus*, but in *Lysis*, 218 A. As for λόγων τέχνη, it is any "art of words," whether actual or ideal rhetoric, dialectic, or even eristic.[577] It is uncritical to press the various meanings which different contexts lend to such a general expression. Rhetoric is called the λόγων τέχνη in 260 D, but Socrates immediately adds that there is no true λέγειν τέχνη ἄνευ τοῦ ἀληθείας ἧφθαι; *i. e.*, without dialectic. There is, then, no inconsistency between this and the use of τῆς περὶ τοὺς λόγους τέχνης in *Phædo*, 90 B; nor can it be said that the λόγων μέθοδος of *Sophist*, 227 A, differs appreciably from the μέθοδος of *Phædr.*, 270 D.[578] Lastly, Natorp's argument (pp. 408–10) that the method of συναγωγὴ and διαίρεσις described in the *Phædrus* does not go far beyond the suggestions of the *Gorgias* and *Meno* is, of course, merely a further confirmation of our main thesis. But when he adds that ἰδέα is used vaguely in 237 D, 238 A, 246 A, 253 B, etc., and not, as in the "later" *Republic* and *Phædo*, in the strict sense of Platonic idea, the reply must be that this vague, untechnical use of εἶδος and ἰδέα is always possible in Plato.[579] Omitting *Theætetus*, 184 D, since Natorp thinks that also "early," we find it in *Rep.*, 507 E; *Philebus*, 64 E, and *Cratylus*, 418 E, where ἀγαθοῦ ἰδέα does not mean "idea of good." Since the transcendental idea is established for the *Phædrus*, of what possible significance is the occasional use of the word ἰδέα in a less technical sense ?

These illustrations might be multiplied indefinitely. They do not establish a universal negative, but they certainly create a presumption against all arguments of the type which careful scrutiny always shows to be fallacious. And the experience of the untrustworthiness of many such arguments creates in the minds of sober philologians a more justifiable "misology" than that which Plato deprecates in the *Phædo*.

---

[576] See ADAM, *ad loc.*

[577] *Euthyd.*, 288 A, ὑμετέρας τέχνης . . . . οὑτωσὶ θαυμάστης οὔσης εἰς ἀκρίβειαν λόγων.

[578] *Cf. supra*, n. 377.

[579] See JOWETT AND CAMPBELL, Vol. II, pp. 294 ff.

THE CRATYLUS

In vivacity and comic verve the *Cratylus* is "early,"[580] in maturity and subtlety of thought "late." Its most obvious feature, the playful allegorical use of etymologizing, is anticipated or recalled in many other dialogues.[581] Admirable is the art with which etymologies recognized to be little better than puns are made the vehicle of a true philosophy of language, and a profound discussion of the relations of language and thought.

With this we are not concerned. We have already seen that the attempt to assign the dialogue an early place in the development of Plato's own thought breaks down.[582] Plato is "already" in full possession of the theory of ideas and of the essential arguments of his polemic against the flowing philosophers.[583] His repudiation of eristic fallacies is as distinct and as clearly, if not as fully, expressed as it is in the *Euthydemus* and *Sophist*.[584]

It remains merely to enumerate, as a part of our cumulative argument, some of the minor resemblances that link the *Cratylus* to its predecessors or successors, and make it a sort of abbreviated repertory of Platonic thoughts and classifications. In 386 D there is a reference to the doctrine of Euthydemus: πᾶσι πάντα ὁμοίως εἶναι ἄμα καὶ ἀεί. In 386 D, πράξεις are an εἶδος τῶν ὄντων; cf. *Theætet.*, 155 E. In 387 B λέγειν is πράττειν, cf. *Euthyd.*, 284 C. In 388 C ὄνομα ἄρα διδασκαλικόν τι ἐστιν ὄργανον καὶ διακριτικὸν τῆς οὐσίας, coupled with the statement, 390 B C, that only the dialectician can use this tool, implies the imagery and doctrine of *Sophist*, 226–31 B, where the κάθαρσις of dialectic and Sophistic is a branch of διακριτικῆς. In 390 B the statement that the user is the best judge recalls *Euthyd.*, 289 D; *Rep.*, 601 D, and is implied in *Phædr.*, 274 E. In 390 C ἐρωτᾶν καὶ ἀποκρίνεσθαι ἐπιστάμενον may be compared with *Phædo*, 75 D. In 390 D the dialectician, as ἐπιστάτης, suggests *Euthyd.*, 290 C; *Rep.*, 528 B. In 392 C the view of the capacity of women is that of *Rep.*, 455 D. With 394 D cf. *Rep.*, 415 B, on the probability that good men will breed true. With 396 C, ὁρῶσα τὰ ἄνω, cf. *Rep.*, 509 D. In 398 A–C the image of the golden race, and the identification of good men with dæmons recall *Repub.*, 415 A and 540 C. In 398 E the rhetorician is akin to the dialectician (ἐρωτητικοί ἔρως, cf. *Symp.*), which makes against Sidgwick's view that in the earlier dialogues the *Sophist* is a rhetorician, in the later an eristic. In 399 C man is distinguished from the brute by conceptual thought, as in *Phædr.*, 249 B. In 400 B the conceit σῶμα σῆμα repeats *Gorgias*, 493 A. In 401 B μετεωρολόγοι καὶ ἀδολέσχαι τινές is precisely in the tone of *Phædr.*, 270 A., ἀδολεσχίας καὶ μετεωρολογίας φύσεως πέρι. In 401 C οὐσία Ἑστία recalls *Phædr.*, 247 A. In 403, 404 characteristic doctrines of the *Phædo*, *Gorgias*, and *Symp.* are implied concerning the naked soul, the invisible world, death, ἐπιθυμία as δεσμός, and the yearning of the soul for pure knowledge. *Cf. Gorg.*, 523 C; *Phædo*, 83 C D, 67 E–68 A. In 408 C the association of λόγος ἀληθής τε καὶ ψευδής with the

---

580 NATORP, however, *Archiv*, Vol. XII, p. 163, thinks the lack of dramatic *mise en scène* a mark of lateness.

581 See JOWETT's *Index, s. v.* "Etymology."

582 *Supra*, pp. 54, 56, 51, n. 373.

583 *Supra*, p. 33, n. 218, n. 539.

584 *Supra*, p. 54.

movements of the All recalls *Tim.*, 37 B C. The quibble ἡμέρα, ἥμερα, 418 D, is repeated in *Tim.*, 45 B. In 418 E ἀγαθοῦ ἰδέα τὸ δέον is explained by *Rep.*, 336 D. In 419 C λύπη ἀπὸ τῆς διαλύσεως implies the doctrine of *Phileb.*, 31 D, and *Tim.*, 64 D. In 422 A στοιχεῖα is used for elements, as in *Tim.*, 56 B; *Theætet.*, 201 E. In 423 C D music is "already" μίμησις. In 428 C the ἐξαπατᾶσθαι αὐτὸν ὑφ' αὑτοῦ is virtually the "voluntary lie" of *Rep.*, 382 A. In 436 D the emphasis laid on the ἀρχὴ or hypothesis (ὑπόκειται) recalls *Phædo*, 101 D, 107 B.

THE EUTHYDEMUS

The *Euthydemus* in subtlety of logical analysis, and in its attitude toward eristic, is akin to the *Sophist* and *Theætetus*.[585] The question, Can virtue be taught? the protreptic discourses, and the quest for the political art resume similar discussions in the *Meno, Protagoras, Charmides,* and *Gorgias*.[586] To the partisans of development the dialogue offers a dilemma. Either this mature logic must be assigned to an early work, or a late work may display comic verve of style and engage in a purely dramatic, apparently unsuccessful, Socratic search for the political art.[587]

A systematic analysis would be superfluous after Bonitz, Grote, and Jowett. But the *Euthydemus*, like the *Cratylus*, is a repertory of Platonic thoughts that link it to "earlier" and "later" dialogues. A few of these may be enumerated: 273 C, αὐτὸν αὐτῷ βοηθεῖν ἐν τοῖς δικαστηρίοις; cf. *Gorg.*, 509 B; 275 D, the captious question, Are those who learn οἱ σοφοὶ ἢ οἱ ἀμαθεῖς? merely illustrates the doctrine of *Lysis*, 218 A; *Symp.*, 203 E; *Soph.*, 229 C, 276 D ff.; do they learn ἃ ἐπίστανται ἢ ἃ μή, recalls the method κατὰ τὸ εἰδέναι ἢ μὴ εἰδέναι of the *Theætetus*,[588] and the distinction between ἐπιστήμης ἕξις and κτῆσις; cf. 277 C and 278 A with *Theætet.*, 197 B; in 276 E ἄφυκτα is used as in *Theætet.*, 165 B; 278 B προσπαίζειν is used for eristic, as παίζειν in *Theætet.*, 167 E; 280 E, τὸ δὲ οὔτε κακὸν οὔτε ἀγαθὸν; cf. *Lysis*, 216 D; *Gorg.*, 467 E; 282 B, οὐδὲν αἰσχρὸν .... δουλεύειν .... ἐραστῇ .... προθυμούμενον σοφὸν γενέσθαι, cf. *Symp.*, 184 C; 284 B, λέγειν is πράττειν, cf. *Cratyl.*, 387 B; 287 A, if there is no error, τίνος διδάσκαλοι ἥκετε, cf. *Theætet.*, 161 E, 178 E; 287 D, πότερον οὖν ψυχὴν ἔχοντα νοεῖ τὰ νοοῦντα. The quibble suggests the metaphysical problem of *Parmen.*, 132 D, cf. *A. J. P.*, Vol. XXII, p. 161; 289 C, the art of the user and the art of the maker, cf. *Rep.*, 601 D, *Cratyl.*, 390 B, 290 A, cf. *Gorg.*, 454; 290 C D, cf. *Polit.*, 305 A, and *supra*, p. 62; 290 C, the mathematician subordinated to the dialectician, cf. *Rep.*, 528 B; 291 B, ὥσπερ τὰ παιδία τὰ τοὺς κορύδους διώκοντα, etc., is the germ of the image of the aviary in the *Theætetus;* 291 C, cf. *Polit.*, 259 D; 292 D, cf. *Charm.*, 167 C, *Meno*, 100 A, *Protag.*, 312 D; 301 A, cf. *supra*, n. 199; 301 B, cf. *supra*, n. 426.

---

[585] *Supra*, pp. 54, 58.

[586] *Cf. Idea of Good*, p. 204; *supra*, n. 97.

[587] 292; cf. *supra*, n. 71. BONITZ, p. 125, protests against the assumption that Plato is really baffled in 292 E, and sensibly adds: "Ich erwähne dies nur, weil diese Art der Folgerung und der Erklärung Platonischer Dialoge weit verbreitet ist. Man sollte doch in Erwägen ziehen, ob denn jene Ruhe und Sicherheit der Discussion einer Frage als Frage für jemand möglich ist, für den sie eben nur noch Problem ist und eine Möglichkeit der Lösung sich nicht dargeboten hat."

[588] *Supra*, nn. 547, 548.

The significance of the closing conversation with Crito is often missed.[589] Nothing, of course, can be inferred from the casual admission (307 A) that χρηματιστικὴ and ῥητορικὴ are ἀγαθόν; or from the "contradiction" of the *Republic* in the statement that philosophy and πολιτικὴ πρᾶξις are both ἀγαθόν, but πρὸς ἄλλο ἑκατέρα. Socrates is speaking to his worthy friend the business man Crito from the point of view of common-sense. We have also seen that the allusion to Isocrates (?) does not determine the date.[590] Plato is defending himself and Socrates against the criticism that such trivial eristic is unworthy of the attention of a man of sense. The dignified rhetorician to whom the criticism is attributed, like Isocrates, confounds eristic with philosophy and proclaims the futility of both.[591] Plato replies (1) that in philosophy as in other pursuits the majority are bad; (2) even eristic may be a useful logical discipline. The second thought is implied rather than expressed. It is implied by the intervention of the δαιμόνιον (272 E) and by the statement that the gentlemen who in Prodicus's phrase[592] hold the borderland of philosophy and politics, and who think the philosophers their only rivals for the first place, are badly mauled in private conversation when they fall into the hands of eristics like Euthydemus.[593] Socrates, on the other hand, though ironically admitting defeat, has shown himself throughout able to do what is postulated of the true dialectician in the *Sophist*, 259 C: τοῖς λεγομένοις οἷόν τε εἶναι καθ᾽ ἕκαστον ἐλέγχοντα ἐπακολουθεῖν.[594] The multitude think such logical exercise unbecoming. But that is because, in the words of the *Parmenides* (136 D), ἀγνοοῦσι . . . . ὅτι ἄνευ ταύτης τῆς διὰ πάντων διεξόδου τε καὶ πλάνης ἀδύνατον ἐντυχόντα τῷ ἀληθεῖ νοῦν ἔχειν. But Socrates, regardless of personal dignity, welcomes every occasion for intellectual exercise: οὕτω τις ἔρως δεινὸς ἐνδέδυκε τῆς περὶ ταῦτα γυμνασίας (*Theætet.*, 169 C).

PROTAGORAS, GORGIAS, MENO, SYMPOSIUM, PHÆDO, AND REPUBLIC

The leading ideas of these dialogues have already been studied, and it is not necessary to analyze them in detail.[595] We may acquiesce in the presumption that the *Protagoras*, *Gorgias*, and *Meno* are somewhat earlier in manner and style[596] without

[589] GROTE, e. g., says: "In the epilogue Euthydemus is cited as the representative of true dialectic and philosophy."

[590] *Supra*, p. 72.

[591] 305 A, καὶ οὗτοι (Dionysodorus and Euthydemus) ἐν τοῖς κρατίστοις εἰσι τῶν νῦν.

[592] See JOEL, *Der echte und der xenophontische Sokrates*, Vol. II, p. 634.

[593] 305 D, ἐν δὲ τοῖς ἰδίοις λόγοις ὅταν ἀπολειφθῶσιν. Cf. *Theætet.*, 177 B, ὅτι ἂν ἰδίᾳ λόγον δέῃ δοῦναί τε καὶ δέξασθαι. The rhetorician is helpless in the hands of either the philosopher or the eristic.

[594] Cf. *supra*, nn. 117, 426.   [595] See Index.

[596] SUDHAUS, *Rhein. Mus.*, 44, p. 52, tries to assign the *Gorgias* to the year 376 between the *To Nikokles* and the *Nikokles*. He is refuted by DÜMMLER, *Kleine Schriften*, I, pp. 79 ff., who proposes other Isocratean parallels, which are courteously, but sensibly, minimized or rejected by

ADAM (edition of *Republic*, index, s. v. "Isocrates"). Obviously, barely conceivable references in Plato to an Isocratean type of thought or a Gorgian style prove nothing. Nor can anything be inferred from coincidence in commonplaces or in ideas that can be found in *Euripides* and *Thucydides*. It would be easy to "prove" by these methods that the *Busiris* follows the *Republic* and precedes the *Symposium* which contradicts it (cf. *Busiris*, 4, with *Symp.*, 198 D). Strangely enough, the very critics who force a reference to the *Helena* upon *Republic*, 586 C, are apt to reject, in the interest of their chronology, the two almost certain citations of Isocrates by Plato, that in *Phædr.*, 267 A (*supra*, p. 71), and that in *Gorgias*, 463 A, where Isoc. κ. σοφ. 17 καὶ ψυχῆς ἀνδρικῆς καὶ δοξαστικῆς ἔργον εἶναι is wittily parodied by ψυχῆς δὲ στοχαστικῆς καὶ ἀνδρείας. Dümmler calls this a "nicht einmal wörtliche Uebereinstimmung in einem banalen Gemeinplatz." But the very point of the jest lies in the substitution of the lower word, στοχαστικῆς, for the term δοξαστικῆς intentionally employed by Isocrates to mark the superiority of his δόξα to the pretended

admitting that there is any traceable development of doctrine.[597]   There is also, as we have seen, no evidence in the thought sufficient to date the *Symposium* and *Phædo* relatively to each other or to the *Republic*, the *Phædrus*, and the *Theætetus*.[598] Pfleiderer thinks the *Symposium* the first dialogue of Plato's "third phase," which includes the *Philebus*, *Timæus*, *Critias*, and *Laws*. He sees in *Symp.*, 209–12, a review of Plato's previous career, with many allusions to the different "phases" of the *Republic* (p. 46). So also Dümmler, *infra*, n. 619. It suffices for our purpose that all these dialogues were written after Plato had attained maturity of years, and presumably of thought—the *Meno* after 395,[599] the *Gorgias* after Isocrates's *Against the Sophists*, the *Symposium* after the year 385,[600] the *Phædrus* probably after Isocrates's *Panegyricus*. That the *Phædo* cites the *Meno* is probable.[601] That the *Republic* alludes to the *Phædo* is possible, but not necessary;[602] and, having other reasons for believing the *Phædrus* to be later than the *Gorgias*, we may assume that *Phædrus*, 260 D, 261 A, alludes to *Gorgias*, 462 B, without, however, admitting the validity of such arguments as Siebeck's suggestion (p. 116) that θρέμματα γενναῖα intentionally characterizes the λόγοι as "etwas Herangepflegtes, Ausgearbeitetes."

But it is idle to pursue this σκιαμαχία further.

The chief witness to the unity of Plato's thought is the *Republic*, the great work of his maturity and the most complete synthesis of his teaching. It is presumably later than most of the minor Socratic dialogues,[603] but it completes rather than contradicts them, and their methods imply its results.[604] It is earlier than the *Laws* and *Timæus*, and probably than all or most of the dialectical dialogues, but they do not contradict it, and they develop no important idea which it does not distinctly suggest.[605]

It is generally dated somewhere between 380 and 370, and we may say, if we please, that it was published when Plato was about fifty-five years of age, but any date between his fortieth and sixtieth year will serve as well.[606]

ἐπιστήμη of the metaphysicians. On the other hand, though the *Phædr.* is in point of fact probably later, nothing can be inferred from its agreement with Isocrates (*Phædr.*, 269 D; Isoc. in *Sophist*, 17) in the commonplace that ἐπιστήμη, μελέτη and φύσις are indispensable to the complete rhetor. They are requisites of the ἱκανὸς ἀγωνιστὴς in any pursuit, as is distinctly stated in *Rep.*, 374 D E. Nor is anything to be learned by pressing too closely the various possible meanings of ἐπιστήμη—knowledge of the Isocratean rules of rhetoric, knowledge of dialectic and psychology that might make rhetoric an art in Plato's opinion, knowledge of the subject-matter of the discourse.

[597] ZELLER says, p. 527, that the *Protagoras*, which assumes the identity of the good and the pleasurable, "must" be later than *Gorg.*, 495 ff., and all subsequent dialogues. But *cf. supra*, p. 20. HORN finds in *Protag.*, *Gorg.*, and *Phædo* the following *Denkfortschritt:* (1) Die Lust ist das Gute. (2) Die Lust ist nicht das Gute. (3) Die Lust ist das Böse! In *Phædr.*, *Symp.*, *Phædo* he sees a falling away in middle life from the youthful faith in immortality to which age returns! Lutoslawski thinks that the discussion about the identity of the tragic and comic poet at the end of the *Symposium* is an apology for the comic touches in that dialogue and an announcement

of the *Phædo.* But PFLEIDERER (p. 92) finds that "das Allegro des *Symposion* . . . . auf die schwermütigernsten Trauerklänge des vorhergehenden Sterbedialogs nunmehr die verklärten Harmonien einer wiedergefundenen Lebensstimmung folgen lässt." It's a poor argument that will not work both ways!

[598] *Supra*, pp. 19, 40 ff., 43.   [599] 90 A.

[600] 193 A. It is, of course, just conceivable that, as WILAMOWITZ affirms (*Hermes*, Vol. XXXII, p. 102), the allusion is to the events of the year 418. But we are still waiting for his proof that Plato commits no intentional anachronisms.

[601] 73 A; *Meno*, 82 ff. It is not necessary, for Plato probably often illustrated ἀνάμνησις by geometrical cross-examination in the school.

[602] *Rep.*, 611 B, οἱ ἄλλοι (λόγοι) need not be the specific proofs of immortality given in the *Phædo.*

[603] SIEBECK, however (p. 126), thinks that the *Laches* is the fuller discussion of courage " promised " in *Rep.*, 430 C, αὖθις δὲ περὶ αὐτοῦ, ἐὰν βούλῃ ἔτι κάλλιον δίιμεν.

[604] *Cf. supra*, pp. 14, 15.

[605] *Supra*, nn. 244, 375, pp. 34, 36, 42, 46, 55, 62.

[606] See ZELLER (pp. 551 ff.), who dates it in 375. The coincidences between the *Republic* and the *Ecclesiazousae*

The relations already indicated between the *Republic* and other dialogues force extreme partisans of "development" to break it up into distinct sections which they assign to different periods.[607] Such hypotheses are beyond the scope of serious criticism, which in the total absence of evidence can neither affirm nor deny them. It can only point out the fallacy of the reasoning by which they are supported. The "arguments" of Krohn, Pfleiderer, and their followers have been refuted in more than sufficient detail by Hirmer, Campbell,[608] Grimmelt, and other defenders of the unity of the *Republic*. They may be reduced, broadly speaking, to a *petitio principii* and a few typical fallacies. The *petitio principii* is the assumption that the numerous connecting links and cross-references that bind together the "parts" of the *Republic* were inserted by Plato as an afterthought. The chief and fundamental fallacy is the application to a great and complex literary masterpiece of canons of consistency and unity drawn from the inner consciousness of professional philologians. The architectural unity of the *Republic* is superior to that of the *Laws*, the *Philebus*, the *Phædrus*, or to that of the parts into which the disintegrators resolve it, many of which plainly could not exist by themselves. Secondary intentions, a prelude, digressions, and a peroration, postlude, afterpiece, or appendix may be expected in so long a work. As Jowett sensibly says:[609] "We may as well speak of many designs as one; nor need anything be excluded from the plan of a great work to which the mind is naturally led by the association of ideas and which does not interfere with the general purpose." It is uncritical, then, to assume a central argument and prune off everything that is not indispensable to its development. The argument might conceivably have started from the restatement of the problem by Glaucon and Adeimantus at the beginning of the second book. Plato might have drawn up a sketch of a reformed state, omitting all mention of the higher education, the rule of the philosophers, and the degenerate forms of government. He might have closed the work abruptly with the demonstration of the main thesis at the end of the ninth book. Or, if he wished to add the myth, he might have omitted or found another place for the digression in which the banishment of the poets is justified on deeper grounds. But these bare possibilities do not raise the slightest presumption that the *Republic* was, in fact, pieced together out of detached and disjointed essays. The different topics were closely associated in Plato's thought. And if they were all present to his mind from the beginning, it

---

of Aristophanes yield at the most a *terminus post quem*. *Cf.* Hirmer, "Entstehung und Komp. d. Plat. Rep.," *Jahrbücher für Phil.*, Suppl., N. F., Vol. XXIII, p. 655; Adam, *The Republic of Plato*, Vol. I, pp. 345–55. Hirmer (pp. 660 ff.) disposes of the attempt to daté the *Republic* by the allusion to Ismenias (336 A), and to Polydamas (338 C), by the supposed allusion to Eudoxus (530), and by Reinhardt's reference of 410 B C to Isocrates's *Antidosis*, 181, and of 498 D E to the *Areopagiticus*. He himself, with as little proof, thinks that 498 D E alludes to the *Euagoras*. He dates the completion of the *Republic circa* 370: (1) because, after Christ, he believes that the protest against internecine war between Greeks (471 A–C) "must" refer to the destruction of Platæa by the Thebans in 374; (2) because the picture of the tyrant (577) "must" fall after the first Sicilian journey and before the second when Plato was on friendly terms with Dionysius the younger; (3) because Christ has "proved" that the eleventh epistle (*circa* 364) is genuine, and the eleventh epistle implies the completion of the *Republic* and the beginning of the *Timæus*.

[607] Pfleiderer, *Zur Lösung d. plat. Frage*, p. 79: "Das Zusammenwerfen ganz verschiedener Phasen in der *Rep.*, wie ich behaupte, musste nothwendig für Jeden, der sonst gerne Phasen und Perioden gesehen hätte, die geahnten Grenzlinien wieder verwischen."

[608] *Republic*, Vol. II, essay III.

[609] Vol. III, p. vii.

would not be easy to suggest a more natural and effective order of presentation than that in which we now read them.

To prove, then, that, as a matter of fact, the "parts" of the *Republic* were composed at different times recourse is had to two other fallacies: (1) it is assumed that what is not explicitly mentioned in any part is not known to the author at the time; and (2) slight variations in phrasing are taken to imply serious differences of doctrine. The application of this method to the theory of ideas and to Plato's psychology has already been considered.[610] A few words may be added here on the second point. Rohde[611] says that the immortality of the soul is ignored in the earliest part, II–V, 471 C; first appears as a paradox in X, 608 D; and is assumed in its sublimest form in VI, VII. But his arguments will not bear scrutiny. "Was nach dem Tode kommen möge, sollen die φύλακες nicht beachten" (III, cap. i ff.), is an unwarranted inference from Plato's polemic against Homeric verses that represent death as terrible to all men, even the good—an idea which Plato would always have repudiated. The sneers in 363 C D and 366 A B at future rewards are directed against low ideals—the μέθην αἰώνιον—or are intended to emphasize the necessity of first proving that virtue is desirable for its own sake. When that is done, it is ἤδη ἀνεπίφθονον (612 B) to add the rewards; and there is no more inconsistency in reintroducing in a nobler form the premiums which the gods bestow upon virtue after death than there is in the withdrawal of the supposition that the just man is to be reputed unjust, and in the affirmation that in fact honesty *is* the best policy, though that is not the sole or the chief reason for practicing it.[612]

The omission of all reference to immortality in the first nine books would prove nothing. It is equally ignored in the first nine books of the *Laws*, and is first explicitly mentioned in XII, 959. Glaucon's dramatic surprise at Socrates's confident assertion of immortality proves nothing for Plato. The idea is familiar to the *Gorgias* and *Meno*. And even if we deny the reference of 611 B to the *Phœdo*, and with Rohde place the *Phœdo* after the *Republic*, the tenth book of the *Republic* knows the ideas, and even the τρίτος ἄνθρωπος, and cannot therefore be placed before the *Gorgias* by those who make use of arguments from development. In speaking of immortality Plato naturally tries to qualify and limit the doctrine of the tripartite soul.[613] He can only fall back upon poetical imagery and affirm his faith that in its true nature the (immortal part of the) soul must be one and simple. It is a waste of ingenuity to attempt to find a consistent chronological development in this point in the *Phœdrus; Rep.*, II–V, X; *Phœdo*, and *Timœus*. It is perfectly true, as Dümmler argues,[614] that

[610] *Supra*, pp. 36, 40 ff.   [611] *Psyche*, pp. 588 ff.

[612] SIEBECK (p. 144) and DÜMMLER (Vol. I, p. 248), it is true, find fault with this too, on the ground that the Socrates of the tenth book does not repeat every point of the hypothesis like a lawyer, and forgets the stipulation that the unjust man was to have the power, if detected, to defy punishment, or the wealth to buy off the gods. Dümmler also objects that "nachdem die Perspektive auf die Ewigkeit als μέγιστα ἄθλα der Tugend bezeichnet war,

kann irgendwelche utilitaristische Begründung nicht mehr interessieren." Terrible logic! Are modern believers in immortality wholly indifferent to utilitarian considerations "als Zugabe"? And had Plato no interest in the psychological proofs that the virtuous life is, even in this world, the most pleasurable, given in the *Laws*, the *Philebus*, and the ninth book of the *Republic?*

[613] *Supra*, pp. 42, 46.

[614] Vol. I, pp. 256 ff.

if the soul is really one, the definition of justice as a relation between its parts loses all meaning. But such "inconsistencies" are inherent in human thought, and prove nothing for the relative dates of Book X and Books II–V. Can any modern theologian produce definitions of the virtues that will apply to man in his earthly state and to the disembodied soul?[615]

Lutoslawski, while rejecting the fancies of Krohn and Pfleiderer, holds it possible to show that the first book of the *Republic* falls between the *Gorgias* and the *Phædo*, and that the remaining books follow the *Phædo* and reveal traces of progressive development of doctrine. The following parallel illustrates the force of his arguments:

P. 277: "This sharp and general formulation of the law of contradiction,[616] not only as a law of thought as in *Phædo*,[617] but for the first time as a law of being . . . . is a very important step."

P. 318: "Here[618] for the first time occurs a formulation of the law of contradiction as a law of thought, while in the *Phædo* and earlier books of the *Republic* it was a metaphysical law."

Lastly, a word must be said of the attempt to trace a development in Plato's treatment of poetry. The contradictions of those who employ this method might be left to cancel one another.[619] But the whole procedure is uncritical. Plato was always sensitive to poetic genius, and there was no time when he might not have praised Homer without conspicuous irony.[620] But he always regarded the poet as an imitator, whose aim is pleasure rather than the good, whose ethical teaching must be interpreted or controlled by the philosopher, and whose fine sayings are the product of "inspiration" rather than of knowledge. The *Apology*[621] anticipates the *Republic* in the doctrine that the poets do not know whereof they speak, and the *Phædrus* in the theory of poetic inspiration. The *Gorgias*, 502 B C D, deals with the moral influence of poetry upon the masses in the tone of the *Republic* and *Laws;* and like *Republic*, 601 B, strips from the body of the poet's discourse the meretricious adornment of the poetic dress. The doctrine that poetry is μίμησις is sufficiently implied in *Cratylus*, 423, where the mimetic value of words is discussed, and where μουσικὴ is classified as μίμησις. The differences between the tenth and the third books of the *Republic* cannot be pressed. The third book hints that there is more to come ;[622] and the tenth book announces itself as a profounder discussion, based on psychological distinctions brought out in the intervening books. But it is begging the question to assume that they were discovered by Plato after the composition of the third book. The fact that

---

[615] *Cf. supra*, pp. 6, 7, and HIRMER, p. 641.

[616] 436 B.   [617] 102 E.   [618] 602 E.

[619] LUTOSLAWSKI says that Plato's scorn of poetry developed after the *Symposium*, and that the tenth book of the *Republic* is therefore later than the *Phædo*, which praises Homer without irony, and earlier than *Phædrus* and *Theætetus*, which take for granted the low estimate of the poet. But NATORP, thinking of other passages of the *Phædrus*, is positive that such a dialogue could not have been written after the rejection of poetry in the *Republic;* while DÜMMLER (Vol. I, p. 269) places the *Symposium* after

the *Republic*, and sees in it a return from the bitter mood of the *Gorgias* and *Republic* to a calmer and more generous state of mind: "Da ist er auch gerecht gegen andere; Homer und Hesiod, Lykurg und Solon sieht er unter sich, aber hoch über anderen!"

[620] *Phædo*, 95 A, οὔτε γὰρ ἄν . . . . Ὁμήρῳ θείῳ ποιητῇ ὁμολογοῖμεν οὔτε αὐτοὶ ἡμῖν αὐτοῖς; *Laws*, 776 E, ὁ δὲ σοφώτατος ἡμῖν τῶν ποιητῶν — in both passages seriously, as the context shows.

[621] 23 C; *cf.* the *Ion.* and *Meno*, 99 E.

[622] 394 D, ἴσως δὲ καὶ πλείω ἔτι τούτων.

in emphasizing the distinction between dramatic and narrative poetry Plato carelessly speaks as if the former alone were imitative, proves nothing.[623]   A far more important new point made in the tenth book is already distinctly implied in the *Protagoras* — the antithesis between the principle of measure in the soul and ἡ τοῦ φαινομένου δύναμις,[624] to which poetry makes its appeal.[625]   The mood of the *Symposium* differs from that of the *Gorgias* and the *Republic*.   But this does not prove either that the *Symposium* is earlier, or that Plato had been mellowed by success.   A banquet at which Agathon was host and Aristophanes a guest was obviously not the place for a polemic against dramatic poetry.   But even here the ironical superiority of the dialectician is maintained, and the inability of the poets to interpret or defend their art is revealed.[626]

CONCLUSION.   IDEAS AND NUMBERS.   THE LAWS

The value of Plato's life-work would be very slightly affected even if it were true that in the weakness of extreme old age the noble light of his philosophy did "go out in a fog of mystical Pythagoreanism."   It is not in the least true, however, and the prevalence of the notion is due mainly (1) to the uncritical acceptance of the tradition concerning Plato's "latest" doctrine of ideas and numbers; and (2) to the disparaging estimate of the *Laws* expressed by those who care only for dramatic charm of style, or by radicals like Grote, who are offended by the "bigotry" of a few passages.   A word must be said on each of these points.

1. Aristotle's account of Plato's later identification of ideas and numbers has been generally accepted since Trendelenburg's dissertation on the subject.[627]   Zeller rightly points out that the doctrine is not found in the extant writings, but adds that for Plato numbers are entities intermediate between ideas and things of sense.   In my discussion of the subject[628] I tried to establish two points: first, that we need not accept the testimony of Aristotle, who often misunderstood Plato, and was himself not clear as to the relation of mathematical and other ideas; second, that the doctrine of numbers as intermediate entities is not to be found in Plato, but that the passages which misled Zeller may well have been the chief source of the whole tradition about ideas and numbers.   The first point is a matter of opinion.   I did not deny the testimony of Aristotle, and no one who chooses to accept it can be refuted.   The relation of ideas to numbers was doubtless much debated by the scholastics of the Academy. Aristotle's reports of the intolerable logomachy do not make it clear just how much of this nonsense he attributed to Plato.   But I do not intend to enter upon the interpretation of the eleventh and twelfth books of the *Metaphysics*.   No reader would

[623] 393 C, 394 D.   [624] *Protag.*, 356 D.

[625] *Rep.*, 602, 603.

[626] 201 B, κινδυνεύω, ὦ Σώκρατες, οὐδὲν εἰδέναι ὧν τότε εἶπον. Καὶ μὴν καλῶς γε εἶπες, φάναι, ὦ Ἀγάθων.   Cf. also 223 D, where Socrates compels Agathon and Aristophanes to admit τοῦ αὐτοῦ ἀνδρὸς εἶναι κωμῳδίαν καὶ τραγῳδίαν ἐπίστασθαι ποιεῖν. This is thought to contradict *Repub.*, 395 A, but the contradiction is removed by pressing τέχνῃ in what follows.   One

man is "inspired" by the tragic muse, another by the comic. If poetry were a matter of science, the poet could use both forms, even as the scientific interpreter of poetry would not, like the "inspired" Ion, be limited to Homer. This we may plausibly conjecture to be the meaning.   But it is only conjecture.

[627] *Plat. de id. et numeris doctrina*, 1828.

[628] *De Plat. id. doctrina*, pp. 31 ff.

follow me, and no results could be won. If Aristotle's testimony be accepted, there is an end of controversy. Plato taught in his lectures the doctrine of ideas and numbers.

But the second point is not so elusive. It is possible to test the argument that the extant writings do not recognize an intermediate class of mathematical numbers, and yet might easily suggest the notion to mechanical-minded students. Now Zeller in his fourth edition confounds the two questions. He gives the impression that he is answering me by a *Quellenbelege* from Aristotle and Philoponos. He wholly ignores my interpretation of a number of specific Platonic passages, which he apparently takes for the mere misunderstandings and blunders of a beginner.[629] I have no hope of convincing Zeller, nor do I wish to force myself into a polemic with the honored master of all who study Greek philosophy. But, as Mr. J. Adam, a scholar whose scrupulous candor makes it a pleasure to argue with him, has expressed surprise in his edition of the *Republic* that I still adhere to my opinion in spite of the mass of evidence, I will endeavor to state my meaning more plainly.

The theory of ideas, the hypostatization of all concepts, once granted, numbers do not differ from other ideas. The phrase, περὶ αὐτῶν τῶν ἀριθμῶν (*Rep.*, 525 D), denotes ideal numbers or the ideas of numbers, and ὁρατὰ ἢ ἁπτὰ σώματα ἔχοντας ἀριθμούς are numbered things, things of sense participant in number.[630] That is all there is of it, and there is no extant Platonic passage that this interpretation will not fit. For educational purposes it is true that mathematical science holds an intermediate place between dialectic and the perceptions of sense. Mathematical abstractions (ἡ περὶ τὸ ἓν μάθησις, *Rep.*, 525 A) are the best propædeutic to abstract reasoning generally. But there is no distinction of kind between them and other abstractions, σκληρὸν μαλακόν (*Rep.*, 524 A ff.). Mathematical science as διάνοια is midway between the pure νοῦς of dialectic and the δόξα of sense. But that is because of its method—the reliance on diagrams (images) and hypotheses. In themselves its objects are explicitly stated to be pure νοητά.[631] The "mathematical" numbers then are plainly the abstract, ideal numbers of the philosopher. The numbers of the vulgar are concrete numbered things. There is no trace of a third kind of number.[632] Those who have not yet learned to apprehend abstractions mockingly ask the mathe-

---

[629] It may be permissible to add that he seems to have read other parts of the dissertation with more attention, since, to mention only two cases, he adds on p. 745 a reference à propos of the τρίτος ἄνθρωπος to Republic, 596, 597, and *Tim.*, 31 A, with the interpretation of their significance given on p. 30; and he omits from p. 547 of the third edition a sentence criticised on p. 49 of the dissertation. Another slight but significant point may be mentioned. Aristotle himself makes a not wholly clear distinction between mathematical ideas (τὰ ἐν ἀφαιρέσει λεγόμενα, almost technical) and other ideas. In illustration of this I objected to Zeller's interpretation of *De An.*, 432a2, ἐν τοῖς εἴδεσί τοῖς αἰσθητοῖς τὰ νοητά ἐστι . . . . τά τε ἐν ἀφαιρέσει λεγόμενα ("die abstrakten Begriffe") καὶ ὅσα τῶν αἰσθητῶν ἕξεις καὶ πάθη. My objection was that both grammar and Aristotelian usage showed that ὅσα τῶν αἰσθητῶν, etc., are also *abstrakte Begriffe* (in the German or English sense of the words),

the νοητά being divided into two classes by τε-καί. The sentence still stands, and I am quite willing to leave the question of *Flüchtigkeit* to any competent scholar, e. g., to M. Rodier, who translates "les intelligibles, aussi bien les concepts abstraits (ou mathématiques) que ceux qui ont pour objet) les qualités, etc."

[630] Adam translates αὐτῶν τῶν ἀριθμῶν, "numbers themselves," which is quite right. My point is that "numbers themselves" are proved by the context and by *Philebus*, 56 E, to be ideal numbers. For Adam's further argument cf. infra, p. 84.

[631] *Rep.*, 510 D, τοῦ τετραγώνου αὐτοῦ ἕνεκα . . . . καὶ διαμέτρου αὐτῆς, ἀλλ' οὐ ταύτης ἣν γράφουσιν. 511 D, καίτοι νοητῶν ὄντων μετὰ ἀρχῆς.

[632] *Phileb.*, 56 D E.

maticians (*Rep.*, 526 A), περὶ ποίων ἀριθμῶν διαλέγεσθε; and the answer is, περὶ τούτων ὧν διανοηθῆναι μόνον ἐγχωρεῖ, coupled with an exposition that recalls the *Parmenides* of the pure idea of unity.[633] Simple as all this appears, it might easily be misunderstood by the pupils of the Academy. Mathematics was intermediate from an educational point of view. In cosmogony numbers and geometrical forms are the mediators between chaos and the general idea of harmony and measure.[634] The expression, numbers (arithmetic), of the vulgar and numbers of the philosopher would lead a perverse ingenuity to ask of the mathematicians, in the words of the *Republic*, περὶ ποίων ἀριθμῶν διαλέγεσθε; Plato's use of "dyad" and "triad" as convenient synomyms for the pure idea of two and three would be mistakenly supposed to imply a distinction.[635] The innocent question (*Rep.*, 524 C), τί οὖν ποτ' ἐστὶ τὸ μέγα αὖ καὶ τὸ σμικρόν,[636] would suggest that it was a *terminus technicus* for some mysterious ultimate philosophical principle, and set students upon hunting it and its supposed synomyms through the dialogues, and, inasmuch as μέγα + σμικρόν indubitably = 2, it might well be identified with the indeterminate dyad and its supposed equivalents, or any other "principle" posited in antithesis to the one.[637] The folly once set a-going, there are no limits to its plausible developments. All the unanswerable questions as to the relation of ideas to things may assume special forms for special classes of ideas. Plato himself shows this for ideas of relative terms in a much misunderstood passage of the *Parmenides*.[638]. The problem of the relations of numbered things, of the supposed mathematical numbers, and of ideal numbers, offered a rich feast for the quibblers and the ὀψιμαθεῖς of the Academy. "Before and after" is essential to number, but there is no "before and after" in the ideas. Multiplicity is inherent in number, but the "idea" even of a million must be one. Other ideas may be imperfectly copied by things, but is not the number five entirely present in five things? Echoes of this pitiful scholasticism are preserved for us in the metaphysics of Aristotle. But what possible reason can there be for attributing it to Plato? Adam himself (Vol. II, p. 160) repeats the disconsolate question: περὶ ποίων ἀριθμῶν διαλέγεσθε ἐν οἷς τὸ ἓν οἷον ὑμεῖς ἀξιοῦτέ ἐστιν, ἴσον τε ἕκαστον πᾶν παντὶ καὶ οὐδὲ σμικρὸν διαφέρον; and asks: "Are we then to suppose that there are many ideas of 'one'?" The answer is: "Yes, precisely, to the extent that there are many ideas of anything." We have already seen (*Rep.*, 476 A) that every idea is *per se* one, and yet, not merely as reflected in phenomena, but τῇ ἀλλήλων κοινωνίᾳ appears many. The contradiction is inherent in the theory of ideas. As against the multiplicity of phenomena, we insist on the indivisible unity of the idea. But when we find the idea involved with other ideas in a number of instances, we are forced to use the plural. Plato does not, however, here

---

633 *Cf. Idea of Good*, p. 222; *Phileb.*, 56 E, εἰ μὴ μονάδα μονάδος ἑκάστης τῶν μυρίων μηδεμίαν ἄλλην ἄλλης διαφέρουσάν τις θήσει.

634 *Tim.*, 53 B ff.; *Phileb.*, 66 A.

635 *Phœdo*, 101 C; *Parmen.*, 149 C; *Phœdo*, 104.

636 Plato is using the terms precisely as BERKELEY does when he says (*Principles of Human Knowledge*, XI):

"Again, *great* and *small*, *swift* and *slow* are allowed to exist nowhere without the mind, being entirely relative, and changing as the frame or position of the organs of sense varies."

637 *De Plat. id.*, p. 37.

638 133 C ff.; *cf. A. J. P.*, Vol. IX, p. 288.

in terms pluralize the "one." He says: Of what numbers do you speak in which *the one, i. e.*, the idea of one, present in each as a constituent and essential part of the more complex idea, etc.? Of course, this implies a multiplicity of units in each number, and still more in all; but only as any idea is multiplied when it appears in a number of others. The multiplication of the idea τῇ τῶν σωμάτων κοινωνίᾳ is more easily evaded than that τῇ ἀλλήλων κοινωνίᾳ, because in the first case we may use the imagery of pattern and copy, while, in the second case, the idea is an essential constituent part of that into which it enters. In the special case of numbers, the paradox is still more glaring. But Plato is not one to be frightened from the path of philosophical consistency by a paradox which he rightly regarded as largely verbal. In the *Parmenides* he amuses himself by showing that the idea of "one" itself apprehended τῇ διανοίᾳ μόνον καθ' αὐτὸ breaks up into many.[639] This does not make it the less necessary for the mathematician to apprehend the pure absolute idea of unity and restore it as fast as it is disintegrated by analysis or the senses.[640]

2. Despite many passages of stately and impressive eloquence, the *Laws* will remain the type of "frigidity" for those who, like Lucian, read Plato mainly for the dramatic vivacity of the *Phædrus* or the artistic beauty of the *Symposium*. Our purpose is not to deny the altered mood and style that mark the masterpiece of Plato's old age, but merely to protest against the notion that it may be safely neglected by the serious student, or that it presents a doctrine essentially different from that of the *Republic*.

If Plato was not to rewrite the *Republic*, it was almost inevitable that his political studies should assume the form of a project of detailed legislation for a possible Greek city. But even here, while recognizing that many of his theoretic postulates will have to be mitigated in practice,[641] he holds fast in principle to the ideals of the earlier work.[642] A harmony of the *Laws* and *Republic*, however, though not a difficult task, would demand more space than can be given to it here. We need not delay to examine the contribution of the *Laws* to our knowledge of Greek institutions, or the very considerable influence which it exercised upon the speculations of Aristotle and later Greek thinkers. One service which it renders to students of the dialogues we have already often noted.

As the years wore on, Plato naturally grew weary of Socratic irony, of the game of question and answer, of the dramatic illustration or the polemical analysis of eristic. Even in the earlier dialogues he sometimes evades or contemptuously explains away an equivocation which elsewhere he dramatically portrays or elaborately refutes.[643] In the *Laws* this is his habitual mood,[644] and in consequence the *Laws* may often be quoted for the true Platonic solution of problems which Socratic irony or dramatic art seems to leave unsolved in the earlier dialogues.[645]

While acknowledging this change of mood, we must be on our guard against the

[639] 143 A, 144 E. [640] *Rep.*, 525 E; *supra*, n. 647. [641] 746. [644] 627 B, 627 D, 644 A, 864 B.
[642] 739 C ff., 807 B. [643] *Rep.*, 436 C D E, 437 A, 454 A; [645] *Supra*, pp. 13, 19, nn. 70, 71, 293.
Cratyl., 431 A; *Symp.*, 187 A; *Euthyd.*, 277 E.

exaggeration of its significance by Grote, Mill, and Gomperz. Grote had little appreciation of Plato's substantive thought at any stage. He cared only for the dramatic illustration of the *elenchus*. This, which for the author was a means to an end, was for him the real Plato. The exposition of positive doctrine he treats as the work of a totally different person—a dogmatic Plato who has "ceased to be leader of the opposition and passed over to the ministerial benches." This view, which appears even in Grote's treatment of the *Gorgias* and *Theœtetus*, is still more prominent in his criticism of the *Republic*. In the case of the *Laws* this feeling is intensified by the deep repugnance aroused in Grote's mind by Plato's whimsical provisions for the conversion or punishment of those who denied the truths of natural religion or traded upon the superstitions of the vulgar.[646] He cannot speak of the *Laws* without alluding to that unfortunate page; and the vision which he conjured up of the aged Plato as the Torquemada of a Pythagorean mysticism makes him totally blind to the real significance of what in wealth of content is Plato's greatest work. This view was accepted by Mill from Grote, and by Gomperz from Mill, and it leads them both to misapprehend the true relation of the *Laws* to the *Republic*. Mill says: "In his second imaginary commonwealth, that of the *Leges*, it [dialectic] is no longer mentioned; it forms no part of the education either of the rulers or of the ruled."[647] Similarly Gomperz:[648] "Plato in his old age grew averse from dialectic. In the *Laws*, the last product of his pen, he actually turned his back upon it and filled its vacant place at the head of the curriculum of education with mathematics and astronomy."[649] These statements, even if we concede that they are true in a sense to the letter, convey a totally false impression, as a slight study of the last pages of the twelfth book of the *Laws* will show. Plato does not care to rewrite the sixth and seventh books of the *Republic*. But he defines as clearly as in the earlier work the necessity and function of dialectic and the higher education in the state. Even in the first book we are forewarned that to complete the organization of the state the founder must set over it φύλακας . . . . τοὺς μὲν διὰ φρονήσεως τοὺς δὲ δι' ἀληθοῦς δόξης ἰόντας.[650] In the twelfth book we are introduced to these guardians who are to possess knowledge and not merely right opinion. They compose a nocturnal council which is to be the anchor of the state.[651] Recurring to the imagery and the manner of the early dialogues,[652] Plato tells us that as the pilot, the physician, the general represent intelligence (νοῦς) applied to the definite ends of their respective arts, so this highest council is the head, the soul, the mind of the state, possessing knowledge of the political σκοπός or true end of rule.[653]

---

[646] 908-10.   [647] *Diss. and Discuss.*, Vol. IV, p. 289.

[648] *Greek Thinkers*, Translation, p. 466.

[649] To like effect Zeller, pp. 955, 956.

[650] 632 C. The parallelism with the *Republic* is obvious. There, too (412 A, 497 C D), there is a similar anticipation of the need of guardians who know as distinguished from the assistants. In *Laws*, 818 A, there is another anticipation of the higher education. Mathematics only is mentioned because Plato is explaining that it is not needful for the multitude to study it profoundly. There is no occasion for mentioning any other element of the higher education. The possessors of φρόνησις will surely be able κατ' εἴδη ξητεῖν (630 E) and will practice the dialectical methods of the "recent" *Sophist*, *Philebus*, and *Politicus*. Zeller's attempt to distinguish between φρόνησις and the νοῦς of the *Republic* is a false point. φρόνησις is used in *Phœdo*, 69 B.

[651] 961 C.

[652] *Protag.*, 311 B; *Gorg.*, 447, 448, 449 E; *Euthyd.*, 291 C; *Rep.*, 333.

[653] 961, 962.

No state can prosper or be saved unless such knowledge resides in some part of it as a φυλακτήριον.[654] The beginning of such knowledge is τὸ μὴ πλανᾶσθαι πρὸς πολλὰ στοχαζόμενον ἀλλ᾽ εἰς ἐν βλέποντα, etc.[655] Now τὰ τῶν πολέων νόμιμα aim at many things—wealth, power, and τὸν ἐλεύθερον δὴ βίον.[656] Our aim is virtue. But virtue is both four and one. The intelligent physician can define his one aim. Must not the intelligent ruler be able to define his? It is easy to show how the four virtues are many. To exhibit their unity is harder.[657] A man who amounts to anything must know, not only the names, but the λόγος of things. And the true guardians, teachers, and rulers of a state must not merely rebuke vice and inculcate virtue, but they must be able to teach ἥν δύναμιν ἔχει.[658] The state may be likened to the body, the younger guardians to the senses in the head, the elders to the brain.[659] They cannot all be educated alike. Therefore ἰτέον ἄρα ἐπί τινα ἀκριβεστέραν παιδείαν τῆς ἔμπροσθεν.[660] This is the education already glanced at in our phrases about the unity of purpose. The essence of the more accurate method is our old acquaintance τὸ πρὸς μίαν ἰδέαν ἐκ τῶν πολλῶν καὶ ἀνομοίων δυνατὸν εἶναι βλέπειν.[661] The guardian must be able to do what Meno could not do—ἰδεῖν πρῶτον, ὅ τί ποτε διὰ πάντων τῶν τεττάρων ταὐτὸν τυγχάνει.[662] And similarly περὶ καλοῦ τε καὶ ἀγαθοῦ and πάντων τῶν σπουδαίων, they must not only know in what sense each is one and many, but they must be able to expound their knowledge—τὴν ἔνδειξιν τῷ λόγῳ ἐνδείκνυσθαι.[663] The thing being so clearly indicated, it would be pitiful quibbling to object that the word διαλεκτικὴ does not happen to occur here. Its omission is possibly due to the fact that the Athenian throughout the Laws talks down to the level of his unsophisticated Spartan and Cretan interlocutors. Mathematics and astronomy, then, are not substituted for dialectic, but are added for a special reason among the σπουδαῖα which the guardians must understand with real knowledge. The multitude may follow tradition. The guardians must be able to demonstrate the truths of natural religion, as we have done.[664] Astronomy, the study of the ordered movements of the heavens, is a great aid to this. With astronomy is involved the necessary mathematics, which also in their relation to music and the arts are of use to him who is to shape the characters and laws of men.[665] He who cannot learn these things can never be a ruler, though he may be an assistant.

In the last two pages of the Laws Plato evades giving a detailed account of the curriculum of the higher education thus indicated—perhaps he was weary, perhaps he did not care to repeat the Republic.[666] In any case, there is no justification for the statement that the Laws ignore the higher education of the rulers or substitute in it mathematics and astronomy for dialectic. On the contrary, the unity of Plato's

654 962 C; cf. Rep., 424 C.
655 962 D.
656 Cf. Rep., 563 A, ἵνα δὴ ἐλεύθερος ᾖ.
657 Cf. Phileb., 18 E, πῶς ἔστιν ἐν καὶ πολλὰ αὐτῶν ἑκάτερον.
658 964 C; cf. Rep., 366 E, τῇ αὐτοῦ δυνάμει ἐν τῇ τοῦ ἔχοντος ψυχῇ ἐνόν.
659 964 E; cf. Tim., 69, 70.
660 965 A.

661 Cf. Phædr., 265 D; and with ταύτης οὐκ ἔστι σαφεστέρα μέθοδος, cf. Phileb., 16 B; Phædr., 266 B.
662 965 D. Meno, 74 A, τὴν δὲ μίαν, ἣ διὰ πάντων τούτων ἐστίν, οὐ δυνάμαθα ἀνευρεῖν.
663 966 B.
664 In Book X.
665 967 E.
666 968 D.

thought is strikingly illustrated by his return in the pages just analyzed to some of the favorite ideas of the *Republic* and earlier dialogues.[667]

It is not necessary to prolong this study. The *Timæus*, so far as it affects our argument, has already been considered.[668] The *Timæus* as a whole I have studied elsewhere.[669]

The object of this discussion and the expression "unity of Plato's thought" may easily be misunderstood. I may therefore be permitted, in conclusion, to repeat that I have not meant to sophisticate away the obvious and inevitable variations in Plato's moods, and minor beliefs from youth to old age. Nor in the study of such development would I reject the aid of a sober and critical method of style statistics.[670] My thesis is simply that Plato on the whole belongs rather to the type of thinkers whose philosophy is fixed in early maturity (Schopenhauer, Herbert Spencer), rather than to the class of those who receive a new revelation every decade (Schelling). And I have tried to show that the method which proceeds on the contrary assumption leads to misinterpretation of his writings. The illustrations given are merely typical. There has been no attempt to catalogue exhaustively the opinions of contemporary Platonists. The polemic is, I trust, not discourteous, and is, I am sure, not intentionally disloyal. In any case, it turns generally on the meaning or relevancy of specific passages and can easily be tested. Some excuse for its prominence may be found in Mill's statement that "there are few, if any, ancient authors concerning whose mind and purpose so many demonstrably false opinions are current, as concerning Plato."

[667] GOMPERZ supports his view of the anti-dialectical tendency of Plato's mind in the *Laws* by the hostility of the *Sophist* to every kind of antilogy. But surely eristic is one thing and dialectic another. The true Socratic elenchus is described and the difficulty of distinguishing it from eristic indicated in a *locus classicus* in the *Sophist* (230 B ff.); and both the *Sophist* and the *Politicus* employ the keenest dialectic in order to meet and defeat eristic on its own ground (*Soph.*, 259 C D). In the *Philebus*, which

Gomperz thinks late, dialectic is still the highest science of truth (*Phileb.*, 58). But Plato had other interests than dialectic, and it is unreasonable to expect him to fill the *Laws* and *Timæus* with repetitions of what had been said once for all in the *Sophist*, *Politicus*, and *Philebus*.

[668] *Supra*, p. 37.   [669] *A. J. P.*, Vol. IX, pp. 395 ff

[670] As, *e. g.*, that of RITTER, "Die Sprachstatistik in Anwendung auf Platon und Goethe," *Neue Jahrbücher etc.*, 1903.

INDEX